D1478532

THE APPEAL
THAT WAS NEVER MADE

THE APPEAL THAT WAS NEVER MADE

THE ALLIES, SCANDINAVIA AND THE FINNISH WINTER WAR
1939 - 1940

BY

JUKKA NEVAKIVI

McGill–Queen's University Press

Montreal 1976

First published in the United Kingdom by
C. Hurst & Co. (Publishers) Ltd., London
Published in North America by
McGill–Queen's University Press, Montreal

Finnish edition *Apu jota ei pyydetty* published by
Kustannusosakeyhtiö Tammi, Helsinki © Jukka Nevakivi 1972

This translation © 1976, by Jukka Nevakivi

ISBN 0-7735-0262-9
Legal Deposit 3rd Quarter 1976
Bibliothèque Nationale du Québec

Printed in Great Britain by offset lithography by
Billing & Sons Ltd, Guildford, London and Worcester

To my son,
born *30 November 1974*

CONTENTS

MAP

FOREWORD

This study was originally intended for the Finnish public in order to bring out in full relief certain factors in the diplomatic background of the Winter War of 1939-40, which is still too often presented as an isolated conflict between Finland and the Soviet Union. The prerequisite for reviewing the Allied attitudes of the time was the opening since 1970 of the official British records on the Second World War, as well as special permission to carry out research in the corresponding Finnish, Norwegian, Polish and Swedish diplomatic archives. The limitations still imposed on research in the last-mentioned archives and the continuing absence of the relevant Soviet material made it impossible to present the problem within a larger framework.

Having had the opportunity to prepare the present English edition I am particularly pleased to include in it some additional material that I have discovered in official French archives, at the Quai d'Orsay, at the Embassy in London, and at the war archives of Vincennes. Although my permission to see them was an exceptional one and I am not allowed to quote or refer to the documents I have studied, I have been able to make essential use of them with a view of dealing with the Allied and not only the British policy during the Finnish Winter War. On the other hand American neutrality, rather solid as it still was during the first year of war, seems to provide a reason for leaving the United States outside my theme, however important its role in the background of the Finnish-Soviet conflict.

The following text is based on my *Apu jota ei pyydetty*, published in 1972 by Tammi, Helsinki, but revised while taking into consideration the few alterations necessitated by errata, new facts found in the French archives, some recent publications, and the additional information needed by a non-Finnish reader. The manuscript was prepared during the past two years when I was engaged as visiting professor at the Université de Sorbonne Nouvelle in Paris, free from my duties at the Finnish Foreign Ministry. I feel obliged to emphasize that everything included in this book, as well as in my original study in Finnish, represents my personal views and not those of my office.

I wish to acknowledge the permission of the Keeper of Public Records to quote from unpublished material in the Public Record Office and from documents published by Her Majesty's Stationery Office, and to express my gratitude to the directors of the archives

mentioned in the bibliography, especially to those of the Archives
of the French Ministry for Foreign Affairs, and of the French Army
Historical Section in Vincennes.

I am deeply indebted to all the private persons who were
gracious enough to help me with interviews and personal papers,
particularly to the late Ambassador G. A. Gripenberg. Mr. Ralph
Enckell, Ambassador of Finland in Paris, contributed to my work by
valuable suggestions and many courtesies. General B. B. Duch
kindly assisted me in selecting the Polish material I have used at
the Sikorsky Institute in London. Dr. David Kirby made many
useful remarks upon the manuscript which my wife translated
from the original into English.

December 1975

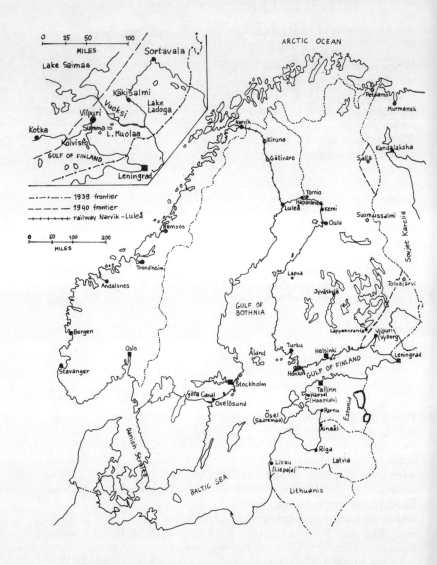

Finland and Scandinavia: the theatre of war 1939-40.

I

THE WESTERN POWERS AND
INDEPENDENT FINLAND

When presenting his season's greetings in 1939 to an old friend at the Admiralty, Winston Churchill found the situation similar to that at the end of 1914. There had been a change from peace to war, but operations both on land and sea had calmed down into silent static warfare: again no news from the Western Front.[1] The *Blitzkrieg* fought in Poland haunted western minds as a frightening prospect, but it seemed too remote and too unreal to force people to recognize a new era. During the winter of 1939-40 the good old days still prevailed in London and Paris. People were hopeful enough to assume that the war would not become total, and that it would not even develop into serious fighting but could be settled by means of diplomacy and blockade; and that, even if a total confrontation finally became inevitable, Hitler would undoubtedly be overcome by the united forces of the two empires.

Less than six months later, in July 1940, the Anglo-French alliance had come to a definite end. Though subsequently renewed, it remained a shadow of its former self: even in the times of Churchill and de Gaulle, the British and French empires were in process of dissolution, and remained definitely in the shadow of the Soviet Union and the United States, the super-powers emerging out of the Second World War.

The first year of war (1939-40) also brought to an end hopes that the conflict might be settled within the boundaries of Europe, by isolating Germany from its allies and sources of raw material. Whatever delusions the unexpected German-Soviet *rapprochement* may have created on the eve of war, it was certain that the days of the classic cabinet policy, when alliances could be changed by enlisting new partners from the opposite camp or from neutrals, were gone for ever. When Italy, after France's collapse in the summer 1940, made the decision to enter the war, it was the last European power to take up arms voluntarily. All the East European and Balkan states that later joined the fighting did so under compulsion. The war grew uncompromising, ruthless and infinite, more total than ever.

In the winter 1939-40 the elderly gentlemen of the Supreme War Council were puzzled by the new and frightening weapons developed by the Germans: the modern *Panzer* tactics, the dive-bombing, and the magnetic mine which was pictured as a more efficient blockading instrument than the submarine. But the west still lacked cogent proof of any of these, and the old strategic concepts, based on the experiences of the First World War, remained unshaken. Even Churchill, though by no means trifling with future perils, admitted as late as at the end of the first war year that "the Kaiser's Germany was a much tougher customer than Nazi Germany".[2]

The dangerous illusion of "the phoney war", *drôle de guerre*, germinated under the shelters of the French Maginot Line, had spread from soldier level to the map tables of the generals. Operations were planned as a pastime, the leading motive being how to win the war without fighting.

As it happened, this vein of thinking was suddenly stimulated by the conflict which, in the shadow of the great European war, broke out between Finland and the Soviet Union, the supposed friend of Germany. Allied concern with what has come to be called the Finnish Winter War exceeded in every respect their traditional interest in that isolated country on the frontiers of Russia. Since these aspects also attracted attention, if not only because of public opinion and private pressure groups, it may be useful to review briefly what Finland had meant to Britain and France during the preceding years.

Let us keep in mind, however, that the purpose of this study is to deal not so much with Allied relations with Finland during the Winter War as with Allied attitudes towards the conflict itself—in other words, with an early stage in the Anglo-French "grand strategy" during the Second World War. Accordingly the introduction is summary, and it is not intended to be an exhaustive account of pre-war relations between the Western Powers and Finland, nor to explore in detail the origins of the Finnish-Soviet conflict which, it is evident, are inseparably bound up with the coming of the great European war in 1939.[3]

1

When Finland became independent, Germany seemed to be accepted as the godmother of the new state.* This fact was not to improve its presentability at the Paris Peace Conference. In comparison with the other novices—the Baltic countries, Poland, Czechoslovakia and Yugoslavia, all hostile to Germany—Finland did not at first

---

* The declaration of independence on 6 December 1917 was followed seven weeks later by the outbreak of civil war, in the course of which the Red insurgents were finally subdued by a German intervention. The Kaiser's government thereby acquired, before its collapse at the end of 1918, extensive influence in the affairs of "White" Finland.

seem welcome in the reinforced European orchestra. France, it is true, had recognized it as early as January 1918, but had withdrawn its consul from Helsinki ten months later, after the Finnish "Rump Parliament"—with no Socialist representatives—had chosen a German prince as the country's king. At the time British recognition was still lacking: the relations between Britain and "White" Finland had been strained to the point where, in the summer of 1918, an open conflict was feared. When His Majesty's Government, together with the United States, at last recognized Finland in May 1919, this was done in such a way which was somewhat humiliating for its "White" regime.*

The aversion towards Finland was accentuated by the ill-feeling which the aftermath of the Civil War had created in Socialist and Liberal circles; this kind of attitude persisted into the following decades. In the early 1930s special attention was attracted by the persecution of the Communists, culminating in the trial of Toivo Antikainen in 1934-6. Finland was often seen as being the contrary of its official façade, a half-Fascist state, where reactionary circles supported by the army and paramilitary organizations were in control, under cover of an ostensibly democratic system.[5]†

Neither did the pointed pro-Germanism of Finns in public positions escape the attention of western officials circles. It is true that in the government there had been a clear change of direction towards the Left as a result of the parliamentary elections of 1936: the "Red-Green" coalition cabinet formed after the elections, with the pro-*entente* Rudolf Holsti, and after him the equally Anglophile Eljas Erkko, as Foreign Ministers, had started to direct Finnish foreign policy into neutral Nordic paths. Still, in London and Paris it was observed with annoyance that the military leadership remained in the hands of pro-German officers, most of whom had had their military training during the First World War in the Royal Prussian Jaeger Battalion 27. Nor did the envoys of the Western Powers in Helsinki entertain any illusions as to the effect of German power policy on Finnish public opinion. "Germany's achievements during 1938", the British Minister T. M. Snow observed in his

---

* In the connexion of the very act of recognition the Finnish Government was urged, in conformity with the decision taken by the Allied foreign ministers at the Paris Peace Conference, to grant an amnesty to the Red Finns who had fought in Allied forces (after their withdrawal from Finland to the North of Russia in 1918).[4]

† "The influence which the I.K.L. (Fascist Party) and the Conservative Party still wield in all branches of administration—civil service, Army, Navy, police and in particular among the so-called 'Protective Guards'—is quite incommensurate with the actual strength of these parties in Parliament. Hence the almost permanent latent danger of a coup." (*Yorkshire Post,* July 11, 1939.)

annual report, "produced in Finland an impression, beyond the reach of propaganda, of German strength, organizing power and ruthlessness."[6]

In certain Western circles the Finnish role was visualized as presented by Sir Walter Kirke to the British public in the summer of 1939: "Today this virile, honest and enlightened people stand as an outpost of Western civilization on the frontiers of the unknown." These circles had not forgotten the goodwill shown towards the planned Allied intervention in Petrograd in 1919 by the then Regent of Finland C. G. Mannerheim, who had led the Finnish government troops in the Civil War. The "White general" was in favour, not least because he had kept a certain distance from the Germans. Mannerheim returned to public affairs in 1932 as chairman of the newly-formed Defence Council, and it was hoped that he would provide a counter-weight against the pro-German General Staff officers. Frequently visited by Western envoys at his home in Helsinki, Mannerheim, for his part, travelled to England three times and to France at least once during 1934-7. Moreover, the then commander of the French armed forces, General Maxime Weygand, and the First Lord of the Admiralty, Duff Cooper, visited Helsinki in 1937 and 1938. Through these contacts Western leaders in pre-war years had frequent opportunities of becoming acquainted with the personality and way of thinking of the man who was considered the first Finnish soldier.[7]

Tourism, especially during the 1930s, as well as the increasing contacts with foreign politicians and journalists, helped to improve the sometimes one-sided image of Finland that had prevailed in Western opinion since 1918. Descriptions in the press and in literature—like Georges Duhamel's *Le Chant du Nord* and J. Hampden Jackson's *Finland*—helped to provide background to the idealized articles later published by the world press on the Winter War. Thus the British and the French had the opportunity to learn that Finland, preparing for the Olympics* but ending up in general mobilization, was in fact an honest, peace-loving, democratic country, displaying its political maturity by loyal participation in the work of the League of Nations.[8]

For the Western Powers one of the surest means of exerting influence on Finland was foreign trade. It was true Finland could not offer anything that Britain or France absolutely needed, nor was it of any great importance for them as a marketing area. Contrary to France, whose trade with Finland has always been relatively limited (less than 4 per cent of the total of Finnish

---

* Planned for Helsinki in 1940.

foreign trade in the 1930s), Britain had an advantage in that the Finns belonged in the Sterling Area. Their main export articles, timber and paper products, were in such demand in the United Kingdom that the British had become — as they have been till the present — their principal trading partner. In 1938 the U.K. share was almost 44 per cent of their total exports and 18 per cent of their imports. The corresponding Finnish share in British trade statistics was naturally more unassuming, in 1938 3.8 per cent of imports and 1.1 per cent of exports.[9]*

The one-sided orientation of Finnish exports was criticized both by Germany and the Soviet Union (the former's share in Finnish foreign trade was nearly 20 per cent, the latter's share only a little over one per cent in 1938). Understandably they assumed that trade follows the flag and *vice versa*. Besides, the Germans were annoyed because one of their firms was refused, obviously for political reasons, a licence for fishing on the Arctic coast at Petsamo, while the Anglo-Canadian Mond Nickel Company was allowed to start exploitation of the nickel deposits in this region.[10]

Petsamo was, of course, of strategic importance as well. In the situation of 1919, when the Allies planned intervention in Russia, southern Finland had seemed to offer a good base for attack against Petrograd. The Royal Navy had then moved into the Baltic Sea — as a matter of fact for the third time within 110 years.† By concluding a naval agreement with Hitler in 1935, however, the British Government had enabled the Germans to build up their naval forces so that, using their new air power, they were again in a position to close the Baltic to outsiders. For this very reason the Royal Navy had no access east of the Danish Straits after the outbreak of the Second World War, even though such a manoeuvre was planned by Churchill in September 1939, after he had been appointed First Lord of the Admiralty.[11]

Thus, once the Germans had closed the Danish Straits, the only access to Finland, the Baltic countries and Poland left to the Allies was by way of Sweden, Norway or Petsamo. Had they been able to use Finnish territory, they would have gained an excellent

---

* For all that, after overseas trade became, at the outbreak of the European war, handicapped by German submarine operations, the importance of the still accessible Finnish and Nordic markets was accentuated. This was the case with British imports of food, like butter and cheese, from Finland, but above all with paper products. According to trade agreements concluded or planned in the autumn of 1939, at least half of all the paper (except newsprint) that the United Kingdom needed in 1940 was to be imported from Finland and the Scandinavian countries.[9]

† The first time during the Napoleonic wars, the second time in the Baltic Campaign of 1854–5.

north-south passage to the Baltic. From the Allied point of view Finland, even if it remained neutral, was in 1939 of more strategic importance than its Baltic neighbours: it isolated the Soviet Union from the Atlantic and Germany from the Arctic — in other words, it prevented a potential enemy expansion to the northern seas.

2

The original purpose of the naval agreement which the British Government signed with the Third Reich in 1935 was of course to contain the growing German menace after Hitler's accession to power. The western reactions to German rearmament were divergent, even contradictory. The pact of mutual assistance with the Soviet Union, negotiated and signed by the then French Foreign Minister Pierre Laval, also in 1935, was concluded to a large extent for internal reasons, in order to persuade the strong French Communist Party into supporting the prolongation of the period of conscription. The behaviour of the French Government at the time of the Czechoslovak crisis gave reason to suspect that the agreement had not been entered into in earnest. The Anglo-German agreement, for its part, was made at the initiative of the British Admiralty for purely military reasons, without consulting the French or the League of Nations.[12]

In Moscow, earlier than elsewhere, Hitler's threats had been taken seriously: shortly after the establishment of the Nazi regime in Germany, the Soviet Government had changed its diplomacy in order to get out of its isolated position, joined the League of Nations, and openly supported the promotion of collective security. But sincere as the Russians may have been, they were prevented from joining the Western European security system; this was mainly due to the bottomless mistrust of their European neighbours, Finland included, and their unwillingness to allow Soviet troops, in case of emergency, to come to their assistance.[13]

Among the Finnish military leadership the prospective understanding between the Western Powers and the Soviet Union met with undisguised suspicion. For instance, Mannerheim, who was in London in January 1936 for the funeral of George V, was rather saddened to observe that the British considered Bolshevism less dangerous than National Socialism. According to him, Edward VIII, not being quite in accord with his Foreign Secretary, expressed his views as follows:

I expressed the personal opinion that whatever one might think of the Nazi movement, it could not be denied that it had put an end to Communism in Germany to the advantage of Western civilization. The King said that he

was of the same opinion, and further indicated that one must not allow
sentimental feelings to influence one's attitude to that country, for one day
the Nazi system would be replaced by another, and the fact remained that
it was an unquestioned gain that the power of the Communists in Germany
had been crushed. The King [too] saw in Communism a danger to the
world....[14]

During the first half of 1937, when Holsti had visited Moscow
and the centrist Agrarian Kyösti Kallio had become President of
the Republic (succeeding the Conservative Svinhufvud), it seemed
for a while that Finnish foreign policy would give way to more
confident relations with the eastern neighbour; this, indeed, might
have facilitated the aspirations of the Western Powers in finding
an appropriate form of alliance with the Soviet Union. But Holsti's
visit to Moscow brought no results. And in Britain, Eden's
attempts to conciliate between the Western Powers and the Soviet
Union failed to receive the support of the Cabinet. When he resigned
in February 1938, nothing tangible had been achieved.

The year of Munich, 1938, which brought a decisive change in
Soviet foreign policy, was now at hand. The annexations of Austria
and the Sudetenland to the Third Reich and the amputation of
Czechoslovakia, even with the consent of Britain and France,
were proof enough for the Kremlin that neither of these powers
was to be trusted in the hour of need. Stalin went even further,
declaring at the XVIII Congress of the Soviet Communist Party
that the policy of the Western Powers gave reason to doubt whether
it was their intention to check German aggression at all, but rather
to direct it eastwards against the Soviet Union.[15]

From this point of view, Finland was seen as part of a dubious
buffer zone, which the aggressor might well intend to exploit.
A clear indication of such suspicions had been received in Helsinki,
when a Soviet diplomat was sent to Holsti to ask for guarantees
that Finland would not assist Germany against the Soviet Union.
By guarantees Moscow meant the cession of certain strategic
islands in the Gulf of Finland, Suursaari (Högholm) being the
foremost objective. The Western Powers, however, did not learn
about these demands until a year later.[16]

During the September crisis in 1938, with the Germans rattling
their sabres on the borders of Czechoslovakia, the Soviet Baltic
fleet despatched unusually strong formations to the neighbourhoods
of Suursaari and Hanko, the southernmost point of the Finnish
mainland. According to the British envoy, this aroused suspicions
in Helsinki that the Russians were now about to take possession
of the bases concerned in order to defend themselves against an
eventual German attack.[17]

In this situation Mr. Snow, evidently at the request of the Finns, asked the Foreign Office on 28 September to make it clear to Moscow that the one and only Finnish wish was to remain neutral, and that there was no reason to resort to any provocative action against them, especially because this might be exploited by the Germans. Three days later he was answered by the Foreign Office that the message had not been forwarded to Moscow, since the Munich meeting had changed the situation. The envoy, for his part, observed the satisfaction felt in Helsinki because the Soviet Union had not been party to the meeting, "a fact which was hailed with relief in Finland, as a proof that the Western democracies had at last severed their puzzling connexion with Russia". Among those sighing with relief was Snow himself, failing to realize that Munich, which estranged Stalin from the Western Powers, was in fact to form the basis for a German-Soviet understanding.[18]

3

The occupation of the remnants of Czechoslovakia by Hitler on 15 March 1939 was more than even Chamberlain could stomach. But even after having denounced the occupation in a powerful speech in Birmingham—an occasion which Churchill later characterized as the definite end of the policy of appeasement—the Prime Minister was pondering over the drawbacks of the remaining alternative:

I must confess to the most profound distrust of Russia. I have no belief whatever in her ability to maintain an effective offensive, even if she wanted to. And I distrust her motives, which seem to me to have little connection with our ideas of liberty, and to be concerned only with getting every one else by the ears. Moreover, she is both hated and suspected by many smaller states, notably by Poland, Roumania, and Finland (Chamberlain's Diary, 26 March 1939).[19]

However, this was no time for inaction in London. As is well-known, a fortnight after the capture of Prague the constantly threatening course of events—the German seizure of the Lithuanian territory of Memel and open threats to Warsaw—made the British Government take the initiative in offering Anglo-French guarantees to Poland. A week later, when Italy attacked Albania, similar guarantees were offered not only to Greece but also to Romania. Finally, as the ominous chain of aggression seemed to have no end, both London and Paris were about to draw the conclusions they had hitherto tried to avoid. Both made moves towards Moscow, though separately.

The Russians met the proposals for co-operation with a positive response on 18 April. Instead of a mere promise of assistance to German-menaced border states, as forwarded from London, they preferred the concrete treaty offer made by Paris. What they proposed was a pact of mutual assistance between all three powers, possibly including Poland; according to their idea, the parties concerned had to guarantee the neighbours of the Soviet Union, from the Baltic to the Black Sea, against eventual German aggression. But the way in which the contents of the Kremlin reply reached, within a week, the ears of outsiders, indicated that certain circles wished the entire project to miscarry. The border states—principally Poland whose very life was at stake—instantly refused to accept the prospect of the Soviet Union being authorized to come to their assistance. The Russians for their part did not accept the British proposal that Moscow should declare itself ready to give assistance only when the Western Powers, because of the guarantees they had given to Poland and Romania, became involved in war against the aggressors.[20]

It was hardly by chance that, when rejecting the proposal to the British Ambassador on 15 May, V. V. Molotov, who had succeeded Litvinov as Foreign Minister ten days earlier, mentioned Finland in connection with the Baltic states. Sir William Seeds immediately remarked that Finland did not belong to this group but to the Nordic one; it would be of extreme importance, he added—echoing Snow's appeals—to avoid any measures that might arouse Finnish suspicions and prevent the country from keeping to Nordic neutrality. Molotov only commented that Finland would not oppose guarantees, if Britain and France were to participate.[21]

As a matter of fact, Seeds' ready wit was the result of what the Finnish Foreign Minister had said to Snow a few days earlier. At the beginning of May, Germany had proposed a treaty of non-aggression to some minor European states, including Finland. When asked by Snow about the Finnish reaction to the offer, Erkko had linked his reply to the Soviet offer of guarantees: if these were to be introduced in one form or another, he had said, it would be difficult for him not to accept the German proposal, because of the pressure of Finnish public opinion. Moreover, Erkko had added, the Finns wanted to be treated as members of the Nordic group and in no other connection.[22]

The reference to Germany was in fact unnecessary. Only a day after the Molotov-Seeds discussion, Finland hastened to refuse Berlin's offer of an agreement, after having made sure that Norway and Sweden were of the same opinion—and thus lost another card in the game in which her neutrality was at stake. With all that, this refusal was not enough to make the Russians more compliant with the fortification of the islands of Åland, when this question, at the initiative of Sweden and Finland, was taken up for discussion at the League of Nations Council.[22]*

When giving Snow an account of his discussions with the Soviet representatives in March, Erkko admitted that the Russians seemed to connect the fortification of Åland with their demands for the islands in the Gulf of Finland. As it happened, a British junior minister, R. S. Hudson,† visiting Moscow at that moment, was given — or himself assumed — the task of assuaging the Finns. Returning by way of Helsinki, he told them on 31 March (being authorized to do so, as he said, by Deputy Foreign Minister Potemkin) that "the Soviet Union would be quite content with an effective guarantee by Finland of the neutrality of these islands". Was this message only a bluff or the last attempt by Litvinov, who was about to retire, to bring up the question of bases in a new form? Be this as it may, and although Hudson reported that on hearing the news Erkko had seemed "relieved", it did not induce the Finns to take any further practical measures.[24]

The British and French seem to have understood, better than the Finns themselves, that Soviet acceptance of the fortification of Åland was ultimately linked with Finnish acquiescence in the Soviet demands for bases in the Gulf of Finland'.[24] The British and French attitude towards the fortification of Åland was, as later expressed by the then Head of the Political Department of the Finnish Foreign Ministry, Aaro Pakaslahti, "completely and purely the outcome of Great Power politics". At least the Foreign Office were fully aware of the positive interest of the Germans in the fortification project, their concern being understandable since the Åland Islands were situated along the iron ore route from the Swedish port of Luleå to their own Baltic ports. Nevertheless, the Western Powers announced that they did not object to the project in principle, provided that all governments concerned, the Soviet Government included, be consulted and that the question be submitted to the Council of the League of Nations.[25]

---

* According to a treaty signed in 1921 under the auspices of the League of Nations by ten European states (excluding Russia), these islands belonged to Finland, provided that they were granted self-government and were demilitarized. In 1938 the Finnish and Swedish governments had decided to propose the revision of the treaty in order to be able to fortify the islands. They had consequently consulted all the signatory governments and also the USSR with the view of submitting the case to the Council of the League.

† Parliamentary Secretary, Overseas Trade Department, in the Chamberlain government.

In May 1939, when the Åland question was finally taken up by the Council, both Britain and France abstained from advocating the case, regardless of Finnish appeals for support. According to Pakaslahti's Swedish colleague, the Western representatives, during a confidential conversation, confessed that they understood Swedish and Finnish aspirations, but "both emphasized—their delicate position in the general political situation with regard to the Soviet Union". The Finns and the Swedes were countered by the Soviet representative, Ambassador Maisky, who pointed out that the contents and implications of the project would first have to be studied. "After Russia, England and France will have concluded their agreements in the near future", Maisky put it nicely to the chief Finnish representative, "peace will be preserved in the Baltic, so there is no reason for Finland and Sweden to rush the fortification of Åland."[26]

4

By the end of May the readiness of the Western Powers to come to terms with Moscow was enhanced by fears of losing the race with German diplomacy. They were now aware of the German-Soviet secret talks which had been started in mid-April simultaneously with the three-power preliminary negotiations. An even more imminent menace was the expansion of the German strategic sphere of influence to the Mediterranean: after the conclusion of the so-called Steel Pact (on 22 May), by which the co-operation between Hitler and Mussolini reached the military field, the Western Powers no longer had any illusions about their chances of checking the alliance between the two dictators.[27]

Five days later the British and French ambassadors presented a new plan to Molotov. They proposed a tripartite agreement which would take effect immediately should one of them be subjected to direct aggression or get into a state of war while assisting a European state—this assistance, however, could only be given with the consent of this state. Molotov rejected the proposal outright. He claimed that the agreements would be too time-consuming and asked for automatic assistance.

Finally, on 30 May, he came up with a new aspect as to the position of the Baltic States and Finland: what should be done if Germany used any one of these countries as its instrument and thereby committed an "indirect aggression" against the Soviet Union? This extremely confusing question proved a dilemma for Western diplomacy. Although the Allied military leadership doubted the likelihood of a German attack in the Baltic area, the Foreign

Office found Molotov's apprehensions understandable. However, the suggestion was, of course, not in conformity with accepted international practice, since the enforced guarantees would imply interference with the internal affairs of other states. Its acceptance would have compromised the position of the Western democracies in the League of Nations as well as the principles on which they were trying to re-establish European security. In fact, the choice was between the League of Nations and the tripartite alliance. Only Winston Churchill, who strongly favoured the latter, did not hesitate to cross the Rubicon.[28] After wavering for a while between the pressure of public opinion in Britain and in France on one side and the increasingly categorical demands from the Kremlin on the other, Chamberlain's Cabinet agreed on 26 June to include the clause on indirect aggression in the draft agreement (referring mainly to the case of Czechoslovakia). It also consented to enumerate the countries covered by the agreement, Finland included, in a separate secret protocol. But as Molotov, a week later, requested in addition the widening of the concept of indirect aggression so as to authorize the guarantee powers to intervene (even if a country covered by the agreement should voluntarily enter political or military agreements with the Germans, or allow the latter to occupy even parts of its territory or to allow their troops passage through it), London was ready to break off negotiations. As made clear by the Cabinet minutes, the ministers were mainly worried by the thought that any Soviet intervention in Finland or the Baltic countries would draw Britain into large-scale war. Only at the end of July, at the request of the French, did they agree to postpone the definition of political conditions until the military experts had completed their own draft of co-operation.[29]

In Finland and the other countries concerned, the guarantee plans aroused growing irritation. After informing the Western powers of Finnish opposition by the usual diplomatic channels, Erkko denounced the plan publicly on 6 June 1939 in an intransigent speech before the Diet. Under these circumstances, the visit to Finland, in the second half of June, of General Sir Walter Kirke, a former military adviser to the Finnish armed forces and recently appointed Commander of the Home Forces, was observed in Helsinki with unusual attention. At one of the official dinners in his honour the general eloquently compared Finland to a much sought-after girl who wants to sit out the next dance, and even assured that Great Britain viewed the girl's attitude with understanding. But, as was disclosed later, Chamberlain's Cabinet had, a day after his speech, agreed in principle to the Soviet demands on Finland and the other border states.[30]

Though formally not on an official mission—he had been invited privately by the Finnish Minister of Defence—Kirke tried to assuage the apprehensions of his hosts. His main argument in the discussions with the Finns was that the eventual guarantees would have no practical significance in the long run, since the Germans would not dare to attack once the Allies had gained enough strength. Mannerheim was not convinced, and pointed out that the guarantees might enable the Soviets to request information on Finnish defence plans. The Field-Marshal* allowed that he fully understood the British point of view, but wanted to stress that, as a Finn, he could by no means accept the Soviet guarantees and that the entire nation agreed with him in this matter. But he and certain members of the Finnish Cabinet would have been in favour of giving up some islands in the Gulf of Finland which were demanded by the Russians. By so doing, Mannerheim maintained, relations with the Soviet Union could be improved and the enforced occupation of the islands averted.[31]

The British Minister in Helsinki observed with satisfaction that Kirke's reception in Finland was exceptionally courteous: Mannerheim took the trouble of accompanying the guest personally to the airport, whereas he did not even turn up a week later when the German Chief of Staff, General Halder, visited Finland as guest of the armed forces. Delighted by what he had heard from Helsinki, Lord Halifax commented after Kirke's return: "Although the Finnish General Staff are undoubtedly somewhat pro-German, they are by no means beyond the reach of other influences."[32] Still, Halder's visit, as well as that of the Head of German Counter-Intelligence Admiral Canaris a little earlier, which had taken place with more discretion, were bound to arouse the suspicions of closer observers: despite the fact that Finland had refused Hitler's offer of a non-aggression treaty, the inveterate pro-Germanism of the Finnish military leadership had still to be kept in mind as a potential adverse factor. Among others, the Head of the Northern Department at the Foreign Office, Lawrence Collier, whose attitude towards Finland was basically benevolent, took a rather sceptical view of the reliability of the Finnish General Staff.[33]

Understandably enough Collier did not discuss these matters with the Finnish Minister, who called on him almost weekly during the summer of 1939. Yet Collier told him a lot that other officials might have suppressed, thus enabling him to keep in exceptionally good touch with the Moscow negotiations. The Minister, G.A.Gripenberg, for his part, was afraid that the information he was sending to

---

* Mannerheim had been promoted Field-Marshal on his seventieth birthday in 1937.

Helsinki was not taken seriously. This was hardly the case, for his outstanding and perceptive reports were of importance during the summer of 1939, at least in giving a basis for Mannerheim's estimates of the situation. We may add that the Minister was related to the Field-Marshal, who thought highly of his competence as a diplomat.

By early July, Gripenberg was aware of two essential facts: the impending Molotov-Ribbentrop Pact loomed large in the minds of the Foreign Office and, in order to counteract this eventuality, the British Government had already decided in principle to give up Finland and the Baltic countries. His conclusions were confirmed on 5 July, when he called on the Foreign Secretary. Lord Halifax phrased his answers neatly, and let the Minister understand that although "the British Government would do their best to defend Finnish interests", it did indeed negotiate in Moscow on an agreement which might possibly "concern Finland in one way or another". The conversation almost had the feeling of farewell: as Gripenberg had once more made it clear that German propaganda might profit from the guarantees, Halifax agreed, but observed that this was unavoidable. The Foreign Secretary concluded the conversation on an ominous note: "If in the long run anything is decided, which is not in accordance with your wishes, you will realize that we felt that greater issues were involved."[35]

The situation having taken such a menacing turn, it was again stressed from Helsinki that the extending of the guarantees to cover Finland would hardly serve the interests of the planned three power alliance. Gripenberg was instructed to write a communication to this effect, which he did, delivering it on 14 July to R.A.Butler, then Parliamentary Under-Secretary at the Foreign Office. The contents and form of the memorandum resembled that presented by Estonia four days earlier; but its wording was more uncompromising, making clear that, whatever happened, the Finnish Government would consider as an aggressor any power that tried to give it armed assistance without its consent.

Towards the end of July, the Swedish *Chargé d'affaires* also called on Butler, expressing, on instructions sent (at the request of Erkko) from Stockholm, his concern as to the planned guarantees which might endanger Finland's relations with the neutral Nordic group. It was now convenient for Butler to assure him that the British Government did not intend to agree to any arrangements injurious to Finland. "Had we given up Finland and the Baltic states", he said, "the pact would have been concluded long ago!"[36]

5

As is known, Halifax informed Moscow, the day before on 25 July, that Great Britain was ready to postpone the settlement of political questions, and to start military negotiations immediately; in the meanwhile the British hoped to stick to a less compromising attitude towards the Russian proposals of guarantees.[37] Even today, after the opening of the official British records, one can agree with A.J.P. Taylor, who wrote in the late 1950s:

> The British Government, in fact, were not interested in solid military co-operation with Soviet Russia; they merely wanted to chalk a Red bogey on the wall, in the hope that this would keep Hitler quiet.[38]

France, for its part, played an active role during the entire tripartite negotiations, seeking an agreement with undisguised ardour. We may presume that she would hardly have been more willing than Britain to give up Finland and the Baltic States, although it is true that France's interests in these countries were fewer; in Poland the positions were reversed, and still Daladier's Government, fully aware of superior German strength, had been ready to urge Warsaw to accept the alarming Soviet conditions at the approach of war. For France, even more than for Britain, the question was now one of life or death. "Bring the agreement with you at any price!", Daladier said when taking leave of his military delegates.[39]

The story of the military negotiations in Moscow, how the Soviet Government let the talks start but meanwhile invited to the Kremlin the German Foreign Minister, need not be repeated here, nor the outcome of these secret negotiations, the Molotov-Ribbentrop Pact, signed on 22 August 1939. Unlike the German ones, the Soviet motives in this understanding are still subject to speculation.

Yet, it is hardly to be expected, even if the archives of the Kremlin may one day be opened, that Stalin would appear—in spite of his well-known miscalculations regarding Germany—as a man who trusted the Fuehrer more than he did Chamberlain and Daladier. The constant delays, the leaks, and the almost blind intransigence of the border states, particularly Poland, gave him ample evidence, suspicious as he was, of the genuineness of the Western intentions. It was for him natural to conclude that Britain and France as well as Germany were engaged in double-dealing. But his main objection to the tripartite alliance was the Western lack of troops and, indeed, of willingness to sacrifice them—as long as German aggression was directed towards the east. Stalin found it safest to ask for time and concrete rights to strategic forward positions, rather than vague promises of a second front, remembering the sacrifice that Russia had paid for its alliance in 1914.

For the Finns this crude turn in great power politics proved costly. The power constellation that Mannerheim, among others, had considered the most dangerous one for Finland, had become a reality.[40] The chief of the Soviet armed forces, Marshal Voroshilov, had, it is true, demanded from the Allied military delegates even more than the Kremlin envoy had asked from the Finns in March: according to British records, Voroshilov had proposed on 15 August that "England and France *must* obtain from the Governments of the Baltic states and of Finland their permission for the temporary occupation by the Franco-British Fleets of the Islands [*sic*] of—

Åland	Ainazi (Latvia)
Hango (Finland)	Archipelago of Ozal (Ösel) and Dago
	Pärnu (Estonia)
Habstal (Hapsal—Estonia)	Libau (Latvia)

with a view to protecting the independence of these States against attack by Germany", and that the Soviet Baltic fleet use these bases together with the Allied fleets. For one thing, the Soviet need for these bases was vindicated by the assertion that it could prevent the transportation of iron ore and other raw materials from Sweden to Germany.[41] This time there was no mention of the islands in the Gulf of Finland or the area of the Karelian Isthmus, the other Soviet demands of which Kirke had informed his guests on his visit to Finland in June.

The final estimate of the Russian demands by Admiral Drax, Chairman of the Military Delegation of the Western Powers, was rather venomous, as might have been expected:

When we have annexed and fortified them, and accepted all the odium for so doing, the Soviet Fleet would graciously join us there and assist us in our naval operations to secure command of the Baltic and defeat the aggressor.

It is still to be kept in mind that these territories were only to be occupied temporarily and *in co-operation with the Allied fleet to be sent to the Baltic*,* no matter how small this fleet might be. This, in any case, differed a great deal from the secret protocol of the Molotov-Ribbentrop Pact, by which the Soviet Union was granted open powers concerning Finland as well as Estonia and Latvia. Lithuania was for the time being (until 27 September) excluded from the German sphere of interest.

The leading principle of Britain in the Finnish and Baltic area—

---

* Moved presumably from the Arctic by way of the White Sea—Ladoga Canal.

secondary as the area was for its own interests, but important for Germany, and vital for the Soviet Union—was not to get too much involved with the destinies of these countries: Finland or the Baltic countries should never be allowed to become a *casus belli*. In the cases of Poland and Romania, of more economic and strategic interest, the British Government had gone further, guaranteeing their integrity, but had to repent its folly: only one week later Ribbentrop returned from Moscow.

In the course of the tripartite negotiations it was never suggested that Finland should assume the role of sacrificial lamb. The country had many advocates, particularly among those in charge of Finnish affairs in the British Foreign Office. An expression of this goodwill was a proposal, made with the blessing of the Foreign Secretary, according to which the Allied Military Delegation in Moscow was supposed to draw Soviet attention to the fact that an enforced occupation of the bases might drive the Finns into the arms of the Germans. Before this argument—a favourite one of Snow's —was taken up in Moscow, the military negotiations were interrupted. The following minutes, nonetheless, reveal that the Foreign Office, at least its Northern Department, had acted in earnest. "I think we must raise this matter as soon as it becomes plain (if it ever does) that there is a real chance of an agreement", Collier wrote on 11 August. "The Russians could not expect us to sign any document without having this vital point cleared up first."[43] Later, even these comments had only formal significance. But they do indicate that, when Stalin made the tripartite negotiations pass into history one week later, the Finnish question remained unsettled.

II

ALL QUIET ON THE WESTERN FRONT
September–November 1939

1

When Hitler unleashed his armies over the Polish borders on
1 September 1939, and the Western powers, in conformity with
their guarantees, entered into hostilities with Germany two days
later, the Soviet Union asserted its neutrality. The initial set-up of
the conflict proved to be exactly as could be predicted after Molotov
and Ribbentrop had signed their agreement the previous
Wednesday. If at that time, a week before the outbreak of war, the
Allied general staffs had still entertained plans based on a two-front
strategy, these had now to be replaced by new ones, better suited to
the actual situation. But the situation was unexpected, and no
means existed for meeting its requirements. This was the terrifying
moment of truth for a bankrupt policy of guarantees.[1]

The Allies were troubled by this dilemma for weeks when at
the end of September, all organized resistance in Poland had come
to an end. What may be called the second sequel of the Molotov-
Ribbentrop Pact had already been carried into effect before the
capitulation of Warsaw, once the Red Army had penetrated into
Poland on 17 September and occupied the eastern territory reserved
for the Soviet Union. But, contrary to what had happened twenty-
five years earlier, the Russian steam-roller did not make any attempt
to proceed further west: commissars and SS officers shook hands in
Brest-Litovsk. This time the battle for France had to be decided in
the west and not in East Prussia or in the Carpathians as in 1914.

When seeking an alliance with the Soviet Union, Britain and
France certainly had no great expectations of the offensive capacity
of the Russian armed forces. In a report drawn up the previous
April, the British chiefs of staff had indeed arrived at a quite
positive estimate of their basic strength. Still they pointed out that
Russian military leadership had been heavily taxed by the purges of
Stalin, and emphasized the lack of organization and the weakness
of the transport system. A Foreign Office memorandum of 22 May
1939, based on this account, concluded somewhat gloomily:

It is true that the Soviet fleet might contain a proportion of German naval
forces in the Baltic, and that the Soviet air forces might be able to render

some assistance. It is, however, unlikely that on land their military effort could be of very much effect, and even in the matter of furnishing...war materials their assistance would be limited by the fact that the Russian transportation system is in an extremely backward state.[2]

Even so, an alliance with Moscow was worth seeking. First, it was only through Soviet territory that the Western Powers would be in a position to support their East European protégés; secondly, it was only by approaching the Soviet Union that they could prevent its co-operation with Germany; and thirdly, as was openly argued in London and Paris, only by being drawn into the conflict could the Soviet Union be deprived of the opportunity of staying out of the war and becoming the leading power in Europe, after the Western Powers and Germany had exhausted themselves.

The fact that Germany had succeeded in assuring herself of the benevolent neutrality of the Soviet Union deprived the Allies of all three advantages, and, consequently, created a fourth disadvantage: the leftist elements in Britain and France, loyal to Moscow, those who really understood Stalin's motives in making an understanding with the Nazis, set about opposing the war before it had even started. In Britain their number was relatively limited, but in France their potential was considerable, even though the French Communist Party, the largest and most powerful in Western Europe, was suppressed in September 1939.*

The worst way by which the Soviet Union could work against Allied aspirations was by obstructing the economic blockade of Germany—in other words, by delivering food and raw materials to her. These shipments, delivered largely on credit, as well as the German imports from the Middle and Far East, transported through Soviet territory, could have been even more important for the war economy of the Reich than they eventually turned out to be.†

---

* A French Communist member of parliament, F.Grenier, who had escaped to England, later wrote that when, during the retreat in June 1940, the false rumour became current that the Soviet Union had joined the war on the Allied side, many French soldiers reformed their units and once more turned to face the Germans.[3]

† In fact Soviet assistance to Germany was relatively negligible during the first war year 1939-40, and never assumed decisive proportions. The example is offered by their oil exports, a big issue at the time, especially from the French point of view: Germany's oil imports from the Soviet Union were only half the amount imported from Romania, i.e. 60,000 tons a month, whereas her total imports and output of oil during the same period were 455,000 tons a month. This does not imply that the importance of Russian oil could not have been greater. The British Industrial Intelligence Centre had estimated to within 5 per cent that at the beginning of the war German oil reserves did not exceed 2 million tons; if Hitler had not managed his 1939-40 operations at lightning speed and doubled his fuel reserves by taking over supplies found in Western Europe, the demands on Russian oil would evidently have been greater.[4]

In addition to these factors, with their immediate effects on the European war scene, British military experts had drawn the Cabinet's attention to the dangers that the Soviet Union could create through its propaganda—or, at worst, through a military offensive—for British interests elsewhere, particularly in Iraq, Persia and Afghanistan ("The Road to India"). It was also feared that, with the Russians allied with the Axis, China would be completely at the mercy of the Japanese. The worst threat, from the Allied point of view, was of course the possibility that the Soviet Union might open its harbours to the Germans on the Arctic Ocean, and perhaps even elsewhere. These fears were not groundless.[5]

The Russian invasion of Eastern Poland and the fact that German-Soviet negotiations were proceeding in Moscow at the end of September* hinted at the possibility that both powers might extend their co-operation into the military field. London and Paris, however, preferred to wait and see. As the utmost expression of their reticence, the Allies did not declare war on Moscow, nor did they even break off diplomatic relations, after the Soviet occupation of the eastern Polish territories. As a formal argument for their omission to come up to their guarantees they stated that these had been given to provide against aggression by "a European power" only.[6]

Churchill, the new First Lord of the Admiralty in the Chamberlain Cabinet, offers an illustration of official British conduct. He had publicly denounced the Soviet action, but in a memorandum addressed to the War Cabinet on 25 September, he emphasized the necessity of keeping up correct relations with the Soviet Union. The mere presence of the Red Army, he pointed out, tied down twenty to twenty-five German divisions in the east. In South-eastern Europe, possibly Hitler's next target, the Allies and the Soviet Union had the common interest of supporting the resistance of the countries concerned. In this case "besides the potential eastern front, a potential south-eastern front may be coming into existence, reaching in a crescent from the Gulf of Riga to the head of the Adriatic":

This policy implies a renewal of relations with Russia as the Foreign Secretary has swiftly foreseen. It also compels our adherence to the policy declared by the Prime Minister of not committing ourselves to particular territorial solutions, and concentrating the whole effort of Britain and

---

* This occasion confirmed the final division of Poland as well as the removal of Lithuania into the Soviet sphere of interest.

France upon smashing Hitlerism, and also of making sure that the German terror is not renewed upon the Western democracies for a long time to come.[7]

Within less than a month, the British Government had aligned its Eastern policy to the lines which the French had laid down in the tripartite negotiations the previous summer. The Allies should by all means strive to eliminate the advantages for Germany of the Molotov-Ribbentrop Pact, by limiting Russia's capacity to give assistance to Hitler and by preventing her territorial expansion. This, however, would have to take place without jeopardising relations with Moscow: the "great alliance" might come true one day, in one form or another. Churchill's insight into Britain's real interests, clear by now, was in due time to affect the British attitude toward the Finnish question, once this had reached the agenda of the War Cabinet.

2

At the outbreak of the European war Finland announced her intention to observe "complete neutrality", according to the rules which the Nordic countries had defined in a joint declaration signed in the previous May. The announcement was confirmed by the statement given at the end of the meeting of the Nordic premiers and foreign ministers on 18-19 September 1939 in Copenhagen. "The Nordic Countries are convinced", it concluded, "that neither of the belligerent parties wants any one of these countries to become involved in the hostilities." Further, this solemn document establish-ed that all the Nordic countries had decided to hold to their rights of keeping up their traditional trade contacts with all other states, including those at war—the three Scandinavian countries had made the same decision in 1914.[8]

As Dr Pakaslahti points out, the document rendered the Finns a service: it once more emphasized that their country belonged to the Nordic group of states, and not to the Baltic group. Such geopoli-tical arguments, of course, no longer meant anything to the Soviet Union. But for the belligerents, the Allies in particular, this assu-rance of solidarity was an obvious intimation. Even earlier the Foreign Office had classified the Nordic countries as "pro-Allied" neutrals—adding, however: "unless coerced into benevolent neutrality towards Germany".[9]

Ever since he had been accredited to Helsinki, Snow had closely followed the Finnish press and the German propaganda it mediated. In the autumn of 1939, after the German-Soviet *rapprochement*, this hardly created any problems. In Helsinki too, as the German Minister von Blücher complained, "there were incidents when Germans were insulted and assaulted". Yet Snow surmised that the Finnish press gave more space to German news material than British, and blamed, to Erkko, the Finnish News Bureau.

The Foreign Minister, for his part, had occasion to complain that the BBC broadcasts from London often gave time to groundless rumours on Finnish-Soviet relations, thus spreading panic and aggravating the position of Finland. These protests, appearing from both sides off and on during the first month of the war, were not fortuitous. What they really reflected was the curious undercurrent which had entered the relations of the two countries and found expression in the irritability of both Foreign Minister and envoy. They implied the fact that Britain had suddenly become an outsider in the Baltic area.[10]

What most preoccupied the British was the decline of their trade with Finland. This trend was apt to lead to the end of political influence as well. Together with the French, they now tried to counteract the Germans, who had sent a special envoy to Helsinki to ensure the development of their trade relations with Finland. Snow hastened, on 6 September, to propose to the Foreign Minister a wartime trade agreement similar to that which Britain intended to conclude with each of the Scandinavian countries. Erkko immediately answered in the affirmative, although protesting that the proposal had not been made to Finland at the same time as to the other Nordic countries. Twelve days later the French Minister came to see Erkko with a similar suggestion. Though accepted by the Finns, this initiative, as well as the British one, remained without any practical outcome since the Finnish-Soviet conflict broke out before any negotiations were set in motion.[11]

Ill-prepared for a crisis, the Finnish Government was worried about getting its pre-war orders of war material delivered. Though the blockade orders, at the beginning of the war, were relatively easy,* only one load of war material was shipped to Finland by the beginning of November, and this from France. Finland was blockaded more effectively by British and French bureaucrats than

---

* According to the British blockade orders, it was possible to transport to Finland under a special freight licence goods from Allied as well as neutral countries, provided that in the former case the exporters had permission to export and that the goods were not forwarded to the enemy. The Germans, on the other hand, promised not to prevent Finland from exporting goods to the Allied countries, if this happened on neutral vessels and did not contain contraband. At the beginning they made clear that the import of war material too, even from Britain and France, was allowed provided that the transports were made on neutral ships.[12]

German submarines.* Neither of the Allied governments was, during the first weeks of war, sufficiently interested in Finland to facilitate its task of preparing for the worst.

During the Polish and Baltic crises the newly-born Finnish neutrality had been put to the test and proved successful. The caution and realistic thinking of the then Foreign Minister are acknowledged by Pakaslahti, who, in other respects, does not give an altogether positive assessment of his personality and policies. He refers to the memoirs of von Blücher, who was highly complimentary concerning Erkko[13]; Snow, for his part, characterized him as "energetic, able and very Anglophile". As for the Russians, they had no reason to praise Erkko in these terms. Thanks to the staunchness of the Foreign Minister, Finland emerged from the first weeks of war in a posture that gave neither belligerent the chance to blame it for partiality. But with the arrival of the months when Finland had to clarify the key problem of its foreign policy—namely, its relations with the Soviet Union—Erkko's idea of neutrality, more legal than political as it was, proved insufficient.

The British and French foreign ministries were convinced that one implication of the Molotov-Ribbentrop Pact was to regulate German-Soviet relations within the Baltic area. The negative attitude of the Soviet Government towards the proposed fortification of Åland, its extensive demands for military bases at the Moscow negotiations and, last but not least, the reports of Allied naval attachés, according to which it was planned that Leningrad should become the main ship-building centre and naval base of the Soviet Union—all were plausible indications that the Russians were not intending to abandon the Baltic to the Germans.[14]

In this situation, any Western counter-measures against pressure on the Baltic states and Finland, inasmuch as such moves were ever considered, were restricted to words. In order to refute the rumours alleging that the Allies, at the Moscow negotiations, had tried to bargain at the expense of the border states, the British legations in Riga, Tallinn and Helsinki were instructed, on 7 September, to inform the respective governments of the real contents of the Soviet demands.[15] After this washing of its hands the Foreign Office maintained a studious silence. Nothing serious was done to disperse the clouds gathering over the Baltic and Finland.

Gripenberg relates in his memoirs that he was not informed until two weeks later that there was still a willingness in London to help Finland. These good tidings were disclosed to him on 21

* See below, p. 35.

September by Collier, who assured him that the Finnish arms
desiderata would now, as well as in the future, be met with no
complications. He added, according to the Minister, that it was
"in Britain's interest that Finland felt itself sufficiently strong
to resist pressure from outside."[16] The same day, *The Times*
published reports from Helsinki of Russian battleships manoeuvring
off the Estonian coast.* "These reports have increased the uneasiness
here over the position of Latvia and Estonia", the report went on.
"Finland does not feel in imminent danger, although travellers have
seen Soviet troops, artillery and munitions moving by road in the
direction of the Finnish frontier."

The same day, 21 September, Collier at the Foreign Office
completed an interesting memorandum. He had been asked to
survey the possibilities of Finland and the Baltic States defending
themselves against the Soviet Union and Germany. According to
his conclusions, the situation was difficult but, as far as Finland was
concerned, hopeful: the Finns, he wrote, were one of the few small
nations in Europe who still had some courage left, and who were
ready to defend their independence and neutrality.

Here Collier expressed for the first time a theme which often
recurred later when the moral import of the Winter War was being
assessed: in holding their own against the aggressor, the Finns
would set an example for minor neutral states and put an end to
the defeatism prevailing in Europe. Moreover, Collier was ready to
assign an altogether thankless task to the Finns: they were to be
encouraged to co-operate with Estonians, so that these two, possibly
together with the other Baltic peoples, would be in a position to
resist the pressure of their powerful neighbours. Britain was to
support them by strengthening her trade relations with Finland
and the Baltic countries, and by providing them with necessary war
material. In other words, she had to safeguard transit through
Sweden, or start using a new supply route *via* Petsamo, where the
Finns were planning to build a railway line from Rovaniemi. As
the first solid measure, Collier proposed that his government should
immediately facilitate the export of strategic goods to Finland and
consider participation in the construction of the Petsamo railway,
if possible by delivering the necessary rails.[17]

In practice the initiative resulted in a request addressed to the
officials, asking these to approve all supply orders coming from

---

* Units of the Soviet Baltic Fleet were at the moment searching for the Polish
submarine *Orzel*, which had been interned at Tallinn but had escaped.

Finland. As for the Petsamo railway, the proposal foundered instantly: the Ministry of Supply considered that it could not afford the amount of steel needed for the construction. Still, Collier's memorandum is worth recording, both for its uniqueness and for its date; the paper indeed does not represent an independent initiative of the Foreign Office Northern Department only.

As it turned out, that very same day a high-level team at the Admiralty began a study on the prospects of the Royal Navy breaking through to the Baltic—this was the so-called Catherine Plan drawn up by the new First Lord of the Admiralty. Gripenberg, who had heard rumours of Churchill's project, connected them immediately with the offer of assistance made to him at the Foreign Office: "I asked whether this was also the opinion of the Admiralty", he noted in his diary, "which was confirmed by Mr. Collier."[18]

During the next few weeks, the political situation changed at such speed that the Admiralty plans had to be scrapped even before they were finished. The Baltic harbours, where as late as in September the British might have expected an enthusiastic welcome, were occupied by the Soviet Navy by the middle of October. Nowhere else, not even in Finland, could there have been such a need to receive Churchill's fleet that the attendant risks of German naval and aerial counter-attacks could be disregarded. Moreover, the Catherine Plan was made useless by the long and severe winter, which forced the German to transfer their loading of ore from Luleå to Narvik, within reach of the Royal Navy.

3

In Helsinki the warnings of the Foreign Office met with a seeming lack of interest. When discussing the political situation with Snow on 16 September, the Secretary General of the Foreign Ministry, Tapio Voionmaa, had pointed out that his Ministry entertained a view "which diverged in many respects" from that of the British. The very next day, though greatly alarmed by the occupation of Eastern Poland, Erkko expressed his satisfaction with Molotov's announcement that the Soviet Union would continue to adhere to its neutral policy towards Finland. The optimism was heightened by the information according to which Moscow was prepared to resume the trade negotiations with Finland which had been interrupted in March.[19]

This turn of events gave the British cause to complain of the wishful thinking and naiveté of the Finns in general, and of Erkko in particular. Rumours of these insinuations soon reached the

Foreign Ministry in Helsinki, occasioning a circular telegram to the Finnish legations abroad, which were cautioned that "the British official propaganda was systematically spreading prejudicial information concerning us and the Russian intentions towards Finland."[20]

In fact, Helsinki had scarcely any illusions as to Russian intentions. One of the earliest alarms had been given by the Finnish envoy in Paris who, in his first comments on the Molotov-Ribbentrop Pact, had reported that the United States Ambassador William C. Bullitt had recommended caution because, to his knowledge, Finland was one of the subjects of discussion in Moscow. The French, on the other hand, saw the situation in a somewhat different light. Magny, who went to see Voionmaa right after the occupation of Eastern Poland, believed that the Soviet Union intended to check Germany's eastward march but would not attack its other neighbours. The French envoy was to maintain this point of view until the very beginning of the Winter War.[21]

But Snow, growing more pessimistic day by day, reported with obvious satisfaction his success in shaking the self-confidence of Erkko. The envoy thus described a discussion with him after the Soviet occupation of Poland: "Mr. Erkko exclaimed: 'Who will save us from this horrible situation?' I replied that I did not see that anyone could relieve Mr. Erkko of the main responsibility of dealing with this problem."[22]

By the end of the month Snow's estimations were proving to have been accurate. On 27 September Estonia, soon followed by the other two Baltic states, acceded to the Soviet demands for military bases. As London had realised, the strategic position of both Finland and Sweden had deteriorated to an alarming degree, now that Soviet aircraft, not to speak of the Red Navy with its submarines, could operate within a short distance of their capitals. The mounting pessimism led to strange reactions at the Foreign Office. Thus Collier, whose Baltic report had lost its relevance in less than a week, even accused the Finns of endangering their own security: "They have put themselves almost beyond help, through not helping the Estonians."[23]

Snow too saw the Finnish situation as beyond hope. The day when the Soviet troops took control of their new bases south of the Gulf of Finland, he prophesied to London that, in case of a Russian attack, Finland would get help from nowhere: the Red Navy would blockade her coasts, and the country would be left to the mercy of the Soviet Union. He concluded his telegram on a dismal note: "I do not exclude [the] possibility that Finns, with Poland as example, may submit to spoliation without resisting."

As Snow reported two days later that even Mannerheim found compromise more advisable than armed resistance, the realism of the Finnish attitude was duly acknowledged at the Foreign Office. "With the Russians installed on the Estonian coast, it would have been folly for the Finns to take any other line than this", D. W. Lascelles, Collier's closest collaborator, commented—with the thoughtful addition: *"But such folly might have benefited us."*[24]

Meanwhile, in Helsinki the authorities were vexed by the panicky words and deeds of the British envoy, who had started clamouring for the evacuation of his countrymen. Erkko soon saw every rumour coming from London as Snow's doing. Accordingly, when the BBC broadcast the news of Erkko's invitation to Moscow for negotiations on 2 October (two days before the invitation was actually issued), he hinted to Snow that the rumour had originated from the British Legation and was expressly intended to endanger Finnish interests.

This discussion, unusually vehement as it was, resulted in a 700-word telegraphic report to the Foreign Office. Snow charged Erkko with going too far, making remarks not only against himself but against Lord Halifax as well. The Foreign Secretary was at fault, because the British Government had engaged in negotiations in Moscow behind Finland's back, and this in spite of Halifax's assurances to the contrary. Mentioning this, Erkko had grumbled that there was "not a single state" that Finland could trust any longer. He had maintained that Lord Halifax had deliberately hindered Finnish arms supplies.* Snow reported:

Minister for Foreign Affairs said that all this showed unfriendly attitude on part of His Majesty's Government, and that instead of latter's doing their best not to aggravate relations between Finland and Russia, British propaganda on the contrary was deliberately trying to make capital of its own out of Finland's plight...[26]

Collier tried to psycho-analyse Erkko's "surprising language," supposing that "he has misjudged the situation, and had better try to put the blame on someone else". But he perceived that the envoy himself, by his evacuation plans, had aroused the indignation of the Foreign Ministry. These plans, having aroused resentment in Helsinki, now enraged the Foreign Office as well, to the extent that Snow's suitability for his post was questioned.[27]

Whatever Erkko had in mind when arranging the interview with Snow, the impact on the envoy was obvious at any rate. With an

---

* A reference to some forty anti-aircraft guns which had been ordered from *Bofors* and which it had then been proposed should be delivered directly to Finland. Halifax had opposed the delivery, insisting that the guns were needed in Britain or by the Allies.[25]

astonishing display of self-criticism, Snow ended by unreservedly
siding with Erkko and by imploring the Foreign Office to take
steps to put an end to false reports on Finland. Now that this
country had been left on its own, the British had better be quiet,
Snow concluded, adding that the Foreign Minister had assured
that he would remain optimistic "if his task was not complicated
from outside"

4

There was a genuine feeling of surprise in London when the Finnish
Government, after having finally been invited to send representatives
to Moscow (on 6 October), ordered mobilization as a sign that it
would rather resort to arms than accept the way of Estonia. At the
Foreign Office Erkko's optimism was now characterized as being
"almost fatuous", being based on the false belief that the German
interest in Finland would keep the Russians at bay. Snow, on the
contrary, reported that he had just met both Erkko and Risto Ryti,
then Director General of the Bank of Finland, and that both of
them had lost all illusions of German support. Had Hitler not
that same day made a speech in the Reichstag, mentioning the
Scandinavian countries as friendly states, but omitting Finland?*[28]

Magny's first impressions seemed less emotional; he believed that
Finland would accept the Soviet demands to the islands in the
Gulf of Finland.† Alluding to the fact that their appeals lacked
resonance in Moscow, both London and Paris agreed not to resort
to pressure. Actually no such support was asked for by Finland:
indeed it would have been contrary to the line of Erkko, who disliked any approach to the belligerents that could compromise
Finnish neutrality. Thus Gripenberg, when addressing a memorandum to the Foreign Office on 9 October, merely called attention to the Soviet aspirations which might endanger the security
of all Northern Europe.[30] This point of view, that the Soviet
offensive would not stop at Finland but continue to comprise
all of Scandinavia, was to be one of the main arguments of Finnish
diplomacy when appealing for Allied and Nordic assistance.

The Russians, in fact, obviously never aimed at Scandinavia,
which was not included in their sphere of interest as delineated by

---

* The exact nature of the Molotov-Ribbentrop Pact was not yet known in
Helsinki. The representative of the Auswärtiges Amt, however, had informed
the Finnish envoy, 9 October 1939, that Germany had left Finland outside
its sphere of interest.[29]
† The Secretary General of the French Foreign Ministry, Alexis Léger (the 1960
Nobel prize-winning author Saint-John Perse) showed Magny's cable to the
Finnish Minister on 10 October.

Molotov and Ribbentrop. What they were out for was to secure, and this time once for all, the outposts for the defence of Leningrad and the Gulf of Finland. By now, however, their claims were much more extensive than they had been in 1937 and 1938. As the Finnish negotiator J. K. Paasikivi, on 12 October met his Soviet counter-parts—none less than Stalin and Molotov in person—for the first time, it was explained to him that they would propose to Finland a treaty of mutual assistance on a similar pattern to those made with the Baltic states. As a reason for Soviet precautions, Stalin gave the possibility that "England or Germany might exert pressure upon Finland in order to force her to participate in an aggression against the Soviet Union."[31]

On the dry reply by Paasikivi that Finland would refuse such a pact because it would not suit her line of Nordic neutrality, the Kremlin leaders put forward some territorial desiderata. Besides the Gulf islands, they demanded the annexation to the Soviet Union of the Finnish frontier zone on the Karelian Isthmus up to the line of Koivisto (Bjorko)–Vuoksi, and the lease for thirty years of a base on the northern coast of the Gulf of Finland, primarily the town of Hanko with its surrounding Territory.* In addition, they argued that the Finnish-Soviet frontier on the Arctic Ocean was not satisfactory, and asked the Finns to cede the north-western part of Kalastajasaarento (or Rybachi) Peninsula. In return for these concessions, they promised Finland a generous parcel of territory in Soviet Karelia.

When returning to Helsinki for consultations, Paasikivi cautioned his fellow-countrymen that this time the Russians might use force to get what they wanted, but he realized that the majority of the Cabinet, supported by public opinion, resisted the idea of consenting to Soviet demands.† In addition to sentimental and political reasons against taking the responsibility for abandoning national territory, there were fears that these claims, as well as those made on the Baltic States, would only be a prelude to the total occupation, if not sovietization, of the country. The cession of Koivisto, the western flank of the Finnish main line of defence on the Isthmus, and above all that of Hanko, a bridgehead on the Finnish mainland, was considered impossible. The only points on which Helsinki was ready to satisfy the Russians were those concerning most of the

---

* Referring to the British nickel concession in Petsamo, they now spoke of a "concession" to be given for military purposes.

† One of the most uncompromising among the Cabinet members was the Foreign Minister, himself the principal owner and editor-in-chief of the country's biggest and most influential newspaper *Helsingin Sanomat*.

Gulf islands, Kalastajasaarento, and the southernmost corner of
the Isthmus at Terijoki (Zelenogorsk).

This, however, was not enough for the Kremlin. The people
there were even more unhappy when Paasikivi took along with
him for the second round of negotiations (from 21 to 26 October) a
man considered notoriously anti-Communist: Väinö Tanner, the
leader of the Finnish Social Democrats. Stalin and Molotov were
still prepared to trade by giving up the original demand for a
pact of assistance and by limiting somewhat their territorial claims
on the Isthmus. On a later occasion Stalin even seemed to abandon
Hanko, on which the Finns were adamant, and to accept an
additional island near the mainland instead.

But the Soviet leaders were obviously in a hurry. Irritated by
Finland's obstinacy and obvious will to resist—as demonstrated,
besides the mobilization, by fortification works and by evacuation
of civilians from the areas near the eastern border—they were
growing impatient. Well before the middle of November, when the
Finnish delegates made a third unsuccessful trip to Moscow,
there were signs on the Soviet side of increasing pressure, such as
activization of anti-Finnish radio propaganda, frontier incidents,
and concentration of Red army units along the Murmansk railway.
Anybody familiar with the power politics of the time had reason to
expect the worst. The situation aroused more attention in London
than in Paris. Of particular interest was Snow's statement that the
Finns took a "purely fatalistic" view of their position, adhering
to their decision to stand or fall defending their rights. This policy—
maybe not the best possible one for the Finns themselves, as the
Foreign Office observed—might, however, serve British interests.
D. W. Lascelles crystallized this view:

In Estonia the Russians have got all they wanted by 'peaceful' means. With
comparatively little shock to world opinion they have converted Estonia
into a virtual Soviet protectorate, which will probably be wholly absorbed
before long. Had Estonia resisted, the final result would have been the same,
but the effect on world opinion would have been very significant. Do not the
same considerations apply to Finland—with even greater force, in view of
the greater interest taken in that country both by the U.S.A. and by the
other Scandinavian states? And would not the armed invasion of Finland
by Soviet forces be at least as likely to embroil Russia with Germany as any
form of temporisation by the Finnish Government? Moreover, any military
campaign by the Soviet Union, even against a country as weak as Finland,
would absorb Soviet oil, food and war material which might otherwise go to
Germany and would—temporarily at any rate—distract the attention of the
Soviet Government from other fields—e.g. Central Asia—where their
expansionist activities would be far more harmful to ourselves. It seems to

me conceivable that a Soviet war of conquest in Finland might sufficiently rouse public opinion in the U.S.A. to bring about, if not a rupture of American-Soviet relations, at any rate an American boycott of raw materials for the Soviet Union; and this would be of great value to us.[32]

In the Northern Department it was proposed that, if the Finns were to be given any advice at all, they had to be informed that it would be more useful in the long run to fight than to retreat. "I am convinced that, if we were to advise the Finns not to resist", Collier observed on 10 October, "we should be playing the German game." Three days later, when the German short-wave stations refused to broadcast Erkko's speech to America, this argument seemed beyond doubt: Hitler wanted nothing else but the surrender of Finland.[33]

The Northern Department seems to have succeeded in convincing the Foreign Secretary of the need for a policy more actively favourable to Finland. This was largely due to the strong reactions which the pressure against Finland had aroused in the Scandinavian countries and the United States. The decision to look for means of helping Finland was certainly not based on sentiment. Chamberlain's private archives, as we are told by his biographer, do not give any indication that he ever gave a thought to Finland, except from the Allied point of view.[34] As far as Halifax is concerned, it is of no avail to look for the name of Finland in his autobiography, which covers his entire period of office up to 1940.[35] We should bear in mind that by this time both ministers were shadowed by Churchill, a member of the War Cabinet since the beginning of September, and that Churchill, to a greater extent than anyone else, represented the opinion, supported largely both by the majority as well as the opposition, that the German-Soviet friendship would be of short duration.

The somewhat lukewarm manner in which Lord Halifax had received Gripenberg's complaints about Soviet behaviour was not likely to encourage Helsinki to believe that the Allies, any more than Germany, would interfere with Moscow's pressure. At about the same time the Finnish Foreign Ministry received a report from Paris pointing out that the Western Powers had refrained from promising the Polish Government that it would guarantee the return of the Soviet-occupied eastern territories: "The French and British Governments are eagerly looking for the opportunity to resume negotiations in Moscow," wrote the Finnish Minister, Harri Holma. "That is why war has not been declared against Russia and that is why France and Britain are doing nothing to help the Baltic countries..."[36]

After the earlier British hesitations it gave Helsinki courage to hear that Halifax had decided to support Finland. Indeed twice in the course of October he stated personally to the Soviet Ambassador that it would be impossible for Britain to improve political and trade relations with the Soviet Union if the latter were to attack Finland.[37] At the same time the Foreign Secretary had taken care to urge the delivery of the war materials needed by Finland. In a letter addressed to the Minister of Defence on 17 October he demanded both the export licence for pre-war orders and the immediate delivery of the artillery tractors recently ordered by the Finns. In this context he put forth the principle which the Foreign Office was to adhere to until the very end of the Winter War:

You will know all the political and strategic reasons that make it urgently desirable for us to do what we can to.strengthen the position of Finland at this time, and I am sure you will do all you can to see to it that as much of this material as can reasonably be spared in view of our own requirements (excluding those of doubtfully possible allies such as Turkey and Portugal).[38]

Meanwhile the Foreign Office was rather vexed to learn that the Finnish Government had requested Americans to interfere. A personal peace appeal to Moscow by President Roosevelt had indeed been sent, but had been rebuffed outright. The British felt fear of losing prestige; it was also conjectured that any attempt to mediate at the moment would only serve German interests.

While trying desperately to interest the British in their case, the Finns, it was felt in London, were lacking in diplomatic tact. Erkko, for instance, had not been altogether true to the facts in "disclosing" to Snow that the Germans had put pressure on him, and threatened that they would occupy Finland and all Scandinavia without hesitation in order to prevent Soviet expansion. Gripenberg, for his part, embarrassed Butler by telling him frankly that the Finns considered the growing Russian strength the greatest danger to Europe, and expressing the wish that Britain would take a more uncompromising stand against Germany.[38] "In these circumstances", Collier concluded on 15 October, "we are under no obligation to do more for the Finns than is needed in our own interests."[40]

For the time being, at least, no one was able to tell what was needed in British interests. At the initiative of the Northern Department of the Foreign Office, the military experts were called to investigate the matter.[41] Meanwhile the question was brought into new light, when the British Minister in Helsinki surprised the Foreign Office by suggesting that, in case the Soviet Union should open hostilities against Finland, Britain should react by breaking off diplomatic relations or by declaring war. Further, he suggested that Japan should be persuaded to attack the Soviet Union.

The Russian demands had by now reached the ears of the Foreign Office. The conditions were considered severe but, as Gripenberg told Halifax, as far as the Finns were concerned, there was room for compromise. The War Cabinet therefore showed no interest in Snow's initiative. At the meeting of 22 October it was generally allowed that Soviet influence and Bolshevism might spread to Scandinavia and the Baltic—a possibility of which Gripenberg and Snow had often warned the Foreign Office. But by now it was also being suggested that Soviet Fleet bases and the strengthening of Soviet positions in the Baltic would tie down a larger part of the German Fleet in the north, which would be most welcome to Britain.[42]

Halifax made use of Snow's initiative in order to have the question dealt with by military experts: the War Cabinet asked the Chiefs of Staff Committee to examine the advantages and drawbacks to Britain of an official or unofficial conflict with the Soviet Union, if the latter were to attack Finland or the Scandinavian countries. The resulting report of 30 October, written by soldiers not by politicians, was to set the trend to British policy towards Finland during the entire Winter War.

The main question put to the Chiefs of Staff was whether the British could safeguard the rear of Norway and Sweden against German attack, if these countries were to intervene in Finland's favour in the event of a Soviet attack. To begin with, the Chiefs of Staff did not believe that the Soviet Union would resort to force: aggression against Finland or Scandinavia, they stated in their report, would be "a very formidable military enterprise" on which the Russians were unlikely to embark at this time of the year. Even so, *if directed against Finland only, the attack would not constitute any military threat to the Allies.*

At the next stage, however, the Soviet Union might penetrate into Sweden and Norway, where it might have as its chief targets the Kiruna-Gällivare ore fields and the harbour of Narvik. Now these important sources of raw material and the supply line might fall into the hands of the enemy. Besides, the security of the British Isles might be threatened by Soviet bases on the Norwegian coast. "*A small British force, say a brigade group, based on the Narvik-Boden railway and operating in support of the Norwegians and Swedes, might have an effect out of all proportion to its size*", the report continued. "*. . We could, however, afford no assistance to Finland against Russian aggression.*"[43]

The Chiefs of Staff suggested that an eventual Soviet invasion of Northern Scandinavia would force the Germans, if only for ideological reasons, to protect the Germanic population of the area by occupying the southern parts of Norway and Sweden. This might endanger the military position of the Allies, without necessarily putting an end to German-Soviet co-operation. Therefore, Britain and France could not afford to break off relations with the Soviet Union under the prevailing circumstances. If it became clear that the Russians intended to penetrate Scandinavia, and Britain wanted to prevent it, the Government would have to make it definitely clear that it had decided to resist the aggressor. On the other hand, the Chiefs of Staff warned, *"no assurance of support should be given to Finland alone, or to Sweden in connection with the threat to Finland."*

The committee report was unanimously accepted by the War Cabinet on 1 November. Halifax said that it was in complete accord with his own views:

It was true that there was a certain amount of support in ideological circles for Mr. Snow's attitude that we should champion Finland as a small state which was being made the victim of aggression. The answer to such criticism was that we must take first things first. The only argument which carried real weight was...whether a stand against Russian aggression would bring us accretions of strength from neutrals.

...We should not be justified in adding to our present burden by declaring war on Russia unless and until the United States of America had definitely ranged herself on our side.[44]

In defence of this view, the Foreign Office formulated the argumentation which Halifax later cabled to Snow as his main instructions. While attempting to protect "a relatively small power" (Poland), it said, the British had become engaged in a life-and-death struggle themselves. If, in this situation, they were now to take in hand more obligations than they could manage, they might be overthrown, and from then on there would be no hope left for any small state in Europe. But if they won the fight, there would be every hope of survival for the majority of small states, Finland included.

Thus, the Foreign Secretary concluded, there is, in fact, *"no real inconsistency between proclaiming that our aim is to end the threat of aggression in general, and refraining from action which might place it beyond our power to win the war, and so achieve our aim."*[45]

---

* Members were the General Chief of Staff (General Sir Edmund Ironside, the Chief of Staff of the R.A.F. (Air Chief Marshal Sir Cyril Newall), and the Naval Chief of Staff (Admiral Sir Dudley Pound; while this report was being composed his substitute was Admiral T. S. V. Phillips).

5

When the Finnish delegates had made their second trip to Moscow, the belief in a peaceful settlement was strong in London. Even the pessimistic British Minister in Helsinki seemed to have changed his mind, declaring that the Soviet Union would not attack. Lord Halifax himself interpreted Molotov's speech on 31 October as proof that the Russians were not inclined to undertake any adventure.[46]

The tone of the Soviet press and radio eluded London as well as Paris, and its increasingly hostile note concerning Finland remained unnoticed. But although the Finns did not return to Moscow after the third trip in the middle of November, most observers believed that nothing would happen. The repeated assurances by the Finns that they were prepared to negotiate, as well as the belief that the Russians were bluffing and not going to start operations with winter coming on, gave reason to trust that the situation would remain unchanged for the time being.

Meanwhile, no consignment of the material ordered by the Finns had been shipped from Britain. Whitehall at first refused to deliver almost all pre-war orders, including the remaining six of the thirty-two small tanks ordered from Vickers, as a result of British pressure put on Mannerheim during his visit to England in 1936. These goods were retained on the same grounds on which the Finns had been refused the delivery of some thirty Spitfire fighters and fifteen to thirty 15-ton tanks the previous summer: Britain was preparing for war and needed all its production for arming herself and her allies. In France it was not even a question of self-interest but of an over-enthusiastic observance of the blockade instructions. Only after long delays did the Finns get some second-hand armament such as old rifles, or the 12-inch naval guns bought from a tsarist battleship interned at Bizerta.[47]

In desperation, Gripenberg had visited the Foreign Office on 25 October, making it clear that Finland would accept arms from anywhere that she could get them, and was even negotiating with the Germans in the hope of bringing in, through their territory, material bought from Italy, Hungary and Yugoslavia. This, however, failed to speed up the British deliveries, since scarcely anybody believed that the Germans were still interested in Finland. On the contrary, German co-operation was likely to endanger Finnish acquisition of arms, since the Allies had every reason to look forward to the opportunity of disclosing German double-dealing to Moscow.[48]

As the crisis showed signs of abating, it was conjectured that the

Russians might try to force Finland to make a choice between concessions and her continuing to mobilize, which would harm her economy. Even in the latter eventuality it was found that Britain would be unable to help Finland financially.[49] The authorities in London were fully aware that the Allies had done nothing to build up the defence of the country. Nonetheless, the Finns were at no time warned by British diplomacy of the riskiness of their venture— on the contrary, they were encouraged. Lord Halifax, as Gripenberg reported on the Soviet demands, '..*considers it improbable that [the U.S.S.R.] would cause a military conflict"* and (10 October); "..*expressed his assumption that we would never agree to a naval base on the Finnish mainland"* (25 October), and "..*his general impression being that Russia would never attack"* (10 November). When Collier, who was present at the last discussion, took the liberty of telling Halifax that he had been more hopeful a couple of days earlier than after Snow's most recent reports, the Foreign Secretary turned to Gripenberg and said that his optimism was based on "other sources of informations."[50]

Were these sources the reports from military attachés? The following cable dated 2 November 1939 gives us an example of similar views:

At lunch British military attaché Colonel Fraser said that *if Finland just says no, USSR will not dare attack*. He based his argument on experiences gained of USSR army in Poland and Baltic countries. He said that apart from its select mechanized forces USSR army had made quite miserable impression.[51]

French military men also continued to encourage the Finns with the usual arguments that the leadership of the Red Army, weakened by Stalinist purges, was not equal to the job before it; that it was not organized for a war of aggression, and that the Russians could not tie their forces down in a country which might keep up resistance even after occupation. In fact, the British and the French were by no means the only diplomatic representatives to express views of this nature.[52]

In Helsinki, the circumstances were exceptional, as we have seen, since both the British and the French envoy pictured the situation rather differently from their respective Foreign Ministries. After the outbreak of war Snow reminded the Foreign Office of the caution he had displayed during the autumn, in a long telegram which may be interpreted as a disguised accusation against London for neglecting to do anything to prevent the war.* As for the French

Minister, he remained optimistic to the end, although he too recommended to the Finns that it would be better to yield. It was in the style of Magny, former Prefect of Champagne and Chief of the *Sûreté nationale*, to stress the internal aspects of the crisis: in the Government, the hard line was represented by the Minister of Defence, the "anti-Russian" Niukkanen who, a Karelian himself, resisted territorial concessions; whereas the Foreign Minister, Magny maintained, was basically opposed to Niukkanen.

At the Quai d'Orsay, Magny's candid remarks to the effect that "the Finns are foolish to take so firm a line" caused a certain irritation.[53] In the absence of French sources, it remains unknown who were displeased. According to Holma's reports, Léger actually shared the envoy's belief that the Russians would not attack, but that Soviet security called for the bases requested—thus the wisest move for the Finns would be to give in. Léger reflected that Finland was in for a long and strenuous period of tension: for her it would be better if the war were to end as soon as possible (in the defeat of Germany), whereas for the Soviet Union it would be more profitable if it went on as long as possible. "Moscow knows", Léger said to Holma on 8 November, "that at the very moment Germany is on its knees or probably being bolshevized—*the Western Powers, which are not yet weakened, with all civilized countries, will launch a joint campaign against Bolshevism and Russia.*"[54]

Holma pointed out that Léger "loves speculation and conjecture." Yet his picture of the future was largely accepted in the leading Allied circles. Their nearest spokesman for the Finns was the British envoy in Helsinki who, in an official telegram despatched to the Foreign Office, had the courage to maintain that "Stalin is a more likely winner than Herr Hitler, and, if left to his own devices, is accordingly possibly the greater menace of the two."[55]

The Soviet Union, Snow pointed out on 20 October to Voionmaa, did not expect its understanding with Germany to last: "If England wins the war and the Nazi system collapses in Germany, England will easily reach a working agreement with Germany. Soviet expansion too will be contained."[56]

Addressed to the Finns, these comments were naturally intended

---

* "Attention was drawn to the shortcomings of the Minister for Foreign Affairs (Erkko) and the country's lack of experience. Emphasis was laid...on the fact that main risk in the situation was the light-hearted assumption by either side that the other would in no circumstances fight. How far any of these conclusions were accepted by His Majesty's Government I have no means of judging, but...the conclusions have all been borne out to the letter by facts, and...Germany and Russia have been acting hand-in-glove." (Snow's tel. no. 230/17.12.1939, to the F.O.; FO 371/23696/7578).

to strengthen their resistance. Faithful to their traditional role of
"outpost", they were once again engaged in the first line of
defence of "western civilization". Yet, from the Finnish point of
view, the situation at the start of the Winter War could not have
been less promising; German power was growing and Hitler's
relations with the Soviet Union were at their height. German
neutrality proved illusory—instead of permitting the transit of war
material to Finland, the Germans volunteered to assist Russian
submarines which were operating against Finnish ships in the Gulf
of Bothnia: for unknown reasons the Soviet Government finally
rejected this offer. But though never effective in the military sphere,
the German-Soviet entente hindered Finnish defence efforts in the
field of diplomacy. There was, of course, always the possibility
that the Russians would threaten to draw closer in its relations to
the Third Reich if the Allies interfered in the Finnish-Soviet
conflict.[57]

The Kremlin's diplomatic offensive seemed problematical—
especially in London, where Ivan Maisky, one of the top Soviet
foreign representatives, acted as Gripenberg's counterpart. The
Russians certainly had no doubts that their position in London was
still quite strong. The British entertained an exaggerated view of
Soviet capacity and willingness to help the German war effort, and
were outlining a trade agreement with Moscow, hoping thus to
direct the principal part of Soviet exports to their own ports and
not to Germany. It was hardly to be expected that the Foreign
Office would lightly put a strain on these negotiations, only
because the Finnish question—"the only cloud in the sky of British-
Russian relations", as Maisky put it—was now growing bigger
and blacker.[58]

Maisky was a welcome guest in London political circles, even
during the troublesome autumn of 1939, not only because he
represented a great power but also because of his personal wit and
charm. Among the public personages encountered by Gripenberg,
he often found ideas which had been implanted by the Russian.
These ideas were not easy to fend off, since Maisky, a former Soviet
Minister in Helsinki, was well acquinted with Finland and the
Finns. For instance Hugh Dalton, who later, as Minister of Economic
Warfare, appeared to be rather reserved towards the Finns pictured
them as follows, the idea obviously originating from Maisky:

A visitor to Finland was being driven a long distance through the country
in a droshky. The driver drove him for twenty miles saying nothing. Then
he pulled up, dismounted and spoke to a man working in a field beside the
road. He asked the man: "How are you getting on?" The man said:

"Pretty well, but the ground is very hard." He was ploughing and there was a frost. The driver then mounted his seat and drove without a word for another twenty miles. Then turning to his fare, he said: "That man was my brother." Then he drove on for another twenty miles in silence. Then, turning to his fare again, he said: "I had not seen him for thirty years", and then without another word, he drove on to the end of the journey. "That", said Maisky, "is what the Finns are like."[59]

One week before the war, Gripenberg still found himself on Maisky's tracks. "I think you should try to reach a kind of understanding with Soviet Russia before the war [in the west] really starts", R. A. Butler said to him thoughtfully during a discussion at the Foreign Office, "for once that happens, it is to be feared that Russia will venture an aggressive action against you."

Butler's advice, which the Finnish Minister felt to be inspired by Maisky, did not concern the immediate future; the Soviet Union, he said, would not attack now, and if it did, Sweden or maybe even the United States would help Finland at least by giving war material. "And ourselves—we would never allow *Scandinavia* to be threatened," he concluded, selecting his words carefully, "*I think you have a very strong position.*"[60]

The following Monday morning, 27 November, it became known that the Soviet Union had accused Finland the night before of shelling Soviet territory at Mainila village on the Isthmus, causing casualties to the Red Army. Halifax summoned Maisky in the afternoon and asked for prompt settling of the incident, referring to information from Helsinki that it was due to a misunderstanding on the part of the Russians. Maisky replied that this was out of the question: the facts had been examined and the Finns were guilty. The dialogue thereby ended in mutual menaces, Halifax threatening a deadlock in British-Soviet relations, and Maisky bursting into bitter charges against the British Government and press which he held responsible for Finnish obduracy.[61]

After this uneasy *tête-à-tête* the Soviet Ambassador failed to appear at the Foreign Office for weeks, leaving the entire field to Gripenberg. In his memoirs he openly confessed the reason:

During the previous seven years of my work in London as Ambassador of the USSR I had lived through quite a number of anti-Soviet storms, but that which followed 30 November 1939 broke all records.[62]

The discussion with Maisky seems to have given Halifax food for thought. Receiving the Norwegian League of Nations delegate C. J. Hambro a few minutes later, he suddenly said: "Do you think, in the North, that the Finnish Government is composed of sensible people?"[63] Halifax had, it is true, negotiated with Germans at Berchtesgaden, but he was still surprised by the Soviet intransigence as well as by the incredible stubbornness of the Finns. He had to give serious thought to the question whether the Finns were not sensible, or indeed whether they were downright crazy, as had been argued among his own officials.

Unlike the Admiralty and the War Office, which showed no concern, the Foreign Office had started outlining the prospect of retaining British influence in the Baltic by means of the Finnish resistance. No illusions were entertained over the final outcome of the conflict, but it was still considered possible that the Finns might delay the penetration of hostile forces into the northern parts of the Baltic, and show their Scandinavian neighbours how to defend themselves.

France had no comparable Baltic interests, and the Finnish situation consequently failed to arouse as much immediate attention in Paris as in London. What finally woke up the French Government was the Finnish resistance and its emotional appeal to public opinion, which for the first time seemed to enable the Allies to mobilize world opinion against the aggressor.

III

THE RED ARMY ATTACKS

December 1939

1

In the early hours of 30 November 1939, Red Army troops crossed the Finnish border at more than twenty different points on the Karelian Isthmus between the Gulf of Finland and Lake Ladoga and along the eastern frontier between Ladoga and the Arctic Ocean. In spite of the darkness of the day, the Soviet air force attacked several targets within Finnish territory, Helsinki included, causing a number of civilian casualties.[1]

Although the action of the Russian land and air forces was backed up by a total blockade of Finnish ports and coasts, the invasion was neither preceded nor succeeded by any declaration of war. Not until the third day of hostilities was the nature of the conflict clarified by the Soviet news media. A "Democratic People's Government" had been created under the premiership of a veteran Finnish Communist emigrant, Otto Ville Kuusinen, and established at Terijoki, by now occupied by Red troops; this government was immediately recognized by Moscow and called for Soviet help in the "liberation" of Finland.

Instead of a *Blitzkrieg* and a quick march on Helsinki, which was generally expected, the Soviet offensive developed into a long and difficult campaign, lasting nearly through the winter of 1939-40. After the first uncertain days of the conflict, the Finnish troops, although poorly equipped, managed to bring the Red Army to a halt, mainly at distances of between thirty-five and seventy-five miles from the border. Besides the occupation of the Gulf islands in the south, it was only in the extreme north that the Russians gained a decisive victory by capturing, with superior forces, the port of Petsamo and the area surrounding it, thus barring Finland's only access to the world's oceans.

In the south on the Isthmus, where the Finns had concentrated the bulk of their ten infantry divisions, they were more equal in numbers with the Soviet troops, good fighters but poorly led (five Finnish divisions against fourteen infantry divisions, one mechanized armoured corps, and three tank brigades of the Red Army*).

---

* For the strengths of the two armies in the last phase of the Campaign, see pp. 100-1.

They were thus able, before Christmas, to put a stop to the enemy's advance in front of their main defence barrier, proudly called the "Mannerheim Line" after the Field-Marshal who, on the first day of the fighting, had been appointed Commander-in-Chief of the Finnish forces. The Red Army was halted there for the next two months, gaining the time needed for regroupment and reorganization before resuming their offensive.

Meanwhile along their eastern border the Finns had made extensive use of their superior ski troops and guerrilla tactics, surrounding and eliminating most of the Soviet divisions, which had tried to make their way into Finland in heavily armoured columns through endless, snow-covered forests. The world press published the news of these seemingly unbelievable victories during the second half of December. But it was not until the following month that foreign correspondents were allowed to witness the feats of the Finnish resistance, and the exotic battlefields of *Salla*, *Tolvajärvi* and *Suomussalmi* became known all over the world.[3]

From London the situation at first appeared obscure. The French Ambassador, during the early days of the conflict, expressed his view that the Soviet Union was not actually fighting a war, but trying to exert pressure on Finland in order to gain concessions; he thought that the Russians were using the same method of limited offensive that they had applied against the Japanese in Manchuria a few months earlier. The appearance of the Terijoki government, as well as a statement given in Moscow on 2 December according to which the Soviet Union was not at war with Finland but was merely assisting its democratic forces, sufficed to prove the contrary. "M. Corbin was wrong like so many others", the Foreign Office observers commented. "Now that the Kremlin has conjured up this puppet government and inspired it with a programme which no decent Finn could accept, all chance of a peaceful compromise seems definitely excluded."[4]

The confusion was increased by the fact that many people connected the establishment of Kuusinen's government with the dissolution of Cajander's cabinet in Helsinki, these changes taking place almost simultaneously. It was reported in London newspapers on 1 December—*The Times* excepted—that the Finnish government was about to surrender. *The Evening Standard* stated half-jokingly that the Finnish headquarters had on the previous day given their first and last communiqué. At the Foreign Office as well as at the Quai d'Orsay, Finland was at first considered virtually lost. On the other hand, both Britain and France ignored the existence of Kuusinen—the only reference to him was made when the two powers refused to accept the blockade of the Finnish coasts, which the Soviet Union had declared "at the wish" of the government of the "Finnish Democratic Republic", on the grounds that they had not recognized the government concerned.[5]

However, during the next twenty-four hours the situation was clarified. The new head of the Government in Helsinki, Risto Ryti, who had maintained good relations with the British Legation ever since his term as Director of the Bank of Finland, received Snow on his first day in office, gave him an account of his programme and asked urgently for war material, especially fighter planes. A similar request was made to France, whence an affirmative reply was received sooner than from Britain. Public opinion certainly reacted to the Finnish distress in a much more spontaneous way. Everywhere except in Germany and the Soviet Union, the press and the radio, suffering from a lack of war news, greeted the news of the Red assault with indignation, taking almost unanimously a moral stand on the side of the Finns.[6]

The War Cabinet considered the situation at its meeting on Saturday, 2 December, and drew the conclusions indicated by the following extract from the minutes:*"Indignation with Russia was likely to increase in this country, and it might be difficult politically to avoid a more open condemnation of her action in Finland in view of its similarity to German aggression in Poland."*[7] The Finnish-Soviet conflict would have no immediate effects on the Allied position, the Cabinet estimated, but "it might be a prelude to further Russian expansion schemes, which might develop later in South-East Europe and in Asia... *If Russian aggression occurred in South-East Europe, we might be forced to declare war upon her whether we liked it or not.*"It is known that the French had similar fears during the first days of the Finnish-Soviet conflict.[8]

In the War Cabinet the view was thus gaining ground that Britain would have to alter its circumspect policy towards the Soviet Union. This caution did not, now or later, hinder the Foreign Office from arguing that Finland should be supported and used against the Soviet Union. The attitude of the Prime Minister on this twilight affair is illustrated in a private letter of 3 December 1939, signed by Chamberlain. After observing that the aggression against Finland had by now produced more indignation than Hitler's attack on Poland, "though it is no worse morally, and its development is likely to be less brutal", the Prime Minister went on:

I am as indignant as anyone else at the Russians' behaviour but I am bound to say that I don't think the Allied cause is likely to suffer thereby. It has added a great deal to the general feeling that the ways of dictators make things impossible for the rest of the world, and in

particular it has infuriated the Americans, who have a sentimental regard
for the Finns because they paid off their war debt."[9]

These were rather cool words from a Conservative, who had
never been able to escape from his sub-conscious anti-Sovietism
sufficiently to be able to start negotiations with Moscow for a
defence alliance. As well as opinion at home, Britain had now to
reckon with that of the Dominions, the United States and the
European neutrals, especially the Nordic states. Furthermore,
when the War Cabinet took up the question once again on 4 December, the Foreign Secretary reported that there had been anti-Soviet
student demonstrations in Rome the day before. In Fascist Italy
such manifestations could hardly have taken place without government approval. On hearing the news, the War Cabinet developed
the idea of immediately approaching both Italy and Japan—the
Axis friends of the Germans—and, by appealing to their
anti-Soviet feelings, thus perhaps alienating them from the
Third Reich.*

After learning of the Molotov-Kuusinen agreement, Halifax
understood that there was no longer any possibility of the Soviet
Union being satisfied with its earlier demands. Yet he told the
Cabinet that the Russians had not acted for the purpose of
bolshevizing Finland but rather, surely, in order to carry their
aggression further west, especially into Northern Norway. Referring
to this eventuality, and to opinion in the Scandinavian countries as
well as the United States, he proposed that the Government at
once agree to deliver the thirty fighters asked for by Finland. The
Minister of Aviation replied that this was impossible, and the Chief
of Air Staff, who was also attending the meeting, did not hesitate to
draw attention to a host of British military targets which were
badly in need of fighter protection, ranging from the expeditionary
force in France to Liverpool and the Tyne. With all that, the soldiers
were silenced by the Prime Minister's dry remark that the Finns
should be helped for "*political reasons*". The first consignment of
material assistance to Finland was thus agreed upon, at least in
principle.†[10]

---

* When deciding to express its indignation at the Soviet aggression not only to
Italy but also to Japan, the Government pointed out that "the Japanese might
be particularly receptive of such an idea owing to their affinity with the
Finns" [sic!].

† The final decision concerning the aircraft delivery was made on 4 December.
The number of planes, however, had been reduced from thirty to twenty, and
they were not to be Spitfires or Hurricanes, as suggested by the Finns, but
older Gloster Gladiator fighters (W.M. 103 (39) 7).

2

It is easy to understand why the Allied high command considered armed assistance to Finland meaningless, not to say unnecessary. Few experts had any idea of the realities of the new front and of the fact, as the French military representative on the spot put it, that in Finland success depended on quality rather than quantity.[11] Notions about the Finnish armed forces were faulty, being based mostly on the reports by military attachés assigned to Helsinki, or by professionals temporarily staying in or visiting Finland, but not on official information: indeed, the Finns had no agreement for military co-operation with either Western power.

Owing to lack of information, the picture of this theatre of war, even among the top military leadership, was unrealistic and even distorted, and this at the time when a possible expedition of assistance was under discussion. Matters were not improved by the fact that senior officers, like the French Military Attaché in London, General Lelong, Generals Gough and Lewin and indeed General Ironside, the Chief of the Imperial General Staff (C.I.G.S.), were all familiar with the Arctic conditions of Northern Russia and Finland, having served there during and after the First World War, and even now, twenty years later, were considered experts in this field.*

The military attachés had had their most recent experience of the Finnish land forces in August 1939, at the manoeuvres at Heinjoki near Viipuri, in which 20,000 men participated, almost the entire peacetime strength of the Finnish army. The foreign observers, as reported by the British Military Attaché Lieut.-Col. Vale, were impressed by the men's excellent physique, but they also did not fail to notice other things: the inadequacy and poor condition of the equipment, the almost total lack of modern armament (very few anti-aircraft and, in particular no anti-tank weapons), not to mention the fact that the leadership of the larger units was unable to handle the troops in unusual situations.

Vale's conclusions gave an unpromising picture of the Finnish army's potentialities:

Although the Finnish soldier appears to have great powers of endurance and to be fired with the definite determination of defending his country, especially against Russia, Finland would be taking a very great risk if she

---

* In 1919, General Sir Hubert Gough was the Head of the British Military Delegation to Finland; Lewin was Chief of Staff of Maynard's force at Murmansk. Ironside as well as Lelong were in Arkangel in 1918-19, the former as Commander of the Allied force operating in the area.

allowed herself to get involved in war against any major power. The training
and experience of the Higher Commanders appears to leave much to be
desired; the equipment and armament of units is in a very bad condition
and the only hopeful feature appears to be the natural difficulties of
the country.[12]

Vale had also had the opportunity in June, together with
General Kirke's party, of getting acquainted with the fortifications
on the Karelian Isthmus. In his report he pointed out that even
the line of defence at Summa, some 20 miles south of Viipuri (the
"Mannerheim Line") lacked a coherent fortified system: it consisted
only of a number of strongpoints, in front of which were erected
portions of anti-tank obstacles and barbed wire.[14] Vale did not
seem too convinced of the effectiveness of the defensive works, but
added that they were executed mainly by enthusiastic volunteers—
"a very good indication", he observed, "of the national hatred
and suspicion of the Soviet Union".[13]*

Even before the outbreak of war, the Allies, as we know, had
feared that Soviet forces might extend their operations to Northern
Norway and Sweden. At the Foreign Office, special attention was
paid to the fact that the Russians had demanded from the Finnish
delegates the north-western part of the Kalastajasaarento Peninsula
on the arctic coast, and had occupied this as well as nearly
all of the Petsamo area during the first days of the war. This was a
confirmation of the opinion that the Russians aimed at isolating
Finland from her last harbour within reach of the Allies, and at
occupying the positions for an invasion of the North of Norway.[15]

It appears from the reports of the Chiefs of Staff Committee†—
that the Gällivare-Kiruna areas and Narvik were considered the
eventual targets of Soviet offensive. Since the British Navy was in
control of the Norwegian coast, the attack could only be launched

---

* Reports of French observers recorded in the Vincennes archives also assess
the Finnish fortification works as rather modest. According to the commander
of the Finnish II Army Corps in the western part of the Isthmus, his sector—
44 miles long— of the main line between the Gulf of Finland and the River
Vuoksi consisted of thirty-nine obsolete (over fifteen years old) and forty-four
modern concrete bunkers surrounded by ordinary field-works, barbed wire
and tank barrier systems. Half of these were concentrated on the most critical
stretch between the sea and Lake Muolaa east of the Viipuri-Leningrad railway,
which in addition was covered by the fire of two heavy coast artillery batteries
from Koivisto. Instead, the remaining 38 miles of the main line eastward
had—besides the formidable natural obstacle of the River Vuoksi—almost no
other fortifications excepting six antiquated gun casemates and twenty pillboxes
flanked by the Ladoga coast artillery.[14]

† See above, pp. 33-4.

by land. The only possible direction of advance would then have been the Finnish "waistline" between Salla and Suomussalmi. The Allied headquarters knew these areas only on the map. They were inclined to identify their own interests with those of Finnish defence, and were wondering, like the French General Staff, why the body of Mannerheim's army was concentrated to the south-east, on the Isthmus, whereas the North of Finland, where the real weight of the offensive was to be expected, was left almost undefended.[16]

Through their military attachés in Helsinki, who had good connexions with the Commander of the Finnish Air Force, Major-General Lundqvist, the British were well informed of the inadequacy of the country's air defences. This weakness was considered the Achilles heel of the Finnish armed forces. Of course, the overwhelming superiority of the Soviet Baltic Fleet was well-known, but the effectiveness of Finnish coastal defences, as well as the approaching winter, seemed to preclude landing operations. At any rate, the decision to attack had to be made at once, otherwise Finland could be occupied by land operations only. Some foreign experts—including the Estonian Admiral Pitka—observed that winter conditions would greatly improve Finnish defence possibilities. The opinion at the Foreign Office, however, was different. No wonder: had the Russians not always proved the best winter fighters in the past—had even Nicholas I not pointed out that Russia had at least two generals whom she could trust—the generals Janvier and Février?[17]

But as it happened, the winter of 1939-40 was one of the coldest in living memory. When, during the campaign, temperatures of 20-30 degrees and occasionally of 30-40 degrees F. below zero were regularly recorded, even those "most reliable generals" turned their backs on the heavily mechanized Russian troops. Only on the Isthmus and the Bay of Viipuri did the exceptionally severe winter help the Soviet tank troops, in the last phase of the war, to develop their attacks over deeply frozen swamps and sea straits, which the Finns had erroneously regarded as impenetrable natural barriers.

There was little doubt that the Soviet Union would be able to use its superior manpower and material, regardless of physical impediments. In numbers its superiority was tremendous: the War Office estimated that at the outbreak of the conflict, out of the total Soviet strength of some 140 divisions, over twenty were posted, with some 2,000 tanks, at the Finnish front; the ten infantry divisions at the Finns' disposal—with almost no armoured troops— were far inferior to corresponding Red Army units in equipment and manpower. Out of the total Soviet Air Force of some 3,000 planes, 500 were concentrated against Finland at the start of hostilities, whereas the number of Finnish fighters did not reach one hundred.[18]

Among military experts, and particularly among the press, the Finnish tidings of victory met with scepticism. As late as 19 December, Gripenberg noted in his diary that the press refused to believe that in Finland over 200 Soviet tanks had been destroyed with the most primitive of defensive weapons including "Molotov cocktails" and did not want to publish the news. Quite soon, however, a different view gained ground. On the third day of the war, London was informed that the Swedish General Staff considered the Finns capable of fighting for six months, if they were promptly supplied with arms. The Foreign Office remained doubtful. Thus Halifax, when visited during these days by a friend of Gripenberg, remarked that the Russians would surely shoot Mannerheim if they caught him—then he asked to what religion the Finns adhered.

But the C.I.G.S., agreeing with the Swedish view, told the War Cabinet that it would indeed take a long time to crush Finnish resistance at this time of the year. Gripenberg confirmed this view by transmitting to Halifax on 11 December the estimate of the Finnish headquarters: the Finns, with the resources available at the moment, could not hold out for more than two months, "*but if . . . certain much-needed supplies could be obtained now and increased in January and February, they could hold out almost indefinitely.*"[19]

Actually Mannerheim's judgment of the situation was not so optimistic at the close of the first week of war. Gripenberg had been instructed, of course, to present this encouraging picture in London in order to cut short the scepticism as to the power of the Finnish resistance to last out, and to get the delivery of war materials expedited. It is hard to believe that Halifax would have taken the envoy's assurances seriously. Nevertheless, he too expressed his optimism in a letter which he addressed, on the same day, to L. S. Amery, one of the first Conservative partisans of intervention in the Finnish-Russian conflict: "We have every hope that the Finns can hold out long enough, at least, to necessitate the consumption by Soviet forces of all the petrol which might otherwise have been supplied to Germany."[20]

Once it was realized that the Finns could in fact resist the Red Army and that there was willingness among the Scandinavians to assist them, attitudes changed. The handling of the requests was speeded up by allowing the Finnish Minister to enter into direct touch with the War Office and other competent ministries. In compliance with his wish, the Ministry of Economic Warfare set up a special committee to study the Finnish needs for such products as fuel, which were not primarily war materials but necessary for the country's defence. The committee included representatives from the Norwegian and Swedish Legations, as was natural, since the Scandinavian countries were assigned a key role in the assistance activities. Above all they were given the opportunity to forward to Finland materials which they had obtained from Britain, on the promise that these items would be replaced by new British exports. Thus it was possible for them, during the first weeks of the war, to deliver to Finland large quantities of fuel, especially petrol for aircraft, as well as other raw materials like rubber, which were badly needed for war industry.

At the same time the War Cabinet hurried up the handling of direct deliveries of war materials. In addition to the ten Gladiator fighters already agreed upon, the Finns asked for a further ten, which they were allowed two weeks later. The Cabinet facilitated the transaction concerning the first Gladiators by guaranteeing to the Gloster Aircraft Company the price, £85,000, which was then to be paid by the Finnish State by instalments; the additional consignment of ten planes was delivered without charge. Simultaneously the South African Government gave up twenty-eight Gauntlet training planes of an old model, which it had already bought from Britain, and presented them as a gift to Finland.* In spite of these speedy decisions, the transport of the dismantled aircraft overseas finally took so long that only a part of the Gladiators, which had to be assembled in Sweden, arrived in time, by the end of February, to be used in the battle for Finland at all.[21]

Otherwise the material assistance to be delivered to Finland before mid-December was more or less humanitarian. Britain was not yet in a position to give up the howitzers, anti-aircraft guns and other heavy equipment requested by the Finns. Machine-guns and anti-tank rifles (13.97-mm.) were promised only in restricted numbers, not more than a hundred of either; at first only 2,000 anti-tank mines were delivered, and 10,000 hand-grenades. On the other hand, such articles as gas-masks, anti-gas ointments and eyeshields were allowed to be sent freely. All in all, this was only a part of the requests cabled to Gripenberg three days after the outbreak of the conflict from Helsinki. This list was soon to have numerous additions.[23]

---

* In addition to the aircraft mentioned, the War Office later presented Finland with 40 ambulances. A full price was paid for the remaining war material delivered by Britain, 25 per cent being paid in cash and the rest on five years' credit in accordance with the contract; due to the later hostilities between the two countries, payments were postponed and finally settled after 1947.[22]

3

Although the Scandinavian countries, from the very beginning of the Finnish-Soviet crisis, had let it be understood that their intervention should not be counted upon, the Allies still retained the hope of forming a joint Nordic front against the Soviet Union. Three weeks after their October memorandum,* the Chiefs of Staff had again discussed the possibility of giving Sweden a guarantee if it would assist Finland against an eventual Soviet aggression. Their answer—in a report dated 21 November—was once more negative: It was concluded that the assistance to the Scandinavian countries could not go beyond the measures required by the defence of the Norwegian coast and the protection of the sea connexions. As far as the land forces were concerned, not even a small expeditionary corps was to be considered. Thus, once again it was confirmed that no Scandinavian country could be guaranteed against a menace coming from the east.[24]

The statement of the military experts seemed to upset the Foreign Office's speculations. The opinion of the Chiefs of Staff was open to criticism since they, as responsible military leaders, had to survey the situation from the most pessimistic possible point of view. In the opinion of the Foreign Office, the eventuality of an open conflict with the Soviet Union was out of the question, but it also believed it possible, as well as the great European war, to have another, minor war being fought in Northern Europe. This conflict might, on the one hand, use up Soviet resources and aggravate the export of strategic products to Germany, and on the other, break off Scandinavian trade connections, especially the export of iron ore to Germany.

While paying a visit to the Foreign Office for the first time after the outbreak of the Winter War, the Swedish Minister Prytz expressed his doubts on the practical feasibility of the two-war theory. Sooner or later the Finnish-Soviet conflict would become entangled with the major European war; this might happen if for no other reason than in the event of Norway and Sweden intervening in the Winter War and thus causing Germany to attack them. At the Foreign Office this eventuality was regarded as highly probable: it was seen as the express means by which the Scandinavians could be drawn into the war. Even if Germany attacked the North, the argument went on, it would hardly be able to conquer Norway and Sweden completely. In addition, the Germans would have to lengthen their front, most likely without

---

* See above pp. 33-4.

succeeding in occupying the Swedish iron mines—at least, in an undamaged condition. Further, the Allies could procure the military support of the Scandinavians and probably the sympathies of other neutrals as well, while losing nothing themselves—not even their good relations with the Soviet Union.[25]

As seen from London, the first reactions to the Winter War seemed unexpectedly promising. Not only Sweden, but Norway also, refrained from making any declaration of neutrality, and by so doing reserved for themselves the right to assist Finland when necessary and opportune. Up to the meeting of the Norwegian, Swedish and Danish Foreign Ministers in Oslo on 8 December, it seemed that the first two countries were ready to intervene on behalf of the Finns, at least indirectly. Thus the question of delivering war material to Finland from outside Scandinavia seemed settled.[26]

It is true that all of them had taken an extremely cautious stand since the beginning of the Finnish-Soviet conflict. Norway had even gone as far as to forbid public fund-raising for Finland and to prevent its active officers from enlisting in the Finnish army as volunteers. Sweden had irritated the British by asking them—out of fear of the Germans—not to give Finland arms free of charge. Yet both in Norway and Sweden there were influential pressure-groups favouring a more outspoken and active policy. The sympathetic attitude of the Swedish royalty and military leaders, in particular, did not pass unnoticed in London, where it was believed, even after the reshaping of Hansson's Cabinet,* on 11 December, that the country would start an all-out intervention in favour of Finland.[27]

As soon appeared, the enthusiasm which had prevailed in Oslo and Stockholm during the first days of December had been based on the false premise that the outbreak of the Winter War had been an unpleasant surprise for the Germans, and that they would not prevent the Scandinavians from giving even more assistance to Finland. As reasons for this illusion there were vague indications, like Goering's stray promise to the Norwegians that Germany would not interfere with the delivery of war material to Finland; or the information that Germany might allow the transit of this material through its own territory.[28]

Such news, and the suspected pro-German sympathies of certain influential Scandinavians such as Norway's Foreign Minister Koht, caused the Foreign Office to assume that it all amounted to a

---

* The main change was the resignation of the actively pro-Finnish Foreign Minister, Rikhard Sandler.

campaign led by Berlin, aiming at the ending of the German-Allied "fraternal war" to the detriment of the Soviet Union. In order to check the effects of enemy propaganda, the Foreign Secretary, shortly after the Soviet attack on Finland, advised BBC and British press reporters to point out with special emphasis that Germany shared the responsibility for what had happened.[29]

Meanwhile, Berlin had reconsidered its attitude towards Finland, an event which deeply affected the policy of both Scandinavian countries during the very same month. In mid-December, the Dutch and French press gave space to the news that fifty fighter planes had been sent from Italy to Finland by road through Germany. In Moscow Molotov immediately summoned Schulenburg and bitterly complained that such transit did not comply with German benevolent neutrality. Ribbentrop arranged that the Italian fighter delivery, by now in Sassnitz, was returned, and the transit permit was withdrawn; Germany never again during the Winter War strayed from its basically negative neutrality towards Finland.*[30]

From the Foreign Office point of view, the German sympathies towards Finland were by no means unwelcome, as a senior official minuted on 13 December at the Central European Department:

We could not wish for anything better than that Germany should help Finland secretly. This will stiffen Finnish and Scandinavian resistance and annoy the Russians (*who are bound to find out*), but at the same time do Germany no good in the eyes of world opinion.[31]

Having vainly expected an exhaustive account from Gripenberg, Halifax had instructed Snow to inquire at the Finnish Foreign Ministry what it all signified. At the War Cabinet meeting of 15 December, he was able to report, on Snow's information, that the Finns had encountered difficulties in trying to have materials transited through Germany, which proved that German feeling toward Helsinki remained cold.[32] By now the situation had grown complicated: contrary to some expectations, Germany was not going to assist Finland against the Red Army, let alone allow the Allies to do so. Her reluctance preordained the stand of Norway and Sweden, even before they were called upon—in the name of the League of Nations—to collaborate in rescuing their Nordic neighbour.

---

* According to the account given by Ribbentrop to Moscow, Germany had granted the mentioned transit permit in October, "when there were as yet no signs of hostilities between Russia and Finland." In the same context it was admitted that some 20-mm. anti-aircraft guns (Niukkanen, 174; there were thirty) had been delivered to Finland by Germany on the eve of war, having been promised the previous summer.

4

One of the first tasks of the new Finnish cabinet, formed on 1 December by Risto Ryti, was to approach the League of Nations, as the instructions cabled to the Finnish delegation in Geneva indicated, "to summon the general assembly on account of the Soviet aggression". Finland was thus reserved a key role at a meeting, which proved to be the League's last, and which witnessed the expulsion of one of the permanent members of the League council, the Soviet Union.[33]

Due to force of circumstances the appeal was made in haste, without any other member-state being consulted. The surprised Scandinavians, as well as the British and French, soon learned that the initiative originated from the League secretariat in Geneva, maybe even from outside the organisation. The Finnish representative to the League, Rudolf Holsti, had in fact mentioned as early as October that the Secretariat was interested in the matter.* Harri Holma for his part reported from Paris that on Tuesday 29 November—twelve hours before the outbreak of Finnish-Russian hostilities—he had met the United States Ambassador, William C. Bullitt, who since the summer had been warning him of the dangers threatening Finland. The Ambassador had on the same day lunched with the Secretary-General of the League of Nations, Joseph Avenol, then on a private visit to Paris, and he now told Holma that it would be advisable for Finland to submit the conflict to the League immediately. When Holma referred to Avenol's well-known reticence, Bullitt said that the Secretary-General had now changed his mind completely and had told him "that if the League will not do anything it is better to close it down."[35]

This change of mind by Avenol, whom Bullitt called the "funeral undertaker" of small states subject to aggression, did not come as a surprise to Finns who were generally familiar with the situation in Geneva. Professor Barros, in his well-informed study on Avenol's period of office at the League, pictures him as a cold and calculating bureaucrat, more interested in his own advantage than that of the

---

* Holsti had proposed that Finland should appeal to the League—on 18 October, the same day as the meeting of the Nordic heads of state opened in Stockholm. He had stressed the necessity of consulting Sweden. For some reason—maybe because the then Foreign Minister considered the submission of the conflict to the League to be a danger to Finnish neutrality—it was never discussed, officially at least, among the Nordic foreign ministers in Stockholm. It appears from the archives of the Finnish Foreign Ministry that the question was not taken up again until 30 November, when Holsti reintroduced it to the ministry.[34]

League. He regards Avenol's attempts to prolong the activity of
the League while seeking the support of the Germans, now masters
of the continent, as the culmination of his final term, which started
in the autumn 1939 and which was as independent as it was
unsupervised by responsible representatives of member-states.*[36]

The secretary-general tried to exploit the Soviet aggression
against Finland and the sentiments which it aroused to activate
the League of Nations, now paralysed by the war. Well trained in
League politics, he quite correctly sensed that the plans for a
general assembly, postponed since the outbreak of the European
War, now had a chance of success; as the French representative
Paul-Boncour later observed, "there was even more readiness
now to condemn the aggression since it came from the Soviet
Union."[37]

Bullitt, himself well-known for his aversion towards the Soviet
Union, was inspired after realizing that the Secretary-General had a
tangible aim in deliberating the Finnish question: "As long as the
Soviet Union remained a member, it was impossible for the League
to operate." As the crisis on the following day was developing into
an armed conflict, the Ambassador had reiterated his point of view
to the Finnish Minister and promised to prepare the ground by
influencing Premier Daladier, both directly and through the White
House. Meanwhile Holma, having now himself met Avenol,
phoned Holsti in Geneva, who in turn got in touch once more with
Helsinki. The following morning, 1 December, Holsti also had the
opportunity to discuss the matter with Avenol, just back from Paris-
and to hear the latter's opinion that the majority of the member,
states would support Finland. Although the League might not be
able to give material help to Finland, the Secretary-General
pointed out, the universal importance of its support was not to be
underestimated.

The decision of the Finnish Government, according to the new
Foreign Minister, Väinö Tanner, and Minister of State, J. K.
Paasikivi, was intended to get the League to mediate peace between
Finland and the Soviet Union, or at least to ask other states to
assist Finland in its war effort. It is obvious that the unreserved
endorsement of this plea in Geneva helped Ryti's cabinet to avert
the Soviet attempt to introduce their puppet, Kuusinen, and thus
procure for his government legal international recognition. *The idea
of expelling the Soviet Union, which originated elsewhere, does not seem to
have been in accord with Finnish interests or expectations.*[38]

---

* Similar evidence is to be found in Finnish sources.

At Avenol's wish, Holsti and Holma tried to get Tanner to come to Geneva. However the Foreign Minister had already discussed the matter on the telephone with his Norwegian and Swedish colleagues and informed Holsti on 6 December that he would stay at home. The latter, together with Holma, was authorized to represent Finland at the General Assembly.

The Finnish appeal to the League of Nations had come as an unpleasant surprise to the other Nordic countries. Fear of Soviet and German reactions, together with awareness of the weakness of their own defence, on one hand, and solidarity with a sister-country subject to aggression, with public opinion clamouring for intervention, on the other, placed the Danish, Norwegian and Swedish Governments in an embarrassing position. Four years earlier, forming the so-called Oslo Group which included Finland, they had announced that they reserved for themselves the right to decide when to apply the sanctions implicit in article 16 of the Covenant.* Now the question was whether they could dissociate themselves from their obligations even if one of the Nordic countries was the victim of aggression.

Tanner helped them out of the difficulty. Having secured his permission by telephone, the Norwegian Foreign Minister, who because of a government crisis in Stockholm came to play a central role at the meeting of the foreign ministers of the "neutral Nordic countries" held in Oslo on 7 December, easily pushed through what was emphatically called the Tanner-Koht proposal. According to this, the League of Nations was to confine itself to identifying the aggressor, demanding that parties to the conflict withdraw their troops from foreign territory, and starting negotiations for finding a peaceful settlement. The expulsion of the aggressor was out of the question, and sanctions even more so.

In the "instructions" given to Geneva by Tanner it was observed that, since poor telecommunications made it difficult to advise the delegates from home, they had to decide on voting alternatives by themselves. The Finns would have to follow the Tanner-Koht proposal, in other words, have the League demand that the aggressor withdraw its troops and start negotiations; but, as far as the expulsion of the Soviet Union was concerned, this possible outcome would not further Finnish interests. To these observations a further detail was added just before the decisive Council meeting, to the effect

---

* The Article obliged the members of the League to break off immediately all trade or monetary as well as personal connections with any state violating the obligations of the Covenant, if the Council proposed participation in armed counter-measures and, in such a case, to allow the passage of the military forces of other member—states.

that the delegates were to abstain from voting on the question of Soviet expulsion.*

5

The expulsion of the Soviet Union, an obsession for Avenol, was finally realised without Tanner's co-operation. The aggression against Finland had created an unprecedented wave of anti-Soviet feeling. This phenomenon was the result of what had happened between Germany and the Soviet Union that autumn, and was not limited to the traditionally anti-Communist, anti-Soviet elements but even included adherents of the extreme Left who had been upset by the Molotov-Ribbentrop Pact and its consequences. Antipathy towards· the Soviet Union and sympathy towards Finland were facts which the governments sending their delegations to Geneva could not overlook.

This applied in particular to France. The press—both on the Right, desiring peace with Germany, and on the Left, basically opposing such a peace—had condemned the Soviet Union ever since the Finnish appeal became known. The newspapers close to the Government, however, warned that the Germans might take advantage of the Assembly of the League to further their own peace offensive. Obviously this was the reason why the Quai d'Orsay at first shunned the Finnish initiative. Even after Finland had made its official appeal to the League, the British Foreign Office was informed that Secretary-General Léger viewed the initiative with reservations, proposing consultations between the two foreign ministries.[40] Yet, four days later, on 7 December, the Finnish Minister in Paris, referring to an official statement, cabled to Helsinki that the Quai d'Orsay had changed its attitude. In fact the French now seemed almost too sympathetic: "*Appui moral* altogether too small a demand. Expulsion of Moscow minimum. If not achieved, better to close doors of League."

As has been shown by Barros, Avenol had discussed the question with Champetier de Ribes, who was later the second French representative at the League meetings in Geneva. Avenol realized that he too favoured summoning the Assembly and the expulsion of the Soviet Union.[41] Obviously Champetier had kept quiet until

* The Scandinavian line openly adopted by Helsinki displeased Holsti, who was afraid it might cause ill-feeling in France as well as the United States. Yet he proceeded in strict accordance with the instructions received from Helsinki and warned the League Secretariat on 9 December that Finland was under no circumstances committed to the expulsion of the Soviet Union. Avenol for his part paid an unexpected call on the U.S. Consul General in Geneva, trying in vain to talk the latter into influencing the Finns to change Tanner's mind.[39]

Léger's uncommitted position had proved wrong. Prime and Foreign Minister Daladier in fact demanded a reversal of policy. The French cabinet was, of course, aware that its right-wing opposition tried to benefit from the situation in its own way. The then Minister of Finance Paul Reynaud later observed that "those who were most ardent in pressing for the breaking of relations with Stalin were the [mainly right-wing] Pacifistes—in other words those who three months earlier tried to find ways to avoid fighting against Hitler."[42] The cabinet decided that France should go to Geneva, after all; her position there would have to be sufficiently anti-Soviet to satisfy the hard-line Rightists at home; but it would also have to be sufficiently anti-German to give the *Pacifistes* little or no freedom of action.

To what extent Daladier's sudden activity was due to Ambassador Bullitt's influence, as suggested by Holma, still remains conjectural.[43] At the session of the Chamber of Deputies on 8 December, where the question of sending a delegation was discussed, Daladier condemned Soviet behaviour in the severest terms. He expressed his satisfaction that the conscience of the world, which already seemed silenced when faced with the use of brute force, now showed signs of awakening for the first time since 1 September. This idealism explains why whether inspired by Bullitt or not, Daladier went so far as to plan to go to Geneva himself, and why, before the final voting, he let his delegates tell the British: *"If the League does take positive measures it is better for France to stay out."*[44]

Meanwhile in Britain the Foreign Office adopted a similarly hesitant attitude towards the summons to the meeting. Halifax told the War Cabinet on 4 December that he himself would stay away from Geneva and send R. A. Butler as the British representative. The Foreign Secretary considered the summons to meetings unfortunate: they would only cause trouble for the world organization itself. Halifax had obviously studied the memoranda of his League of Nations expert, A. W. G. Randall, who proposed ways of getting the meeting over with the least possible damage.

The British had many causes for worry, from the League budget to the Polish and Czechoslovak credentials (of which the Foreign Office was ready to accept the former but not the latter), and finally to the actual political content of the agenda. There was a danger that the problems of Palestine and the Chinese-Japanese war would be revived at the Council, and that the Soviet Union, besides eventually taking up the Czechoslovak question, would accuse the Western Powers of leaving Albania and Ethiopia to the mercy of the aggressor; Poland might call the Soviet Union to account; someone might even take up the conflict between Germany and the Western Powers, with all the complications involved. Or, as Randall warned regarding the Polish question: "The Assembly may at once be in full cry after a hare we have tried to keep safely caged!"[45]

At the Foreign Office the possibility of Kremlin counter-measures caused headache. In addition to the possibility of growing German-Russian co-operation, a common cause for anxiety to all the Allies, there were worries about the British oil interests in the Middle East, the Suez Canal and India—all within reach of the Red Army. It also occurred to Randall that if the Soviet Union were expelled, the financing of the League would depend on the Western Powers. The breaking of diplomatic relations, not to speak of war, was out of the question. "The more I think about it, the less I like the idea of the expulsion of Russia," Halifax wrote to Butler on 7 December. "Try to prevent it.. if you can. But if you fail, I don't think you can help voting for it."[46]

At this stage the Foreign Office was considering a moderate resolution, along the lines of the one accepted in 1937 on the Chinese question, stating that the aggression had taken place, expressing the moral support of the League for the victim, and urging the member-states to assist in repelling the attack. When talking to the Swedish minister on 5 December, Butler admitted that each member-state would be allowed to assist in accordance with its own interpretation (Article 16 of the Covenant). Prytz for his part pointed out that the object was only to provide a moral background for assistance to Finland. This occasioned Butler to engage in the following play of images:

We agreed that this background might be rather like that of the old-fashioned photographer who depicts his subject as leaning against a sham pillar or against a bridge over a rustic stream. The Minister said he hoped that the subject of the portrait would not fall into the stream.[47]

The leading idea of the British in Geneva was to co-operate with the French and to keep possible disagreements from the public. When the pressure of their allies finally forced them into a situation when they had no other choice than to vote for expulsion, they assured themselves that the Soviet Union would not retaliate by declaring war, maybe not even by breaking off diplomatic relations. Yet, as to the sanctions, London remained intransigent regardless of the insignificant material issues concerned: they were "not practicable".

It is obvious that the British Government at this point did not seek to take full advantage of the situation. If the Allies had already been planning to ask the Scandinavian countries for transit permission, a man of Butler's standing, a junior minister close to the inner circle of the Cabinet, would not have spoken thus on the 16th Article—at least not to the Swedish Minister. If the British had been so far-sighted they would hardly have objected to the sanctions either. When in the end they voted for the expulsion of the Soviet Union (the powers to this effect approved by the War Cabinet were conveyed to Geneva on 14 December, only a couple of hours before the decisive vote), they did it obviously less for practical reasons than for the principles of League morality and Allied solidarity.[48]

6

The preliminary meeting of the League of Nations Council on 9 December went off in full accordance with the wishes of the Secretariat. In the absence of the Soviet representative Maisky, the Council was in a position to take its decisions unanimously: it subjected the Finnish question to the General Assembly. Open discussion was restricted to a minimum in order to avoid delay in taking up the appeal and the appearance of other more delicate themes for discussion. On the first day of session, 11 December, the General Assembly heard the speech of the Finnish representative and subsequently elected a special committee to deal with the question. The wording of the final resolution was outlined by the thirteen members of this committee behind closed doors, and the draft was then never questioned at the sessions of the General Assembly or the Council. As a matter of fact the very composition of the committee predetermined the subsequent nature of the resolution.*[50]

---

* In preparing the meetings, Avenol was assisted by the Norwegian representative C. J. Hambro, an ardent partisan of the Finnish cause, whose views on international issues differed rather radically from the "hundred per cent neutrality" line of the Nygaardsvold-Koht government. Ever since the outbreak of the European war, while working as chairman of the Control Commission of the organization, Hambro had occupied a key position in the League. At Avenol's wish he tried to enlist Ireland's Eamonn de Valera, who had been elected chairman of the 19th General Assembly, to come to Geneva, since the latter would have been authorized to summon the postponed General Assembly with no further formalities. When de Valera was informed about the plans of expulsion, he refused to come (five years earlier he had been one of those engaged in getting the Soviet Union to join the League) and the session had to be arranged as a completely new meeting, the 20th. Hambro, against the wishes of his government, but supported by Avenol, was elected chairman of the new Assembly.[49]

When the General Assembly at long last met for its final meeting in the morning of 14 December, the only thing to arouse general interest, even exclamations from the press ("cowardly!"), was the statement made by the Swedish representative Undén, on behalf of his own government as well as the governments of Norway and Denmark. The Scandinavians proclaimed that they would abstain from voting on any proposals for the resolution if these pertained to the sphere of sanctions. The decision to expel the Soviet Union was then transferred to the Council.

The play directed by Avenol could be brought to its close, without unexpected diversions, during the same afternoon. With the support of France and Britian, with China, Greece, Yugoslavia and the newly-elected Finland (as the party concerned) abstaining, the Council accepted the second proposal with the support of the seven other members at 6 p.m. In the terms of the resolution, the Soviet Union was no longer a member of the League.

The Finnish attitude in voting was later subject to criticism. *"Tanner did not seem interested in the expulsion of the Soviet Union,"* Hambro observed later when analysing the sequence of events. *"He clearly believed that it would be easier to negotiate with Russia in the future, if the Nordic countries were not—compromised."*[51] Hambro and his fellow-activists were even more annoyed by the evasive attitude of Norway and Sweden. As he pointed out, assistance to Finland was decisively handicapped by the fact that the Scandinavian countries had dissociated themselves from the obligations of the 16th Article of the Covenant. To drive the point home, Undén had let it be understood, even before the final vote, that he refused to countenance any reference to this Article. Should it be referred to, he had threatened, Sweden would point out that the Soviet Union—according to its own statement—was not at war with Finland.[52]

In France the resolution caused general satisfaction. The moderation of the neutrals and the consequent reticence of the League met with criticism, it is true, both in the press and in official circles. "We can guess how this purely moral sanction affected Stalin!", Georges Bonnet, the former (Munich period) foreign minister, later wrote.[53] In Britain too, dissident voices made themselves heard. Aneurin Bevan, for instance, criticized the fact that the League had taken such severe measures against the Soviet Union, while doing nothing to help Albania and China, and no longer allowing Haile Selassie to enter its corridors.[54]

As far as Finland was concerned, the results came up to expectations. Once it became obvious that the Soviet Union would refuse to make peace through the mediation of the League, the Finns were mostly interested in finding out how much their war effort would be supported from Geneva. Thanks to Avenol, who now found occasion to show that the League was still equal to its task, a great deal was achieved within a short time. The General Assembly commissioned the Secretariat to co-ordinate humanitarian assistance to Finland, and moreover its recommendation facilitated the procuring of actual war material for Finland. Three members of the Foreign Affairs Committee of the then Finnish Government have verified this fact in their memoirs.[55]

Those most eager to put the recommendation into effect were the British and French governments, not through the Secretariat of the League, but directly. The Foreign Office in particular tried to keep Avenol out of their assistance to Finland. His attempt to come to London at the end of December was prevented, and his inquiries met with a surly response. Sir Alexander Cadogan found Avenol's interference an example of the League's helplessness and described his proposals—that the Allies should announce publicly in what ways and to what extent they assisted Finland—as being "excellent but silly in practice."[56]

The recommendation of the League provided a useful background —as is known, Butler and Prytz had discussed this concept—when the Allies started using the Finnish-Soviet conflict for their own purposes. At least as far as Britain was concerned, the Geneva resolution was made with no such motives in mind. Nevertheless, the assistance, which later developed into an open attempt at intervention, was launched immediately after the resolution. The same evening (14 December), even before the Foreign Office had had time to study the resolutions passed in Geneva, the French Ambassador called, proposing co-operation in assisting Finland and tying the Soviet forces down in the north.

In other respects the resolutions made on account of the Finnish appeal had no political consequences. Most of the hopes and fears which they aroused, in both the Allied and the neutral European states, came to nothing; the Soviet Union failed to declare war or to break off diplomatic relations with its expellers, Germany did not react in any way, and Spain, Italy and Japan remained as hostile to Geneva as before. Avenol himself seems to have realized that the expulsion of the Soviet Union, the League's last resolution, had been a mistake.[57] In practice this had to be admitted by C. J. Hambro who, in his capacity of chairman of the last General Assembly, had the honour of welcoming the Soviet Union at the closing ceremonies of the League of Nations in 1946.

IV

FINLAND AND THE IRON ORE QUESTION
December 1939 (2)

1

The Geneva resolution had caught the British unprepared. The decision to assist Finland had been made and even confirmed prior to the League of Nations appeal: at its meeting on 11 December the War Cabinet had reached the conclusion that it was in British interests to help Finland as much as possible. All the same, the practical measures taken so far, as the Foreign Office pointed out, had amounted to no more than expressions of friendship, which could not be expected to influence the War's final outcome. There had not been time, nor perhaps the courage, to decide how extensive the support to Finland should be.[1]

Among the British public, it is true, Soviet aggression had aroused rather vigorous anti-Soviet reactions, but the Chamberlain Government adopted a cool and calculating attitude towards the conflict. Only after the first sensational defeats of the Red Army did it arrive at the conclusion, under French influence, that advantage should be taken of the situation by the Allied war effort: it was now or never that the Western Powers had to seize the initiative, win over world opinion, surround the enemy and win the war.

From mid-December this line of policy was promoted in the War Cabinet by Halifax and Churchill, even though by differing and partly contradictory proposals. The Foreign Secretary suggested, in accordance with the view which his ministry had established in the course of the autumn, that Finland should be supported in order to engage the Soviet Union in a prolonged conflict and to protect Scandinavia from Russian and possibly also German aggression. When answering Amery, who had suggested that Stalin and Hitler, the "two gangsters", were to be drawn in Scandinavia into the decisive battle of the great European war, Halifax had repeated his earlier view: the Allies, while assisting Finland, must not become engaged in a conflict with the Soviet Union, *unless they were in a position to enlist the support of the majority of the neutrals.**

---

* See p. 48. "Remember that Russia has always been weak at the extremities," Amery wrote to Halifax on 6 December 1939: she would be seriously held up over the Finnish war while Germany, if attacking the North, would be beaten and finally exhausted "over the immense area of Sweden's lakes and forests, just as we beat Napoleon over the vast area of Spain—in each case with the help of a patriotic population."[2]

At the Cabinet meeting of 15 December, Halifax commented in a similar vein on Snow's latest initiative that Japan, Italy and, eventually, the United States as well should be invited to form a common front for the rescue of Finland: not only vigorous diplomatic support but also intensified armed assistance were necessary for Finland, but this involved risks still to be clarified. Halifax had already covered some of the groundwork, since the memorandum on the North European situation asked for by the War Cabinet had been finished the same day.[3]

The Foreign Secretary had been asked to study the possible consequences for Allied interests of the Soviet attack on Finland and the eventual spreading of the conflict to the Scandinavian countries. Unlike Norway, which had done nothing for Finland, Halifax observed that Sweden had helped her neighbour in every possible way and was liable to Russian pressure in the event of prolonged war. Germany was not really interested in the Finnish situation, but would possibly support Sweden if the latter got into trouble with the Soviet Union. Thus, neither Norway nor Sweden seemed in imminent danger from the Soviet Union or Germany, as long as Finland continued to fight. It was in the Allied interest that such a dangerous situation should not be allowed to develop, Halifax concluded. All in all, Finland had to be assisted by all possible means in order to make it an effective barrier between the Soviet Union and the Atlantic Ocean.[4]

The analysis, as we now know, failed in that it underestimated Soviet strength and German interest in Scandinavia. Moreover, its author did not discuss the proposals for a more active Scandinavian policy which the dynamic First Lord of the Admiralty had been urging since September. When Halifax, presenting his memorandum to the War Cabinet on 18 December, asked what was to be done if the Soviet Union put pressure on Sweden, and Germany, worried about its ore interests, interfered. Churchill became irritated and turned the whole problem upside down: *it was not in the interest of the Allies to keep Norway and Sweden outside the conflict, as Halifax had suggested, but to draw them into the war!*[5]

While the question was submitted, with Halifax's memorandum as a starting-point, to the Military Co-ordinating Committee, the Cabinet received for its consideration Churchill's strongly-worded memorandum on Scandinavian policy, and the Ministry of Economic Warfare report on the ore question. These documents immediately turned the Cabinet's attention from the eastern border of Finland to the western coast of Norway.

2

Churchill's interest ever since the first weeks of the war had been fixed on the Baltic and the western coast of Norway with a view to cutting off German supply routes from Scandinavia. He was convinced, with the Ministry of Economic Warfare, that it was possible to rock the economic foundations of the enemy by checking its imports of oil and iron ore. It was calculated that the Finnish war would indirectly aggravate the supply of both these basic raw materials: Germany was expected to run out of oil, as the Soviet Union would consume its surplus in the war against Finland. The question of iron ore seemed even less complicated: if German ore transports from Scandinavia were cut off, the M.E.W. pointed out, the Reich's industry would find itself in difficulties by April.[6]

It was well-known that German steel production, even before the war, had been dependent on the high-grade iron ore imported from Sweden. Since France had cut off its ore exports, this dependence was increasing.* By the end of the first year of war German ore supplies had decreased to 2 million tons, and its steel industry had consequently been cut to half its earlier capacity, even though the imports from Scandinavia continued.[7]

The bulk of the Swedish ore was transported from the Gällivare-Kiruna mining area, first by rail to Luleå, then via the Gulf of Bothnia and the Baltic to Germany. During the period when the port of Luleå was frozen, generally from mid-December till mid-April, ore was shipped from ice-free Narvik, which was a shorter railway distance from the mining district than Luleå. A smaller quantity of the ore, coming from the Grangesberg mines, was mostly loaded on ships at Oxelösund (some 60 miles south-west of Stockholm) and it could safely be shipped, practically throughout the year, to German Baltic ports. This ore, however, was not sufficient for Germany. At best, the Grangesberg shipments amounted to 330,000-350,000 tons — a strong argument for believing that the closing of Narvik could prove fatal for the German war economy.

New evidence in support of these estimates was found in the French memorandum sent to the French Premier by Fritz Thyssen, a German steel magnate exiled in Switzerland, who described the Reich's iron ore penury in dramatic terms. The M.E.W. also received reports from Norway and Sweden, according to which ore

---

* In 1938 German ore imports were estimated at 22 million tons, France accounting for 5 million and Sweden for 9 million tons. (*Medlicott*, 1952, p. 31.)

exports to Germany were to be increased and a growing number of shipments centred in Baltic ports, out of Allied reach.[8]

This seemingly reliable information justified the initiative taken by Churchill in September, two weeks after being appointed to the Admiralty. He had in fact taken up the project of cutting off German transports along the Norwegian coast, by laying mines in the territorial waters as had been done in 1918.[9] At first it seemed possible to attain this goal without offending the Scandinavians. Churchill had indeed suggested that the Norwegians be asked to loan the bulk of their commercial fleet to the British and that the Swedes be asked to sell the iron ore to them, since it could not be shipped elsewhere because of the blockade. But as the attempts to convince Sweden and Norway by means of diplomacy miscarried, the First Lord went back to his original blockade plan. The ore flow had to be cut off immediately, if necessary by force.[10]

After having suggested to the Cabinet a number of alternatives, ranging from limited navy operations to sabotage, Churchill proposed, in mid-December, that the ore question could be solved, on the pretext of assisting Finland, by a military expedition to Scandinavia. Although he claims in his memoirs that he "sympathised ardently with the Finns and supported *all* proposals for their aid", his practical measures were, in this respect, limited to those which he considered to be in the British national interest. An illustration of this is the advice given in January 1940 to his friend Harold Macmillan, who was then leaving for Finland, that Britain might have even greater interests than helping Finland, however desirable and laudable that particular cause might be.[11]

The League of Nations resolution provided Churchill with a welcome excuse for confuting those Cabinet members who had considered his suggestions as perilous to Britain's reputation. In a new memorandum, dated 16 December, he put forward, in addition to his earlier request that the western Norwegian coast be closed immediately, the demand that the ore transports from Swedish Baltic ports be checked by means of magnetic mines laid down by submarines in Luleå, and by sabotage in Oxelösund. But not one word in support of assistance to Finland is to be found in the memorandum. Instead, at the end of the document, there is a reference to the League of Nations, which is in striking disagreement with Nordic legal principles and traditions of neutrality. These lines by the future Nobel laureate, quoted before but worth repeating in all their eloquence, give us some insight into the political morality which was to demand even from the neutrals a good deal of sweat, blood and tears, while leading Britain towards victory:

The final tribunal is our own conscience. We are fighting to re-establish the reign of law and to protect the liberties of small countries. Our defeat would mean an age of barbaric violence, and would be fatal not only to ourselves, but to the independent life of every small country in Europe. Acting in the name of the Covenant, and as virtual mandatories of the League and all it stands for, we have a right, and indeed are bound in duty, to abrogate for a space some of the conventions of the very laws we seek to consolidate and reaffirm. Small nations must not tie our hands when we are fighting for their rights and freedom. The letter of the law must not in supreme emergency obstruct those who are charged with its protection and enforcement. It would not be right or rational that the Aggressor Power should gain one set of advantages by tearing up all laws, and another set by sheltering behind the innate respect for law of its opponents. Humanity, rather than legality, must be our guide.[12]

3

In France the Finnish situation gave rise to stronger reactions than in Britain, due perhaps to temperamental reasons but also to political ones. The opposition, as mentioned previously, exploited the conflict for its own political ends. The Right, the *Pacifistes*, many of them Daladier's former supporters, found in the situation created by the Finnish war an opportunity to identify a new enemy. When the League of Nations resolution became known, the then chairman of the Senate Foreign Affairs Committee, later one of the men of Vichy, Pierre-Étienne Flandin, called for the breaking off of relations with the Soviet Union. The government was not ready for such drastic measures, instructing the censor to remove articles favouring the break from the press—the extreme Right-wing *L'Action Française* was actually banned for a few days—but, after a week had elapsed, there was a change in the official attitude. Accordingly, a representative of *Le Figaro* told the Finnish Minister that "he had been amazed when, around Christmas, we were allowed to write about it."[13]

This new turn reflects the marked development in Allied policy toward Finland during the week before Christmas, a change which bears the personal imprint of the French Prime Minister. Daladier probably viewed the question with the wisdom of an old politician, as Gamelin claimed in his memoirs, that is without unnecessary fervour.[14] When Holma—together with Colonel Aladár Paasonen, who had come to Paris to deal with the question of military assistance—called on Daladier for the first time on 15 December, the Premier stated that he was prepared to break off relations with Moscow as soon as the British did the same. The French, nonetheless, were to prove more cautious than their allies in this matter: while Sir Walter Seeds left Moscow at the end of December to remain indefinitely on "sick leave", the French Ambassador Paul-Émile Naggiar stayed on for another month. Relations were never severed, although there are indications that the French government later tried to goad the Soviet Union into taking the first step towards a break.*[15]

Daladier had the gift of convincing both his allies and the Finns of his sincerity. His actions in the matter of assistance to Finland seem to have been calculating but purposeful and effective. From the time of the Geneva resolution—with the exception of an interlude in mid-winter—until the beginning of March 1940, when he announced his personal decision to send 50,000 men to Mannerheim's aid, the French Premier in fact held the initiative in Allied policy towards Finland. One is indeed tempted to ask what might have happened if he had not had a fall from a horse in early January and been obliged to remain in bed for several weeks, at a time when the intervention project was in full swing.[16]

Characteristically enough, Daladier was quick in exploiting his initial success at Geneva. On the very day (14 December) the French Ambassador was instructed to present Daladier's proposal to the Foreign Office. Daladier asked the Secretary-General at the Quai d'Orsay to tell the United States Ambassador that the French had taken the lead in assisting Finland, had decided to despatch thirty of their newest (Morane Saulnier) fighters there immediately, and had proposed that the Allies offer the Scandinavians their support in resisting the Soviet Union. By this disclosure the French were naturally hoping to make the greatest possible use of the help to Finland in their national propaganda.[17]

Two days later the French Ambassador met Halifax in London and succeeded in persuading him to accept Daladier's initiative. At the same time the foreign secretary had the opportunity to convey his own views to the French government. The British preferred to aid Finland, he said, by rapid and extensive deliveries of war material, and simultaneously by taking measures for securing the co-operation of the Scandinavians. In fact they considered that these countries, Sweden foremost, would probably become subject to Soviet pressure before long.[18]

When the matter was taken up at the Allied Supreme War Council in Paris on 19 December, Halifax was surprised to find that the French were intent on going further. Daladier even handed

---

* See below, pp. 111-12.

him a ready-made proposal for a message to be sent to Stockholm and Oslo. Chamberlain and Halifax at once noticed that the French proposed nothing less than guarantees to the Scandinavians against eventual Soviet or German attack. Besides, Daladier categorically added, it was not enough to send war material, but an expeditionary force for Finland was also necessary. The League of Nations resolution provided the Allies with grounds for interfering in the conflcit and for requesting transit permission from Norway and Sweden· To cap it all, Daladier took up Churchill's favourite idea, the cutting off of iron ore deliveries to Germany. In this respect too his line was brutally frank; in fact he proposed that the ore route be closed in conjunction with intervention in Finland, which, however, he did not consider merely as a pretext, as Churchill did, but as an end in itself.[19]

The proposal of the French Premier, who on this occasion also gave an account of Baron Thyssen's ore report, seems to have made a deep impression on both Chamberlain and Halifax. At later discussions on the subject they referred to Daladier and Thyssen rather than to Churchill and the Ministry of Economic Warfare experts. The British delegates still managed, it is true, to avoid the proposal of sending troops. The Council decided temporarily to give all possible material help to Finland unofficially, through the good offices of private arms dealers—as it was known that the Scandinavians wished the aid to be sent in this way. On the other hand, they readily accepted Daladier's idea that the Geneva resolution be used as an argument for a proposition to Norway and Sweden—with the basic purpose of isolating these two countries from Germany in one way or another.[20]

The news of what had happened in the Supreme Council created a sensation in Helsinki and inspired the Finnish Government, for the first and in fact the last time, to appeal to the Allies for military assistance. At a dinner after the Supreme Council meeting, Holma had met a number of well-informed Frenchmen, above all Champetier de Ribes. Having been briefed by these and the American Ambassador, he cabled Helsinki that the Council had decided to send Allied troops to assist Finland, provided that Sweden and Norway would join the war on the side of the Finns. In consequence, apparently as a result of the emotions prevailing in Helsinki after the recent Russian general offensive on the Isthmus, the Finnish Legations in London and Paris were instructed on 22 December to make clear to the Allied governments that outside military assistance was of paramount importance to Finland. In simultaneous telegrams to Oslo and Stockholm, the Finnish diplomatic representatives were requested by their Foreign Ministry to inform the Scandinavian governments that the Allies were planning to send troops and that Finland welcomed such assistance.[21]

In his memoirs Pakaslahti admits that these instructions "were undeniably somewhat vague and—ambiguous": he doubts whether the Foreign Minister, when accepting the drafts, had "understood the far-reaching consequences" of the cables. Gripenberg's diary, however, is explicit that *Tanner had personally affirmed the basic idea of the cables by telephoning to London one day later that Finland needed help in the form of troops.*[22]

This, as well as many other curious December incidents, was left without mention in Tanner's memoirs. Even a month later, when the peace preparations were afoot, Tanner was observed to complain about the envoy in Paris, who, together with the "dangerous" Colonel Paasonen (to quote Tanner, who was afraid of the Colonel's direct contacts with the President of the Republic and the Finnish army headquarters), worked tirelessly for an Allied intervention. Tanner had perhaps not realized that, in addition to his personal enthusiasm, Holma had official grounds for such activities in Paris: the cable from the Foreign Ministry of 22 December 1939, which could be interpreted as general instructions, especially as it had never subsequently been revoked or clarified. The situation was different in London. On visiting the Foreign Office, Gripenberg found that the sending of troops was still undecided. He reported to Helsinki that for the time being the British Government was not ready to make up its mind.[23]

The electrifying effect of the Supreme Council discussions was felt at the meeting of the War Cabinet Military Co-ordination Committee on 20 December, which was attended by Admiral Lord Chatfield and General Ironside, both freshly back from Paris. Churchill had not been to Paris, but he was flattered to hear that the Supreme Council had shown interest in the ore question. He was consequently ready to give up his demand for the sea blockade of the Norwegian coast and to consider a new "larger plan". He was encouraged by the estimate of the C.I.G.S., according to which the actual target—the mining areas of Northern Sweden—could be occupied and held with relatively small forces—three to four thousand men able to ski—and that a Red Army attack on these regions would not be feasible until late winter at the earliest.

Accordingly, the possibility of the intervention leading to hostilities with the Soviet Union in fact seemed slight. The danger did, of course, exist, as Churchill observed, at least in certain respects. But since this represented a unique opportunity of depriving Germany of her vital supplies, it had to be exploited even at the price of great risks. One of these, the Military Co-ordination Committee admitted, was the possibility that the Allied intervention might "stimulate Germany into increased activity, and the whole tempo of the war would speed up." The Committee nevertheless ended by recommending intervention, leaving the practical planning to the chiefs of staff.[24]

Ironside had only a few days earlier jeered at Churchill's activity, but now, himself inspired by interventionist zeal, rushed to see the director of a London mountaineering club in order to find men who could ski. Even he seemed to share Churchill's opinion that too much attention should not be paid to the German menace: "Germany was inexperienced in combined operations," he told the War Cabinet. "An invasion of Southern Scandinavia would be an enormous commitment for her."[25]

All the same, when the question was taken up by the War Cabinet on Friday 22 December, Churchill had to resort to Sir Samuel Hoare's previous idea that the Scandinavian countries should be offered guarantees against Soviet or German attack to counterbalance all the help they could possibly give to Finland. A similar paragraph had been included in Daladier's draft communication to the effect that the Allies were "prepared to consider in what circumstances and in what form an assurance could in practice be given to Sweden and Norway."[26]

Churchill demanded that the gurantees should be given immediately, in order to have his earlier plan for the blockade of the west coast of Norway put into effect without delay. But Halifax evasively argued that the measures proposed by Churchill might endanger the success of the larger intervention plan or, in other words, make the Scandinavians unwilling to consent to the transit. Chamberlain was also of the opinion that excessive haste might ruin the enterprise:

It was essential to get Sweden in on our side. It would be impracticable to put in a force through Narvik to stop supplies to Germany from the Gälivare minefields unless we had the good-will of Sweden, and if we had Sweden's good-will, Norway would probably fall into line.

Since the Prime Minister had taken sides with Halifax, Churchill had to give way. The "minor" plan, the extension of the sea blockade to Norwegian territorial waters, was postponed until the Chiefs-of-Staff had considered the matter and a reply had been received from the Scandinavian countries. Besides the measures necessary for the defence of Sweden and Norway, the Chiefs-of-Staff were assigned the task of investigating what *indirect* help Britain might send to Finland immediately.[27] No sending of troops, of course, could be considered for the time being, only war materials and technical experts. However, in the light of the recent appeal for help from Helsinki, the military experts, if any, one understood that the success of the planned intervention in Scandinavia did very much depend on the endurance of Finnish resistance. "The solution rests with Finland," as Ironside admitted in his diary on Christmas Day.[28]

At the Foreign Office it was generally agreed that the aid to Finland should be intensified without delay. One of the first promoters of the idea of sending Allied troops to Finland, Under-Secretary Sir Orme Sargent, expressed his thoughts concisely:

There is a great deal to be said for adopting a forward policy in this matter in the hopes of thereby saving Finnish independence, instead of allowing Finland to collapse and then having to intervene in worse circumstances to save Norway and Sweden. If we do intervene there is a great deal to be said for doing so while we can still count upon the resistance of the Finnish Army.

Sir Alexander Cadogan, the Permanent Under-Secretary, had objected to Sargent's intervention proposal by referring to the lack of troops, but he too did not believe in the prospect of the Allies getting involved in war with the Soviet Union: the Finnish war, like the recent Spanish war, could be the subject of discreet intervention. Sargent for his part was terrified at the thought of aggression against the Scandinavian countries putting the guaranteeing Allies into as awkward a position as that brought about by the attack on Poland four months earlier. Sweden, in opposing the guarantee offers, made the same comparison.[29]

The Foreign Secretary returned to the question at the Cabinet meeting after Christmas. After a long and strenuous discussion it was decided, as he had proposed, to delay the blockade measures until the following week in order to give the Scandinavians time to decide freely on the offers of co-operation now before them. The offensive of the Red Army having come to a standstill, the German menace now attracted more attention than the Soviet one. The bringing up of the ore question, according to Halifax, would have endangered the acceptance of the offer, and consequently the assistance to Finland as it had been planned by the Allies.[30]

Daladier accepted the postponement "provided that the Allies now make a really decisive effort to assist Finland and to persuade Sweden and Norway to co-operate to this end." Accordingly, the French once more emphasised what they considered the main motive of the initiative.[31]

5

The War Cabinet had discussed the possibility of reinforcing the *démarches* to be made in Oslo and Stockholm by sending a Cabinet representative. The idea was rejected since a ministerial visit was considered too conspicuous. The proposals were eventually delivered through diplomatic channels, reaching their destinations on 28 December.

The memorandum presented to the Swedish Minister in London did not in fact contain anything sensational. At this stage there was no question of sending troops, only indirect assistance—"technical experts" (this is what made the Scandinavians suspicious) and material—being considered. The deliveries were to take place *unofficially*, as requested by the Swedes, on a commercial basis, or at least thus disguised. The most confusing paragraph in the document, that concerning the guarantees, came at the end. In addition to this, the Norwegian and Swedish representatives received verbal confirmation that the Allies proposed to their governments military contacts at General Staff level, to prepare for eventual mutual co-operation.[32]

The British Minister in Helsinki received instructions to inform the Finnish Government and to inquire what steps they proposed to take to persuade their two neighbours. In fact, the Finns had already expressed a similar wish on their own initiative in Stockholm and Oslo less than a week earlier.* The replies received in Helsinki had shown that the Scandinavians saw the situation in far more dramatic colours than could be imagined in London or Paris, or even in Helsinki. Thus in Stockholm, according to Erkko's cable:

Boheman said if troops are sent, end to independent existence of Finland and Sweden. The Scandinavian countries caught between Russia and Germany, and the West have small opportunity to send troops.[33]

The official Swedish answer was delivered in Paris on 4 January and in London one day later. It implied that Sweden was prepared in principle to facilitate the assistance operations of Britain, France and other states. It was, however, expected that the assistance would take place, as Prytz put it in London, in such a way "*that it did not give the impression of Sweden taking part in international activities,*" that the deliveries of war material would be carried out in the form of Finnish purchases from abroad, and that any eventual accompanying technical personnel would consist of volunteers travelling to Finland as private persons, and that the assistance would be kept secret.

---

* See above, pp. 68-9.

After giving an affirmative reply to the first part of the proposal but with conditions that were not negotiable, the Swedes refrained from the offer of guarantees, observing that the best they could do for the Finnish cause and for the interests of Europe as a whole was to remain neutral. In the instructions to Prytz, the Swedish Foreign Ministry asked that he should add verbally, when delivering the reply, that although it was appreciated in Stockholm that the Allies understood the Swedish position, the *hypothetical situation* chosen as a basis for the offer could not be discussed.*

Even though the Swedish answer failed to come up to expectations, it was not considered as altogether negative. Halifax even paid attention to Prytz's use of the word "now" in saying that the offer could not be discussed: "I note the word 'now' as of some interest." He also understood that Allied material could thenceforth be transported through Sweden to Finland under all circumstances.[34]

While the Swedish reply had left Halifax with some hopes, these were soon dispelled by the reactions aroused in Oslo and Stockholm by the news of Allied intentions in Norway. In Oslo, Koht had delayed answering the Allied offer, although he had been aware of the transit plans (informed as he was by the Finnish representative) since Christmas Eve. His reply was made easier by the announcement given to the Norwegian Minister in London on 5 January that the British sea blockade would be extended into Norwegian territorial waters. Norway protested, followed by Sweden, arguing that the plan would violate its neutrality and endanger the security of all Nordic countries. A protest cable despatched to London by the Swedish Foreign Ministry was followed by a message from King Haakon of Norway to King George VI, in which it was predicted that the plan, if put into effect, would lead Norway into war and distress.[35]

The interest in the Finnish war in London and Paris, arising mainly out of anti-Soviet sentiments, had by late December reached

---

* In the reply Britain was given a pungent reminder of the fact that it no longer had anything to say in the Baltic. Now only the Soviet Union and Germany were referred to as "Great Baltic Powers": "Collaboration between the two great Baltic Powers may lead to such measures that effective assistance to Finland may be prevented, at least temporarily...An eventual action by the two great Baltic Powers would, in addition to other consequences for Sweden herself, with great probability lead to a speedy breaking down of the resistance of Finland, without, as far as the Swedish Government can see, the Powers outside the Baltic being able to prevent this" (Memorandum dated 4 January 1940 by the Swedish Minister; Appendix No. 2 in Lord Chatfield's memorandum "Assistance to Finland", FO 371/24797/676).

new proportions. There was an increasing tendency to use the conflict as a weapon against Germany, which after all was regarded as enemy number one. The diversity of Allied aspirations complicated the formulation of a clear and effective policy in Finland, and as a result the Allies lost within less than a month their opportunity to exploit their initial success. The aggressive policy of Churchill, whose purpose was to isolate Germany, made it difficult to persuade the Scandinavians that they should assist Finland with the support of the Allies; it also neutralized the softer, somewhat anti-Soviet line represented by Halifax, which aimed at prolonging the Finnish resistance for as long as possible.

By now it was already realised in Oslo and Stockholm that both these alternatives were intended to get the Scandinavians involved on the Allied side and, sooner or later, into the world war. This observation made both governments increasingly aware of the political dangers which the Finnish war posed to the entire area, and increasingly eager to prevent the conflict from spreading. In London and Paris the assistance and intervention plans were continued with, but from now on the limits drawn by the Scandinavians had to be considered. This was the beginning of the development, during the second month of the war which, despite active Allied efforts, ended two and a half months later in disillusionment for the Finns.*

---

* See below, p. 95 and fn.

V

INTERVENTION PLANS
January 1940

The failure of the Norwegian and Swedish governments to respond positively to the Allied initiative made it highly unlikely that assistance for Finland and the cutting off of ore transports to Germany would meet with the approval of the Scandinavians. At Whitehall, plans for intervention were nevertheless developed, starting from the assumption that they could be carried out only with the co-operation of the local inhabitants. Technical reasons were the determining factor behind this assumption. As the Scandinavians still remained obdurate and the activists at home demanded action even if it provoked resistance, the soldiers made it clear that intervention under these conditions would be impossible without new and prolonged preparations.

The actual purpose of the reports of the Chiefs-of-Staff Committee, presented to the War Cabinet on 2 January 1940, was to study the possibilities of cutting off iron ore transports to Germany.[1] The defence of Finland was considered a mere secondary objective—but a necessary one, in order to keep the Russians as well as the Germans away from Narvik and the ore fields of Northern Sweden. On the other hand, the occupation of these regions by Allied forces would have opened a supply route to Finland.

The Chiefs-of-Staff suggested that intervention through Northern Sweden should be carried out by one or two brigades, between 4,000 and 7,000 men, by the end of March—at least before the break-up of the pack-ice in the Gulf of Bothnia offered the Germans the opportunity to send their own troops to the north in spring. In addition to an expeditionary force consisting of elite units familiar with winter conditions, such as French alpine troops and possibly Canadians, it was suggested that one or two infantry divisions might be sent to Narvik to secure the port and the railway leading to Sweden. For protecting Southern Sweden and Norway against the Germans, four to six Allied divisions were considered necessary.[2]

The Chiefs-of-Staff thought it possible that the Germans would try to get to Luleå and would occupy the Åland Islands as their first stage of operations. They also warned that the *Luftwaffe* might take immediate counter-measures, regardless of the season, in the Narvik-Gällivare areas, and subject them to air attacks with bombers operating within a radius of 600 miles: with the advance of the Red Army offensive the Germans might even have access to air bases on the Finnish side, for instance at Kemi at the head of the Gulf of Bothnia.

But, as the military experts observed, Finnish resistance showed no signs of collapse at that moment. A Soviet advance towards the North of Sweden and Narvik seemed unlikely for the time being. At worst, light formations of the Red Army might cross the Swedish frontier in April. Even if the Russians finally succeeded in occupying Finland and then repaired the damaged rail network of the country, they were not able to concentrate more than ten, and probably only four or five combat divisions at the Swedish border, and after midsummer at the earliest. Even then, it was concluded, the Allies ran no considerable risk of meeting the Soviet forces; they could indeed take charge of the Swedes along the border as well as the Finns retreating west of Tornio and use them for guerrilla operations against the Russians.[3]

In contrast to these somewhat illusory considerations, the Chiefs-of-Staff showed a striking sense of realism in giving little value to Churchill's suggestions that the ore transports could be stopped simply by means of sabotage. In his heart of hearts, Ironside viewed these proposals with ironic detachment, observing that they were imaginative beyond all measure; in his diary he recounts how Churchill, even in late February, played with the idea that the ore route on the Gulf of Bothnia could be closed with sea mines sent secretly by rail from Narvik to Luleå. As the First Lord had been unable to explain how this was feasible, someone had remarked he should have some handy assistant to help him in concocting such ideas, like Friday for Robinson Crusoe.[4]

Finland was obviously designed to serve as a base for the sabotage preparations. The War Cabinet had agreed on 27 December, before the discussion of the Chiefs-of-staff reports, *"that the railway sabotage personnel should sail forthwith for Finland"*. The special personnel were to travel to Finland in the guise of commercial agents, and their task was to cut off the Murmansk railway from the direction of Finland. They were to be British because, as was stated, there was no chance of training Finns for the task in such a short time. The main objective actually seems to have been the Swedish ore ports and the Gällivare-Luleå line rather than the Murmansk railway: for sabotaging the latter the Finns surely had no lack of specialized men familiar with winter conditions.[5]

The Chiefs-of-Staff admitted that the ports of Luleå and Oxelösund could be destroyed for several months; but single agents would not suffice for the task, and it was scarcely possible for the necessary special troops with large amounts of material to be transported to the spot. The destruction of the Gällivare railway, on the other hand, seemed absurd at this stage: repairing it would have been exceptionally difficult because of physical impediments, and might of course seriously retard the carrying out of the planned intervention.[6]

It was clear to the military experts that the measures proposed by Churchill could imperil the larger intervention plan and, while damaging Finland's supply connections, hasten her collapse. Even a limited plan for laying mines in Norwegian territorial waters and blockading Narvik might provoke a German counter-attack, when the situation could slip out of Allied control. Though this might be avoided, the Scandinavians would then hardly consent to co-operate in a more extensive intervention.

All the war games played at Whitehall had one thing in common: that almost every factor—operational terrain, climate, time, enemy, even forces available—was unknown. Necessary reserves were unavailable. Even if the expeditionary corps to be sent to Scandinavia had been assembled simply by thinning the defence of the Western front, the bulk of it, untrained and with insufficient supplies, would have been unfit for the exceptional conditions north of the Arctic Circle. The attitude of the Norwegians and the Swedes was highly questionable: the Chiefs-of-Staff, as we have seen, never thought of the operation without the participation of the Scandinavians. And, last but not least, there was the question whether the Red Army, once Finland had collapsed, would stop at the river Tornio or cross it. This was the reason why the Allies were aiming at Northern Sweden—the pretext might now turn into terrifying reality.[7]

In any case the attitude of the generals had changed decisively: they no longer worried even about the possibility that the Allies would get involved in a war with the Soviet Union.[8] While preparing their plan they were apparently hypnotized by Daladier and Churchill, believing that this would indeed be a turning-point in the war. In the first paragraph of their report, the following lines express the magnitude of changes involved in the planned expedition:

It must be realized that to embark in Scandinavia in the spring of 1940 represents a fundamental change in our policy. Up to date that policy has been to remain on the defensive on land and in the air, while our armaments are increased. The plan under review, however, would enable us to initiate, in March, offensive operations which might well prove decisive. The opportunity is a great one and we see no prospect of an equal chance being afforded us elsewhere.[9]

2

Even before Christmas, the War Cabinet had expressed fears that the halt of the Red Army offensive in Finland would have a soothing effect on the Scandinavians and would make them less and less willing to join the battle.[10] The fact that the Russians had failed to clarify their war objectives in public fed the misgivings, actively spread by Finnish diplomacy, that their final objective was the Atlantic coast. In this situation, with the other Nordic countries showing such obvious lack of fighting spirit, it seemed to be in the British interest for resistance in Finland to be strengthened, as long as this was still desired. Sir Orme Sargent, drafting a reply to Snow, observed that a great change of mind had taken place in the War Cabinet:

Up till now we have, I fear, given Mr. Snow very little reason to suppose that we attach any real importance to the continued existence of Finland as an independent State. The war material that we have sent, and are sending, to Finland is obviously not going to affect the final issue and is merely a gesture. But, unknown to Mr. Snow, opinion has recently been crystallising here to the effect that we ought to save Finland if only because she constitutes a barrier between Russia and her control over the Swedish iron ore and her ambitions to reach the Atlantic.[11]

The Soviet threat to Scandinavia had been stressed since mid-December when the cutting off of German ore transports was under discussion. As expressed by the report of the Chiefs-of-Staff, political aspects relating to the assistance to Finland were not neglected either. They attracted increasing attention, especially in France, for the reason that General Weygand was planning an offensive from the Levant against the Soviet Union, with the intention of destroying the Caucasian oilfields.* Meanwhile, as a French document written at the turn of the year put it, "the Finnish front meant the same advantage to the Allies as the Macedonian front in the 1914–18 war"— in other words the possibility of diverting German attention elsewhere away from France.[12]

The view that Soviet military power had proved hollow and that the Allies did not necessarily have to fear a conflict with it, even while the war with Germany was still going on, was gaining ground. During the very first week of the Finnish war, this point of view was expressed, surprisingly enough, by Sir William Seeds himself. His French colleague, M. Naggiar, disillusioned by the pro-German policy of the Soviet Government, was of the same opinion and

---

* See below, pp. 110-11.

indicated, in a report sent from Moscow, that the Allies should not stop half way once they had started the assistance to Finland. According to a January report by the French Ambassador in London, even Sir Alexander Cadogan at the Foreign Office expected that the Allies would soon decide whether it would be more advisable to declare war on the U.S.S.R.; in the latter case, Cadogan had argued, the Swedes would prefer to appeal for Allied help, if the Russians were to continue their advance over the western border of Finland.[13]

By now the military experts readily followed the diplomats. After drawing attention to the inefficiency displayed in Finland by the Soviet forces, especially the air force, the Chiefs-of-Staff concluded:

(a) We think it likely that Russia will persist in her attempt to conquer Finland and that she may thus become involved in a large commitment in Northern Europe.

(b) Such commitment is likely to diminish her ability to threaten British interests in the Middle East.

(c) We believe that if we went to war with Russia, our action would be welcomed by the majority of neutral states throughout the world, as being evidence of our determination to make a firm stand against unwarranted aggression.

(d) We recognise that war with Russia may throw an additional, but not insupportable, burden upon our control of sea communications.

(e) On balance it appears that *the disadvantages of open hostilities with Russia should be accepted in preference to losing the chance, and perhaps the only chance, of achieving the early defeat of Germany.*[14]

With such an atmosphere prevailing, more active anti-Soviet action on the British side might have been expected during early 1940 than was actually the case. It was a matter of lacking means rather than willingness. As far as land and air forces were concerned, Allied resources were limited, and the transport of larger units to Finland was made impossible by the opposition of the Scandinavian countries. The use of naval forces, asked for by Finnish authorities in December, was controlled by the reluctant Churchill. The supply of arms was the only way to strengthen Finnish resistance.

It might be expected that, after the political decisions to assist Finland had been taken, the Finns would have received the war material they lacked quickly. However, the negligence in delivering their orders, especially in Britain, considerably diluted Finnish defence efforts. In the War Cabinet the most consistent supporter of assistance was Halifax; he gave ready assurances of his sincerity, as for instance when Gripenberg came to ask him for fighters: "I wish I had aeroplanes in my pockets. You would get them all!"[15] The most effective obstructionists, on the other hand, were the ministries responsible for the British war effort; they had no difficulty in justifying their unwillingness to share their meagre weapon stocks with the Finns, a sufficiently prescient attitude in view of the situation only six months later.

Every single request for war materials was haggled over. "Always the same game", Gripenberg sighed, "first they refuse, valuable time is lost, and then something is given."[16] It must be added that the incompetence of the Finnish officials in charge of war material purchases often aggravated the difficulty of these activities. Daily, confused requests arrived in London from Helsinki—these could be large or small, and were either qualitatively too exigent or quantitatively too inaccurate, with the common feature that all were to be carried out immediately. By demanding certain supplies in small amounts, time and again, and others in almost unlimited quantity, the Finns often gave a misleading picture of their real needs.[17]

Thanks largely to the energy and skill of the head of the small Finnish Legation in London, a considerable part of the deliveries were carried out. Since a planned inter-ministerial co-ordinating body never came into being, the export licences for the war materials had to be procured separately from the ministries concerned.

To top it all, some mistakes, which for one reason or another took place in the deliveries, hindered the prompt arrival of the material, especially aircraft, at the front: the Gladiator fighter aircraft were without repair equipment; the special calibre machine-guns were sent without the necessary ammunition; the Blenheim bombers lacked radios with frequencies used in Finland, and were not equipped with bomb-racks suitable for the bombs in use there.[18] The prohibition on the use of British flying personnel hampered the air transportation of the most urgent materials, even the transfer of planes delivered to Finland; on the long flights by way of Norway at least five planes were lost, apparently because the Finnish pilots were unfamiliar with the new models.[19]

The majority of the fighters and other heavy equipment had to be transported by the few available Finnish freighters to Norway. From there the dismantled planes were generally taken to Sweden for assembly and testing, while the rest of the material was transported by rail to Finland—with reloading on the border at Tornio.* Waiting for transport licences and convoys often delayed the deliveries so much that the time taken to deliver a single consignment from Britain to Finland averaged one month.[20]

British assistance did nevertheless produce results which in the last phase of fighting were seen and felt even at the front. The first

---

* The Finnish and Swedish railways have different gauges.

considerable reinforcements were a dozen long-nosed Blenheim bombers, of which only ten actually reached Finland by air in January. The decision to give the Blenheims had been taken shortly before Christmas, when Snow had sent a cable on 19 December saying that Ryti had asked for them. According to the envoy, Ryti had said that Finland needed the planes for bombing the Murmansk railway as well as Leningrad and Moscow, "*as a counter-threat to secure cessation of air raids on Helsinki, and secondly, on account of the moral impression in Russian cities, which he thought might be very far-reaching.*" The order for the next dozen Blenheims and thirty new fighters was entered by Gripenberg soon after Christmas. These deliveries, however, took longer. Only the Blenheims arrived in time, thus raising the total of the British planes taking part in the Winter War to fifty-two.[21]

In January the Finnish land forces too were promised new and heavier equipment: twenty-five 105-mm. howitzers (150 had been asked for) with 25,000 rounds; twenty-four heavy 76-mm. anti-aircraft guns with 72,000 rounds; twenty-four artillery tractors for 6-inch guns; and four 6-ton armoured cars—most of these items were promised with immediate delivery. Further, in addition to the consignments delivered in December, export licences were granted for fifty anti-tank rifles (with 10,000 cartridges), 8,000 anti-tank mines and 40,000 hand-grenades.*[22]

As far as France was concerned, she had sent to Finland by the beginning of February a number of fighter aircraft, but no bombers: besides the thirty Morane Saulnier 406 fighters—an excellent model though poorly armed—seven antiquated Caudron 714 fighters had been despatched and seventy-six others promised. None of the Caudron planes arrived before the end of hostilities—rather luckily for the Finnish pilots. Moreover, the Finns were promised Koolhoven co-operation planes, eighty in all. Besides the Morane fighters, at least fourteen shipments of French war material reached Finland before the end of hostilities.

The artillery sent by the French was perhaps more important in quantity than quality. In addition to twelve 75-mm. field guns with 24,000 rounds, which were shipped early enough to be used at the front, the Finns were supplied with twelve 105-mm. and twenty-four 155-mm. howitzers (with some 50,000 rounds) and with over one hundred of the 80-155-mm. recoilless

---

* To the list of materials granted British export licences after December may be added: 5 searchlight reflectors, 45 tons of hexachlorethane, 1,300 field telephones, 250 field telephone switchboards, 2,000 miles of field cable, 100,000 uniforms and overcoats, 50,000 pairs of boots, 5,000 large tents, 300 field kitchens, 1,000 saddles, 5,000 horse blankets, 150,000 haversacks. These items, among many others, are worth noting, since most of them arrived before the Winter War was over.

de Bange guns, mostly dating from the nineteenth century (with abundant ammunition). Somehow, the Finns still regard these old-fashioned cannon as symbolic of all the foreign assistance provided to Finland during the Winter War. Much of this armament, the French observers reported, remained unserviceable because no instructions were provided for the Finnish armourers and gunners, and because of the errors and omissions in packing committed by those responsible for delivery.*

The French infantry weapons shipped to Finland before the beginning of February included one hundred 81-mm. mortars with 100,000 shells, fifty 25-mm. anti-tank guns with 25,000 rounds, 200,000 hand-grenades, and over 5,000 light machine-guns with some 20 million cartridges.† According to an estimate, found in the Vincennes military archives, the total value of the equipment and armour delivered by the French during the Winter War had amounted by 12 February 1940 to 433.5 million francs. In addition, the French had made Finland a gift of military goods worth nearly 33 million francs. Moreover, by readily allowing transit to Finland through French territory of a considerable number of foreign (especially Italian and Hungarian) arms consignments and volunteers, France greatly helped the Finnish war effort indirectly.[23]

As indicated by the decision of the British and French governments in March, the Allied aid to Finland might have been more effective. Few Britons and Frenchmen, and even fewer Finns, harboured any illusions about securing the continuation of Finnish resistance, especially as spring was approaching and assistance remained so scanty. The liaison officer of the Imperial General Staff, Brigadier Ling, and his French counterpart Lieutenant-Colonel Ganeval, after spending a fortnight at Mannerheim's headquarters were soon fully aware of the realities of the situation. "Have you come here", the Field-Marshal greeted the latter on his arrival, with undisguised bitterness, "only to prolong our agony?"[24]

On 13 January Ling warned London that the Finns needed modern fighters immediately to protect the country from air raids. In addition, their land forces needed—in the following order of importance—long-range guns, anti-tank weapons and ammunition for the field-guns. But, worst of all, even the most effective material assistance could not make up for the loss of human materials. Ling

---

* More artillery was later promised and even despatched, but it did not reach Finland before the Winter War ended. See below, p. 127.

† Here may be added 100 field telephone switchboards, over 3,000 miles of telephone cable, 200 tons of barbed wire, 500 flashlights, 20,000 signal rockets, as well as important field observation and fire control equipment.

reported Mannerheim as saying that he needed 30,000 new able-bodied soldiers before the winter was over. Ganeval, returning to Paris a week later, described the situation even more pessimistically. "He gave me the impression", Gamelin writes,

....that the resistance of the Finnish army was approaching its end, not because the losses had been great but because, due to the length of the front, all forces were engaged, and the troops in the front line could not be changed nor local points of breakage be reinforced: there are no reserves....[25]

3

Ling's report in the middle of January created the basis for the War Cabinet decision to intensify assistance to Finland. In addition to the relatively important materials delivered hitherto, the Cabinet agreed in principle to the enlistment of British volunteers and started discussions on the formation of an expeditionary force of regular troops which, contrary to the earlier Narvik force, were intended expressly for Finland. The middle of January may thus be regarded, from the point of view of British policy towards Finland, as the turning-point of the Winter War. Besides the strategic considerations described above,* the new decisions were due to the fact that even a number of members of the War Cabinet had begun to see assistance to Finland as an end in itself. The first person to ask for it in the inner circle of the War Cabinet was the Lord Privy Seal, Sir Samuel Hoare, who had been Foreign Secretary during the Ethiopian crisis. His memorandum, read at the War Cabinet meeting on 27 December, emphasized the necessity of inducing the Swedes to join the war, which Hoare considered feasible by exploiting "a very strong anti-Russian feeling in Sweden".[26]

The question was discussed again by the Cabinet on 1 January after Halifax had received from Prytz advance information as to the nature of the answer to be expected from Sweden. The Cabinet seems to have paid little attention to the negative tone of Swedish opinion. Everybody was excited by the news, published during the last two days by the press, that the Finns had beaten the enemy at Tolvajärvi and Suomussalmi.† Halifax even reported that there had been bread riots in Leningrad. *"Finnish resistance, if sufficiently supported"*, the Secretary for War, Hore-Belisha, observed, *"might result in a defeat of Russia."*[27]

---

* Ling's report stressed the fear that the occupation of Finland would result in the partition of all the three Nordic countries between the Soviet Union and Germany.

† Cf. above, p. 42.

The Lord Privy Seal then returned to the question of whether the "great occasion" afforded by the Finnish situation had been sufficiently exploited by the Allies, and proposed that in addition to material assistance, manpower should also be sent to Finland. The Cabinet instantly agreed, giving him the task of studying, together with the Military Co-ordinating Committee and the Foreign Office representative, all the possible ways of assisting Finland, direct armed intervention excepted.[28]

At the meeting of the Co-ordinating Committee on the same day, 4 January, the question of sending volunteers to Finland was taken up for the first time at an official level. The attitude of the Prime Minister and Foreign Secretary as well as the C.I.G.S., as expressed in various contexts, was somewhat reserved. The Secretary for War, on the other hand, was in favour of granting permission to those wishing to go to Finland whether they were military personnel or not.* (Chamberlain still viewed the sending of soldiers with special aversion.) The question had not been taken up earlier, it was observed, because "the Finns, who had been very precise in their demands, had so far confined these to material and had as yet never asked for men—not even technicians".†[29]

For the military high command the situation was made less complicated by the Cabinet decision of 12 January, according to which Churchill's "minor" plan was definitely given up. The Foreign Secretary, the plan's main opponent, argued that the Australian Prime Minister had been outspoken against forcing the neutrals. Halifax also said that he had been warned that Swedish pro-Allied opinion might react very strongly if the neutrality of the Nordic countries were violated despite their objections. His informant, the well-known Swedish banker Marcus Wallenberg, Jr., who was in London for trade negotiations, had also called attention to the fact that the Allied plans made assistance to Finland more difficult: the Swedes, Wallenberg had said, had delivered 20-30 per cent of their war material supplies to Finland, receiving continued replacements from the Germans; if the British were to try to stop the ore traffic by force, even this form of support would come to an end.‡[30]

---

* The meeting turned out to be the last involving the temperamental liberal, Hore-Belisha, as Secretary of State for War; Prime Minister Ryti had the odd impression that he was an opponent of assistance to Finland (see, e.g., cable No. 20, 9-1-1940, of the U.S. Minister in Helsinki, Schoenfield to the Secretary of State; FRUS, 1940, I, p. 275). His successor, Oliver Stanley, adopted a far more reserved attitude toward the Finns and objected to the idea of assisting them at the expense of other considerations of defence.

† On later discussions on the question of volunteers, in Britain, see below, pp. 174-6·

‡ Cf. p. 52.

Meanwhile the alarming news brought by Ling from Finland called the Cabinet's attention to the need for further intensification of assistance. On 16 January Gripenberg visited the Foreign Secretary with the report that Finland urgently needed sixty modern fighters—Hurricanes, if not Spitfires. As revealed in his diary, he acted in understanding with Ling, whom he had met at a luncheon given by his old friend Kirke, and who had advised him to put pressure on Halifax. Ling had even given him the number of fighters needed: about two squadrons, fifty-four planes in all. The brigadier for his part, when making his statement before the Military Co-ordinating Committee, had stressed the fighter shortage of the Finnish air force and maintained that Finnish pilots were fighting virtually with the remnants of the material they had had at the start of the war; no more than thirty fighters were still fit for use, and the Gladiators sent from Britain a month earlier were only now arriving.[31]

Although the Cabinet members were thus informed of the seriousness of the situation, it seemed impossible to meet the request. However, the R.A.F. Chief-of-Staff reported that twelve Hurricanes could be released, and the Admiralty promised to deliver twenty Skua fighters (suitable for dive-bombing) and thirteen Roc co-ordination planes.* Finally the Finns were to receive only the Hurricanes, of which only eight arrived a few days before the end of the war, too late to take part in operations.[32]

In any case, a more favourable attitude towards Finland had gained ground in the Cabinet. The most conspicuous convert was the First Lord of the Admiralty, who had offered Finland the navy planes despite his customary stand against such extensive war material deliveries. The same day, he had given another even more remarkable demonstration of his goodwill by suggesting, in disagreement with the military representatives, that the needs of the defence of the British Isles be reconsidered so that the heavy anti-aircraft guns asked for by the Finns could be delivered.[33]

Considering the events of less than six months later, even a limited concession of this kind signified for the British an undeniable, and indeed foolhardy, self-sacrifice. Even so, concrete expressions of sympathy were not enough to solve the dilemma of Finland's rescue. During the next two weeks Chamberlain's Cabinet continued to discuss this dilemma from a new starting-point, but in the

---

* Furthermore the Cabinet took a favourable view of Gripenberg's initiative that the $10 million loan obtained from the United States for foodstuffs could eventually be used so that the goods procured from America by the Finns would be shipped to Britain and an equivalent number of fighters, ordered by British from the Lockheed factories, could be shipped straight to Finland. Since the deliveries took too long, the transaction was never realized.

old way: asking for more reports, statements and accounts, subjecting it to this and that committee, back and forth, forgetting that "delays have dangerous ends".[34]

Finally on 2 February the War Cabinet at Hoare's suggestion took up the question of assistance as a whole. The resolutions of the meeting were to form the basis for the position adopted by the British delegation at a new meeting of the Allied Supreme War Council three days later. According to them it was "extremely important" to prevent the Soviet Union from conquering Finland during the coming spring. For this reason it was necessary *to send to Finland considerable reinforcements by way of Norway and Sweden, these troops consisting of trained regular soldiers in the guise of volunteers*—a practice adopted by the Italians in Spain.

The Foreign Office was instructed not to mention the ore question this time when asking for transit permisssion in Oslo and Stockholm; instead, it was to reiterate that the Allies were prepared to guarantee the safety of Norway and Sweden against a German offensive. It was also recommended that the Scandinavians be told that, if they refused to accept the Allied proposal now, the responsibility for an eventual annihilation of Finland would devolve on them. Accordingly, as if to stress the fact that the only possible road to assist Finland was by way of Narvik and Gällivare, the Cabinet rejected—at the recommendation of the Chiefs-of-Staff—the French plan for sending an expeditionary force to Petsamo.[35]

4

Despite its remoteness, Petsamo held a great attraction for the Allies. For one thing, it was the only Finnish port free from ice and immune from total German blockade: it was the only route by which Finland could be assisted without permission being sought from outsiders. For one reason or another, it was thought that an expedition to Petsamo would not provoke the Germans into attacking Scandinavia. Further, this region would provide a base for observing the Murmansk coast and the movements of German vessels in the Arctic. The Allies knew from experience that Petsamo was a useful base, since during the last year of the First World War their naval and land forces had been stationed there to secure the Allied supply route to Murmansk. Finally, the British presence in the region could be justified, if for no other reason, by the safeguarding of their interests in the nickel mines.*[36]

---

* As reported by Pakaslahti (op. cit., 228), the concessionaires of the Petsamo nickel company were kept informed by the Finnish Foreign Ministry of the military operations in the North with the purpose of "using even this means for

The actual initiative to intervene at Petsamo did not come from London or Paris, however, but from Helsinki. Two weeks after the outbreak of the war, on 13 December, Snow cabled to the Foreign Office that *the Finnish Foreign Minister had expressed the serious wish that the Allies should open up a supply route to Finland by sending Polish warships to Petsamo*. It is not surprising that Tanner fails to mention a word of this initiative in his memoirs or his diary (in a later context, it is true, he admits that such an operation was planned but that he disliked it).[37] Nevertheless, the following letter written by Tanner in his own hand to Gripenberg, apparently in December 1939, constitutes another piece of evidence on his role in inviting the Poles to Petsamo:

It seems most difficult for us to hold our own up north, especially in Petsamo. This gave rise to the idea to try to interest Britain in the defence of this corner of the world. Since Britain herself may want to avoid war against the Soviet Union, we came to think of the Polish navy. Could it not be sent up there? I mentioned this idea to Snow and he became very enthusiastic about it.[38]

The Polish vessels concerned, three destroyers and two submarines (one of them the famous *Orzel*), had escaped from the Baltic in the autumn and were still sailing under the Polish flag, even if in close contact with the Royal Navy. After Gripenberg had raised the matter, on personal instructions from Tanner, with the Polish envoy in London, the latter quite correctly foresaw that the Admiralty would never approve the plan. On 18 December the Admiralty indeed pronounced against the operation, since, as it maintained, the project lacked significance and it might lead to hostilities with the Soviet Union. The official explanation for not accepting the proposal was that the Polish ships were not fit for use on any ocean.[39] The Finns soon realised that they had been over-hasty and, when the situation cooled down, returned to the difficult road of neutrality—thenceforth avoiding direct contacts with the Polish government in exile. Apparently Germany had not got wind of the mistake, or at least it failed to react. For the time being, however, Helsinki remained adamant. On 21 December Premier Ryti proposed to Snow that the British should use their own navy at Petsamo. The Finnish Minister in Paris was instructed to put the matter before Daladier as well as the head of the Polish government in exile, General Wladyslaw Sikorsky. The General instantly approved of the idea,

gaining support from the Anglo-Saxons". The representative of the Mond Company, on the other hand, as mentioned in Gripenberg's diary (4 Jan. 1940), privately contributed £5,000 to the assistance of Finland.

disclosing to the Finn that the earlier request had been turned down by Churchill because the British feared a war against the Soviet Union.[40]

Daladier, understanding Churchill's embarrassment, for his part favoured the idea of using the Polish navy: one of the advantages of the plan, he observed to Sikorsky, was precisely the possibility that Britain, being in charge of the Polish ships, *"would thus be drawn into direct anti-Russian activities"*; he assured London that "this kind of an operation did not differ greatly from delivering war material to Finland and, if the Russians were looking for a pretext for attacking the Western Powers, they already had one."[41]

From the French archives it appears that the chief of the naval forces, Admiral Darlan, even sent his representatives to London immediately after Christmas to discuss the proposal with the Admiralty. After trying in vain to convince their ally, the French, apprehensive because of the Soviet strength in submarines and the threat that the Red Army might represent in relation to British interests in Asia, on 16 January initiated a plan for an expedition to Petsamo, based on Admiral Darlan's memorandum. Though originally French, it was worked out as a joint Allied operation so that the intervention would not involve the Western Powers in hostilities with the Soviet Union. In a letter to Corbin the following day, in which the Ambassador was asked to bring the matter to the notice of the Foreign Office, Daladier wrote:

By means of supply ships, disguised as Polish, the strategic importance of the operation could be increased. Within the planned scope, in other words, of a Finnish-Polish operation it could no doubt easily be carried out as the responsibility of the proponent governments with our all-out assistance, either direct or indirect. Now almost three weeks have passed since this matter was taken up for the first time, and yet it is subject to negative examination and criticism only.[42]

The operation plan, drawn up under Darlan's direction, seems to have followed in detail the lines laid down in an *aide-memoire* by Col. Paasonen, dated 24 December 1939 and handed to Daladier a few days later. According to this document it would be enough to cut off the sea connections to Murmansk in order to defeat the Soviet division which had occupied Petsamo. The Finns actually fighting on the Petsamo front (a battalion in strength) could have been released for other duties. Several Finnish reserve regiments—there were still quite a number without arms—could have been equipped with the eventual war booty. "This would undoubtedly be the quickest way to help," the author concluded.[43]

But Paasonen's proposal went even further: it was necessary to study the possibilities of *a joint offensive across the Soviet border (towards Kandalaksha in the north and towards Lake Olonets in the south), in order to separate Eastern Karelia from Russia*. In military terms this would have resulted in the blockade of the land and sea forces stationed in the Murmansk area and the Kola Peninsula, in the shortening of the Finnish front, and the securing of its connections to the Ocean. But even to the Allies the plan offered tempting advantages:

....Petsamo and Murmansk would provide a starting-point for British troops in more favourable conditions than in 1918. The political advantage offered by such military operations was also considerable. There were thousands of political exiles interned in the Murmansk and Karelian areas, where the concentration camps were ready to rebel against the oppressors. Finally *Karelia could form the base, where anti-Stalinist national forces could gradually gather.*[44]

Apparently Paasonen drew up his memorandum without instructions from Helsinki. His wide-ranging expansionist perspectives were probably presented as a bait for the anti-Soviet French interested in the new "crusade", and —who can tell?—even for Finnish politicians. The purpose was indeed to outline a grand strategic move, with the promises of a Greater Finland and of a more successful Allied intervention than that of 1918-19 in Northern Russia. The colonel estimated that it would be necessary to have a strong concentration of air power (up to 300-400 planes in order to gain air supremacy), and three or four light divisions of land forces familiar with winter conditions to carry out this operation. No tactical advice, however, was given, especially regarding disembarkation at Petsamo.

Admiral Darlan, as already mentioned, had suggested that the naval unit to carry out the operation should be formed of Polish warships, possibly with the support of Polish-Finnish occupied armed cargo ships which were to transport the invasion force: a French brigade of Chasseurs Alpins, two Foreign Legion battalions, four Polish battalions, and one or two British brigades: 13,000-17,000 men in all. These, together with the Finns attacking from the south, were to beat the Soviet troops, then cutoff their supply lines and open the way to the south.[45]

An expeditionary force, sent to assist the Finns—according to the French proposal, "a few divisions"—was then to cross the Soviet border, at the latitude of Kandalaksha, under Allied cover to cut the Murmansk railway and surround the enemy troops (estimated at four divisions) still left in the north. The plan was even discussed at a political level: for example, the then Chairman of the Chamber of Deputies, Edouard Herriot, told Holma on 17 January that he had heard of the plan from Gamelin and that he was excited at the idea of cutting the Murmansk railway, "a railway that we have built".*[46]

The Chiefs-of-Staff in London criticized the plan as being inaccurate and irrational. The French had ventured to suggest that a landing force be disembarked in one of the fjords (presumably at Kirkenes) on the Norwegian side, in the event that the Finns attacking Petsamo from the south failed in their operation. As the British remarked that this would imply a violation of Norwegian neutrality the French answered that "landing in some lonely fjord would be a less serious violation than landing in Narvik".[47] To the argument that the Petsamo operation would not lead to the main Allied objective—the cutting off of German ore transport—Léger in person presented a rather extraordinary counter-argument: an attack on Petsamo might provoke a German offensive against Scandinavia, in which event the Allies would be justified in hastening to the assistance of Norway and Sweden. As for the Soviet Union, the Secretary-General continued, it would not have *any right* to oppose the Allied ships penetrating to Petsamo, since these were coming to Finnish and not Soviet territory, with the consent of the Finns and with the support of the League of Nations resolution: "On the contrary, if the Russians should oppose, they would be guilty of opening hostilities and the Allies would be entitled to retaliate by destroying their oilfields in Baku."[48]

But it was for political reasons rather than because of military weaknesses that the French, too, finally gave up the Petsamo plan. It was Daladier's idea, as we know, that both main objectives—the assistance to Finland and the cutting off of the ore transports—could be obtained by a single military operation. This made the French give up Petsamo in favour of Narvik. In London, it is true, there was still discussion of endangering Soviet supply routes to Petsamo by other means, such as by laying mines; at one time it was even thought that ocean-going submarines, including their maintenance crews, could be placed at the disposal of the Finns. These possibilities were then discarded after the larger intervention plan came to the fore in early February.[49]

The mere strength of the Soviet naval forces on the Murmansk coast was enough to make the success of the operation unlikely, especially as the massive co-operation of the British could not be counted upon: in the Arctic alone, the number of Soviet submarines

---

* A reference to the Anglo-French financing of the construction of the Murmansk railway during the First World War.

was estimated at twenty-six.[50] The limited capacity of the Petsamo harbour, the continuous flank threat of the Soviet divisions at Murmansk, not to mention the unfamiliarity of the landing forces with Arctic conditions—all these factors make it appear doubtful that the plan could ever have succeeded. Lieutenant-General K.L. Oesch, then chief of the Finnish general staff, and Lieutenant-General A.F. Airo, chief of operations, have told the present writer that they considered Allied chances in the north hopeless. The commander of the Finnish forces in Lapland, Major-General K.M. Wallenius, is less categorical, but he too refers to the exceptionally severe snow-storms occurring in Petsamo in early spring, which would have made the operations difficult.

Harold Macmillan mentions in his memoirs that the British military attaché in Helsinki, newly returned from Mannerheim's headquarters, told him in February 1940 that the Finns planned, in the event of sufficient reinforcements from abroad becoming available, to attack Kandalaksha, maybe even Petrozavodsk; according to this information, the Finnish chief of general staff and the chief of operations believed in the success of such an offensive.[51] The former does not recall this plan, but General Airo observed during our discussion that such a plan was indeed prepared in anticipation of the Allies' arrival. Mannerheim for his part admitted that he had studied the plan with Ganeval and considered it worth carrying through.[52]

Likewise, according to an official Finnish report, Mannerheim had belittled the significance of a couple of Allied divisions in Petsamo for the outcome of the conflict, and pointed out the danger of German counter-measures. On the other hand, he is reported to have told Ling that the operation might have "a greater, maybe more decisive effect, if it were directed deeper by way of Archangel". The Field-Marshal could hardly have suggested this seriously if he had not been aware of more extensive anti-Soviet plans. Considering that the statement was given before Ling's return to London in January, he must have been informed of the matter before it, probably by Ganeval—if not by General Weygand, with whom he had exchanged letters during these days.

It is clear that Mannerheim entertained the idea of exploiting the anti-Soviet sentiments growing in Britain and France and of tempting the Allies to direct their Arctic operation so far to the east that Finland would escape the danger of becoming a battlefield for the Great Powers, as he argued:

An independent operation on Arkangel carried out farther from our border would be of considerably greater importance for us while still not drawing us directly into world war.[53]

5

The plans for a Petsamo expedition had offered to Daladier a welcome back door, when the delay of assistance to Finland had aroused criticism and threatened the prestige of his government. This might partly explain why information on the plan was leaked at its initial stage. Was Daladier serious, or was Petsamo for him only a political bluff? The preparations for intervention seem to have met with obstruction from London. The delivery of war material to Finland, especially that of fighter equipment, had been impeded by transport difficulties. Something had to be done quickly, in order to show the world that France, at least, was not sitting with her hands folded. "The deputy Foreign Minister [Champetier de Ribes] told me yesterday", Holma reported on New Year's Eve, "that Daladier speaks of nothing else [but assistance to Finland], thinking of new plans all the time and letting his assistants study their feasibility." The pressure on him was strenuous, further increased by the fact that he had concentrated the duties of foreign and defence minister on himself, and was tied down in budget negotiations for a week after Christmas, then to his bed for almost a month after New Year with his foot in plaster.[54]

The initiative displayed by the French Premier, and continued after a break of a week or two even from his sick-bed, was actively encouraged by the Finnish envoy in Paris. Holma, as has been mentioned, had interpreted the instructions of his ministry literally, and paid one visit after another to Daladier together with Colonel Paasonen, who was equally dedicated to the cause of intervention. A good example of their activating influence was their visit to Daladier cn 14 January for the purpose of accelerating the Petsamo operation: it was after this discussion that the Premier urged Gamelin and Darlan, who came to see him next, to prepare within two days a preliminary plan for a landing in Petsamo.[55]

Holma showed naive trust in Daladier's assurances of French assistance to Finland. For him it was difficult, especially during the final stages of the war, to distinguish between the interests of the *entente* and those of Finland. What the envoy perceived was the tremendous public sympathy towards Finland, but did not seem able to understand the political struggle for power that was going on in France at the time and in which the emotions aroused by the Soviet aggression were being unscrupulously exploited.[56]

By comparison with Holma, Gripenberg had an easier time in London: British policy toward Finland was in the first place Cabinet policy: cool, reserved and carefully guarded against outsiders. As a rule Gripenberg learnt of the Supreme War Council plans only from Paris. Halifax refused to give him anything but studied allusions. The political atmosphere in London was not stimulating and failed to inspire initiative, all the more so since the British, unlike the French, had direct contacts with Helsinki. On the other hand, the Finnish Foreign Ministry was often presented by its man in London with an over-smooth, Finland-centred and optimistic image of prevailing opinion. Gripenberg also failed to discern in time the different strands of British policy, especially the resources and the willingness to assist Finland. The awakening was painful, as he admits in his diary: "I said [to Collier on 9 March] that if this great empire cannot produce fifty aeroplanes, it is difficult to have proper confidence in its will and capacity to assist."

Both Finnish legations had to function in relative isolation throughout the Winter War, Paris obviously even more so. Well-informed visitors were scarce, communications scanty and unreliable.* Instructions from Helsinki were ambiguous and inadequate, but tended to give the idea that the Finnish Government was genuinely interested in intervention. Thus, for example, on the eve of the decisive Supreme War Council meeting of 5 February, the following cabled instructions signed by the Foreign Minister in person were sent to Gripenberg and forwarded to Holma: "We hope that [the intervention plan] is being continuously prepared with British co-operation, in order that its realization, according to how the situation develops, will be possible at a more favourable moment."[57]

Holma's zeal for intervention irritated the Norwegians and the Swedes who, like Boheman, accused him of carrying on "his own foreign policy". For the Finns it is more difficult to blame him for lack of loyalty, even if Tanner's memoirs do not come far short of such an accusation. The then Foreign Minister admits that "although even in earlier reports Holma had indicated that something of this character was afoot, I had deliberately left him without instructions so that I might not prematurely bind the

---

* The Finnish Foreign Ministry had on several occasions warned the legations in Geneva and Paris that, since their telephone contacts went through Germany, the handling of confidential matters on the telephone should be avoided. This rule, however, was often broken in urgent cases, even in Helsinki, but especially at both legations; this inevitably led to certain essential secrets being disclosed to the Germans. The leaks were made public at the press conference given by the German Foreign Minister on 27 April 1940, during the early stages of the occupation of Denmark and Norway. Ribbentrop indeed quoted a telephone communication of 12 March 1940 from Paris, in which Holma had revealed detailed information on the Allied intervention plan. Cf. Auswärtiges Amt Documents 4/1940: Documents rélatifs à la politique franco-anglaise d'extension de la guerre. Berlin 1940, p. 6.

Cabinet to any plans with which we were unacquainted." In fact, it was for this very reason—because he was not given any additional instructions or information on the peace discussions—that he was not in a position to understand the policy of his government. He probably failed to realize that Tanner basically approved of intervention simply as a threat, to bring pressure on the Russians in order to seek more tolerable peace terms.[58]

After meeting Daladier on 14 January, Holma could no longer complain of the former's waning enthusiasm, of which he had detected signs in Paris at the beginning of January. Only one day after this interview Léger told the US ambassador that his Government would not break diplomatic relations with the Soviet Union or declare war on it, but would *destroy it if possible—using cannon if necessary*. The statement seems extravagant and was perhaps made to impress the anti-Soviet American. French policy, however, was at a turning-point. It is a fact that about this time Daladier was considering the recruiting of a voluntary force made up of foreign emigrants. He also thought of forming an élite unit of regular forces to be sent to Finland—if not under the French flag, as he had boasted to Bullitt, at least in such a manner that there would be no doubts of the colours represented by these "volunteers."[59]

The battalion of Chasseurs Alpins reinforced by a mountain artillery regiment, earmarked for the task on 8 January and formed three weeks later, corresponded to the Premier's idea. The élite nature of the detachment is reflected by the fact that, in addition to the appointed commander Colonel Antoine Béthouart, who had been a training instructor in the Finnish army in 1919-20, and completed his successful military career as a general, three of its few other surviving officers became generals.* Later (22 February) the French expeditionary force was strengthened by two Foreign Legion battalions and an armoured car company equipped with light Hotchkiss-39 cars. The formation was called by the simple covername "mountain brigade". Its training and armament received particular attention. Thanks to motorized equipment its mobility was considered exceptional, as was its firepower. Nevertheless, Béthouart observes that the Peugeot light trucks, which were to be its basic vehicles, were too weak to be used in the north.†[60]

---

* Including the then Captains Faure and Koenig: of these the former took part in the Algerian military revolt in 1962 as a divisional commander and ended his career in prison, while Koenig, the hero of Bir Hakeim, has remained in official military history as one of the great soldiers of "Free France".

† Béthouart's detachment of two half-brigades included, in addition to the brigade staff and four Chasseur battalions, a reconnaissance platoon, an anti-tank company, three motorized artillery groups—each comprising two batteries

In mid-January 1940 both British and French policy towards Finland underwent a marked change. The alarming reports brought by liaison officers from Mannerheim's headquarters provided government circles for the first time with an opportunity to study the cold realities of the Winter War. Now that the victorious communiqués from the Finnish eastern border had ceased, the Allies began to understand that Finnish resistance could not continue for ever if Finland did not receive substantial support.

However, for six weeks the Allies had been planning their domestic strategy—and Daladier even his domestic policy—on the assumption that the Finns would hold out. Giving up earlier considerations, according to which the preservation or destruction of Finland would not affect vital Allied interests, Britain and France now realized that the conflict was closely bound up with their own strategic and political problems: Finnish defence became important as an end in itself. From these premises the Allies reached an agreement in early February to start preparations for a joint intervention in Finland before the arrival of the thaw.[61]*

---

of 75-mm. guns and one battery of 105-mm. guns—one battery of anti-tank guns, small-calibre anti-aircraft equipment, etc.

* Footnote 61 is printed on p. 212 below.

VI

THE FINNS AT THE CROSSROADS

February 1940

1

When presenting their Petsamo plan the French had referred to the gloomy appraisal of the situation given by Ganeval after his return from Finland, and suggested that the Supreme War Council meet at its earliest convenience to discuss the question of assistance as a whole: "As Daladier says, time is slipping on and we are doing nothing but talk," Ironside observed when preparing for the preliminary negotiations with the French on 29 January. "Winston is mad to start something....." Two days later the C.I.G.S., together with representatives of the naval and air forces, left for the French general headquarters at Vincennes to agree on the draft plans which were to be approved at a political level by the Supreme War Council on 5 February.[1]*

The news arriving from the Karelian Isthmus suggested that the large-scale Soviet offensive predicted by Ling and Ganeval in their reports had begun. If Finland fell, the Allies would have no acceptable reason for intervening in Scandinavia; and if they failed to do so, the Germans would be able to concentrate all their forces on the Western Front. In this situation Daladier gave up Petsamo—for reasons of interior policy, as Chamberlain alleged—and returned to the idea of a larger operation, provided it could be carried out without delay.[4]

---

* British and French sources reporting on this rather important meeting of 29 January are by no means consistent. Ironside, for instance, reported after his return home that the French commander-in-chief had no objections to the newly-formed British troops being sent to Scandinavia instead of to the Western Front. According to him, Gamelin had even accepted that one division of the British Expeditionary Force in France might be detached for a northern expedition. "General Gamelin," he added, "*was now no longer convinced that the Germans would attack in the west this year.*"[2] To counterbalance this official statement of 2 February 1940, Gamelin maintains in his memoirs that his words in this context were as follows: "General Gamelin observed that a severe winter is often followed by an early spring, and supposed that *it might be in the German interest to speed up the events and to attack [in the west] as early as March.*"[3]

The fact that the Supreme War Council, less than a week later, agreed without difficulty that at least five divisions should be sent to Scandinavia before the middle of April, should be sufficient indication that no attack was expected on the Western Front in early spring.

Daladier, whose leg was still in plaster, proved less energetic than usual and failed to shake the resolve of the British delegation, which had come well-prepared. Apart from the Foreign Secretary, Chamberlain was accompanied by the cabinet members representing the three armed forces ministries. After crossing the Channel in a cheerful mood and enjoying a good dinner in Paris at the residence of the British Ambassador, the delegation was lively and in the best fighting spirit at the opening of the council meeting on Monday morning, 5 February.[5]

During this meeting, which lasted no more than an hour and a half, the British managed to get through all the resolutions which the War Cabinet had approved three days earlier with the exception of the final abandonment of the Petsamo plan. At their insistence, all efforts were concentrated on intervention at Narvik, because this would be less likely to lead to hostilities with the Soviet Union and would have the immediate advantage of depriving the enemy of iron ore. At Daladier's wish, however, it was decided that the Petsamo plan should be left under consideration and developed further, so that it might be used in case Norway and Sweden refused to allow the execution of the larger plan. The French also agreed that the command of the Allied Scandinavian forces should be entrusted to a British general. "The French are handing an operation over to us and are sitting back pretty," Ironside observed. "But it couldn't well be otherwise because we know so much more about the North."[6]

The movement to France of the four British reinforced divisions during the previous autumn had taken a month. The Supreme War Council decision of 5 February called for the transfer of a bigger army over a distance more than a hundred times the width of the Channel, and furthermore its vanguard, passing through the North of Norway and Sweden, was intended to reach the River Tornio before the Finns collapsed. While committing itself to support the Finnish war effort, the Council at the same time risked having to thin the defences of the Western Front. Instead of a problem which could be solved by a few dozens minelayers and destroyers, as originally conceived by Churchill, Scandinavia had now developed in the imagination of the Allied High Command into a principal theatre of operations.[7]

The plan approved in Paris on 5 February, based on the memorandum drawn up by the British Chiefs-of-Staff, was divided into two parts. The force directed north to the Narvik area was called "Avonmouth", and the troops to be sent to Central and Southern Norway and Southern Sweden "Stratford". In short, the operational orders were as follows:[8]

1. Force 'Avonmouth'

The first echelon directed to Narvik was to comprise at least two brigades of troops well trained in northern conditions, including among others the British 24th (Guards) Brigade and a half-brigade of French Chasseurs Alpins. These were to move up the railway to Sweden, to occupy the Gällivare ore fields, to secure and if necessary destroy the port of Luleå—in the event of an eventual German landing operation at the north end of the Gulf of Bothnia. This formation was also to take care of the delivery of supplies to Finland and to set up, for this purpose, an expeditionary corps consisting of, as was originally planned, the French Chasseurs Alpins as well as the two Foreign Legion battalions (which were to arrive in Narvik with the later echelons) and possibly four Polish battalions. According to the operations report of 22 February, these troops to be shipped from France would have totalled 13,100 men. Since the expeditionary force destined for Finland would also have included at a later date the British 24th (Guards) Brigade (about 3,500 men), its strength would have risen from two to three brigades to one division which, because of poor transport facilities, was considered the absolute maximum.[9]

The expeditionary corps was, if necessary, to be used in the defence of Northern Finland, in the area north of a line drawn east and west through the town of Kemi, with the Salla front as the most likely area of operations: "Operations in the South of Finland or in the Suomussalmi areas are ruled out", the Chiefs-of-Staff emphasized, "by the distance involved and the threat to the communications of the force which might develop from a German landing on the shores of the Gulf of Bothnia."[10]

2. Force 'Stratford'

Five British territorial battalions were to occupy the Trondheim-Namsos area and possibly Bergen as well, and secure—or destroy if threatened by the enemy—the strategically important airfield at Stavanger. Additional British troops, up to four divisions in all, were to be sent through these Norwegian ports and thence across the border to Southern Sweden in order to take care of the defence of that region against the Germans.

The Chiefs-of-Staff had estimated that the time needed for the northern force to disembark at Narvik and to occupy the ore fields and Luleå was at least one month before an eventual German seaborne expedition could be expected to reach the northern end of the Gulf of Bothnia. Since it was estimated, on the basis of the ten previous years' records, that the port of Luleå would become navigable on 26 April, the arrival of the first echelon of Allied troops at Narvik and at Trondheim was proposed for 20 March. This implied that the vessels carrying the equipment of the expeditionary forces would have to leave Britain on 12 March and the ships carrying the troops three days later.

Considering that a reply had to be received from the Scandinavians before the departure of the first transport echelon (i.e. 12 March), and since preliminary negotiations were estimated to require at least a week, Finland was asked to make an appeal for assistance not later than 5 March.[11] This appeal, although a formality, was considered necessary in order to justify the Allied intervention.

Chamberlain was still of the opinion that the consent of the Norwegians and Swedes was necessary before the Allies could proceed with the enterprise. Daladier seemingly disagreed: "If Norway and Sweden were to refuse—it would be ridiculous not to proceed after all these preparations." Yet, for reasons of security this time, it was decided not to approach Oslo or Stockholm until the military preparations were completed.[12]

The Supreme War Council decision gave a great deal of concern to the C.I.G.S., who in the next six weeks had to raise the main part of the expeditionary force, its equipment and escorts. The arming of the divisions required was possible only at the expense of deliveries intended for the western front. The air Cover reserved to assist the operation was limited to two bomber and two army co-operation squadrons (to be used by the northern force) as well as the four heavy bomber squadrons stationed in Britain. The main reason for the scarcity of the air cover available was the assumption that there were not enough usable bases in the area. However, the Royal Navy was to bear the brunt of the operation: in addition to forty destroyers and twenty-five trawlers and patrol craft for escort duties and the naval defence of the base ports, the Admiralty had to mobilize the transport tonnage for the transfer of 100,000 men and 11,000 vehicles from Britain to Norway. It was indeed foreseen that the protection of the convoys would be the main preoccupation of the Home Fleet throughout the operation.

In agreeing to the French initiative to make assistance to Finland a priority item on the War Council agenda, the British Government had implicitly agreed that this question had, if necessary, to be dealt with at the expense of other military objectives. A strikingly new feature in the decision of 5 February was the fact that *the Allies were now prepared to send their regular troops to Finland, even if this involved fighting the Russians.* The British Chiefs-of-Staff had never gone so far, not even in their draft plans for the Supreme War

Council meeting drawn up in late January.[13] Certainly no doubts were felt over the respective importance of assistance to Finland, on the one hand, and defending the ore fields on the other. Yet the practical differences, compared with the earlier considerations, were obvious. Whereas the plan drawn up in January implied the sending of a maximum of 3-4 per cent of the expeditionary force to Finland, the new plan called for using approximately one-tenth of the total strength of the 100,000-150,000 men.

Taking into consideration the fact that the Soviet Army had concentrated more than forty divisions against the Finns, who had barely thirteen, the ultimate strength of the expeditionary corps—one division at the most—would not on its own have altered the balance of military forces involved in the Winter War. From the Allied point of view, however, the decision to intervene was particularly important. It meant a challenge, since by sending a force of this size to Finland they risked their military prestige—for the first time during the Second World War. The re-evaluation of objectives is clearly reflected in a joint memorandum by the Foreign Office and the Chiefs-of-Staff concerning the timetable of the plan: it was indispensable to accelerate the preparations, not with the Germans in mind, since two months were left before the thaw in the Gulf of Bothnia would begin, but because "*every day's delay would mean a day lost in going to the help of the Finns*".[14]

With the intention of enhancing Finnish resistance, the War Cabinet accepted Halifax's proposal that it was urgent to make clear to Helsinki that the Allies were prepared to intervene in favour of the Finns, to "give them a chance of beating the Russians rather than having to accept unfavourable terms of peace".[15]

2

When this comment was made, on 17 February, the Red army had resumed its advance in the western sector of the Karelian Isthmus. The offensive, intended to capture Viipuri and to defeat the bulk of the Finnish forces, had been carefully planned under the new front commander S. K. Timoshenko, newly returned from Poland.* The concentration of troops greatly exceeded those hitherto available in the Soviet north-western front: in addition to the original Russian force in the Isthmus, the now considerably strengthened 7th Army, Timoshenko was given the 13th Army.

---

* Commander of the Soviet troops in Poland in 1939, in the Karelian Isthmus in 1940, and in Bessarabia the same year, Timoshenko was subsequently promoted Marshal of the Soviet Union and assigned, as People's Commissar for Defence, the task of reorganizing the Soviet forces in 1941.

Both formations, reinforced with a great quantity of artillery and armoured and special troops, consisted of some twenty-five divisions against which the Finns on their Mannerheim line could muster seven infantry divisions and some special units, all desperately short of artillery, especially anti-tank and anti-aircraft guns.

The Soviet troops all along the northern front were given new reserves, in order to keep the Finns busy on their 650-mile-long eastern frontier. The Red Army divisions encircled in Kuhmo and on the north-eastern Ladoga front resisted vigorously while the decisive battle would be joined in the Isthmus. Mannerheim had no more reserves; towards the end of the fighting, Soviet superiority in numbers of troops alone probably approached four to one.

The offensive on the Isthmus had been started at the beginning of February with ten days of minor preliminary attacks and artillery barrages, with the intention of tiring out the Finnish forces. The Russians, who were in no doubt of their air superiority, intensified their raids against the Finnish outposts as well as the rear. The main attack against the key positions of the Mannerheim Line at Summa, fifteen miles south of Viipuri, began at dawn on 11 February, with the thunder of thousands of guns. In three days the Finns were driven out of their positions and, fighting desperately, had to begin their slow but irrevocable retreat northwards.

Meanwhile in London the task of informing the Finns of the Allied intervention offer was entrusted on 7 February to Brigadier Ling who was about to return to Mannerheim's headquarters. He was instructed, essentially for political reasons, not to disclose the plans to anyone other than the Field-Marshal:

The Finnish Government had been toying with the idea of negotiating peace terms with Russia, and it would be better to make any approach on the lines suggested by the Foreign Secretary to Field-Marshal Mannerheim himself.[16]

Two days later the Prime Minister, on the grounds of security, tried to have the decision revoked: the Finns might pass the secret on to the Scandinavians, he said, and maybe even to the Germans. Churchill, however, together with Halifax, finally succeeded in winning Chamberlain over, and Ling was sent off with the original instructions. He was to tell Mannerheim that the Petsamo plan had been dropped and that the troops could now be sent to Finland only through Norway and Sweden, within the scope of a larger plan.[17]

All the same, on 12 February Halifax told the Cabinet that he knew that even the Finnish envoy in London was quite well-informed on the Paris negotiations. This should have shown that the attempts to conceal the plan from Helsinki were absurd, if not hazardous.[18] There were several reasons why the Finnish Government and particularly the Foreign Minister were mistrusted in London. Tanner was more inscrutable than his anglophile predecessor Erkko, who also spoke perfect English. A Labour delegation visiting Finland in February had to some extent made him known in London as an individual and for his ideas.* This, however, was never followed up: Snow, who never seems to have come into contact with the Foreign Minister, was about to leave Finland, and his successor, Vereker, hardly had any chance to extend his knowledge of Tanner beyond mere acquaintance.

As far as the French were concerned, the situation was even more hopeless: Tanner in fact treated their envoy, who had lost his grip on Finnish affairs, somewhat mercilessly. After Magny, too, had been sent home, his replacement was someone with whom Tanner at least had a common language—German! But this was not until March, when the time for decisions was running out.[19]

As surmised in London, the inner circle of the Finnish Cabinet—Ryti, Tanner and Paasikivi—had been active during the previous weeks trying to establish diplomatic contact with Moscow.† Tanner had in fact received the first information on the Supreme War Council resolution on 7 February after returning from Stockholm from a meeting with the Soviet Minister there, Alexandra Kollontay. London and Paris, however, so far had no idea of the peace feelers being put out from the end of January onwards through the Soviet Legation in Stockholm. The Kremlin had indeed, on 29 January, announced that it had no objections in principle to making a peace "even with the Ryti-Tanner government". In giving up the Terijoki government it had created the necessary conditions for a negotiated peace and made it clear that its aims were limited. The Swedes for their part had given signs that they might extend their military assistance by sending the Finns heavy artillery and perhaps even regular troops. Thus the Finns seemed to have three promising possibilities: (1) peace, possibly with quite reasonable conditions, (2) continuation of the war with active Swedish assistance, and (3) continuation of the war with Allied support.[21]

In his diary Tanner observed that the situation was intricate, but he failed to conceal his satisfaction with the options now available: had Kollontay not suggested that even Eastern Karelia

---

* For details on the visit of this delegation, see pp. 167-9

† The attempt at mediation through the Germans, initiated by Minister Blücher and with Tanner's blessings, had failed, or—more correctly—had never started, because Count Schulenburg's démarches in Moscow during early January had aroused no response. News of this had reached London by way of Copenhagen, but Halifax had been satisfied with the Finnish envoy's explanation that his government had nothing to do with it.[20]

might be considered as compensation for the territories demanded from Finland.* According to Tanner, everybody, including the other members of the "peace triumvirate", Ryti and Paasikivi, had been in optimistic spirits: "We have all the trumps in our hands", the Premier Ryti had said, "if we can only use them correctly and *bring pressure on both the Soviet Union and Sweden by means of the Western offer of assistance.*" As a result, the Prime and Foreign Ministers, together with the representative of the Commander-in-Chief, General Rudolf Walden, decided, on the same day, 8 February, that the reply to Kollontay would have to wait. Meanwhile the Allied plan, regarding which Mannerheim had recommended the "utmost caution", called for additional information.†[23]

The Field-Marshal, in fact, was painfully aware of the continuing Russian pressure on the Summa front. When the Prime and Foreign Minister visited headquarters two days later, he convinced them that it was of vital importance for Finland to seek peace. The Allied offer of assistance, he observed, was "inadequately prepared"; if it were to be invoked, its planning, manner and time of realization called for joint negotiations between the Allied and Finnish general staffs. But the final decision as to war or peace was to be made on a political level.[24]

As had been outlined by Premier Ryti, it was decided that the Allied offer of assistance should be utilized to the full when it came to making a final decision. Consequently, when reporting the discussions of the headquarters to the President of the Republic, Tanner, accompanied by Ryti, presented the text of a communiqué, which was published by the press in his name the following day, 12 February. After denying that the government had resorted to German mediation, Tanner openly threatened that if Finland failed to obtain peace on reasonable terms, she would continue the fight with recourse to assistance from elsewhere. "It is possible", he concluded, "that the rumours concerning the peace mediation have been circulated only in order to discourage assistance from abroad."[25]

On the same day, 12 February, the Foreign Affairs Committee of the Cabinet had a meeting at which Tanner once more initiated discussions on peace. The "peace triumvirate" succeeded on this occasion in winning over President Kallio, but the three other

---

* This in spite of Molotov's assertions that the promises given to Kuusinen's government concerning the annexation of Karelia to Finland were no longer valid.[22]

† It was strange but characteristic of the unconstitutional state of affairs then prevailing in the Finnish inner circle, that it only decided now to notify the President of the Republic of the peace contacts.

committee members remained adamant in insisting on the continuation of fighting. The only result of the discussion was that the
Foreign Minister was sent to Stockholm once more.[26]

During this short trip to Stockholm the following day, Tanner
received two unpleasant surprises: Moscow had just announced
that it would no longer be satisfied merely with a parcel of the
Karelian Isthmus, nor with Hanko, but wanted the territory of
all Southern Karelia up to the north-eastern shore of Lake Ladoga;
and Sweden for her part made it clear that she could not increase
her assistance or allow Allied transit to Finland. Having returned
to Helsinki during the night, Tanner heard from Ryti the third and
most disagreeable surprise: the Red army had broken through the
main line of defence at Summa. "Shocking news", he ended his
diary entry, "this 13th has been unlucky in every respect."[27]

The almost unbounded illusions regarding Finnish capabilities
which had prevailed in the Cabinet during the first days of February
were soon dispelled for ever. Following a newspaper disclosure,
Premier Hansson and King Gustav publicly declared that Sweden
could not compromise her neutrality even for the sake of Finland.
In Helsinki it was now concluded that it was no longer possible to
defy the Russian demands. On 20 February the Finnish *Chargé
d'affaires* in Stockholm was instructed to ask the Swedish Foreign
Minister Günther, "in the interest of Sweden, since it is otherwise
to be feared that Finland will turn to the Western Powers", to
start mediating peace between Finland and the Soviet Union.[28]

Three days later General Walden, returning from headquarters,
again reported that the High Command had reservations about the
Allies' capacity to help Finland effectively, doubted the strength
of the Isthmus front, and recommended a serious study of the peace
prospects. At the Cabinet meeting in the morning of 23 February,
attention was drawn to the inadequacy of transport facilities which,
as emphasized by Tanner, might result in a situation whereby
"before the reinforcements are here, all of Southern Finland may be
conquered". Apart from Walden, only the Prime and Foreign
Ministers, as well as the Minister of Defence, Niukkanen, were
present. "After Niukkanen had left", Tanner concluded, "we
remaining three decided to strive energetically towards peace, even
if this should cost us certain losses." Ling apparently had not come
in time.[29]

3

In studying the answers received from Oslo and Stockholm in early
January, the British Cabinet had concluded that the Scandina-

vians were reluctant because of the suddenly real danger of German aggression. Up till then, enemy operations against the Nordic countries had been considered improbable, since they would be contrary to German interests. Now the situation had changed: if the Germans were to attack first, the Cabinet observed, they would incur the charge of infringing Nordic inviolability, and so the Allies could enter the scene as defenders.[30]

Meanwhile, the two Scandinavian governments had received a note from the Kremlin protesting against their military assistance to Finland and warning that direct as well as indirect support would have undesirable consequences for their relations with the Soviet Union. Sweden and even Norway, whose Foreign Minister had been woken at 3 a.m. on 6 January to receive the note, had taken the warning calmly, and there was no recurrence of Soviet pressure. After the offensive of the Red Army came to a halt in Finland, both governments believed that their main enemy was no longer the Soviet Union but Germany.[31]

Since January the Scandinavians had been quite well aware that what the Allies really wanted was not transit to Finland but Swedish ore. In London the discussion on the blockade question with the emotionally inclined Norwegian envoy had been "irksome", to use Halifax's expression. In Oslo the Secretary—General of the Norwegian Foreign Ministry had asked the British Minister how the Allies would feel if, in forcing their way through the Scandinavian countries, they were placed in the position of the Russians, whom the whole world had condemned for their attack on Finland. In Stockholm, Boheman humiliated Mallet's deputy by pointing out that the British Government already had on its conscience the fate of too many smaller states which it had guaranteed and failed to protect.[32]

The British Cabinet's policy had till now been based on the idea that, if not pressed overmuch, Sweden might assist Finland more effectively, and perhaps even consent to Allied transit. On 12 January, Churchill had suggested the contrary approach: action first, negotiation later. He believed that, faced with a *fait accompli*, the Swedes would content themselves with protests and that the Norwegians would follow their example. At Chamberlain's suggestion the Chiefs-of-Staff were then advised to study the possibilities of intervention *even if the Scandinavians were to offer open resistance.*[33]

In their reply five days later, the Chiefs-of-Staff warned that intervention without the consent of the local governments would be foolhardy. Even by means of passive resistance, sabotage of port and railway equipment, removal of rolling stock, cutting off of electricity and so on, the Scandinavians could frustrate the operation, since in the meantime the Germans might intervene. By now, the military experts considered a German counter-offensive undesirable. Chamberlain, referring to the appeal received from the Australian Prime Minister who feared that coercion of the Nordic countries might have an unfavourable effect on the opinion of the other neutrals, dealt a final blow to Churchill's proposal. The Cabinet turned to Halifax, authorizing him to continue wooing Norway and Sweden by using normal diplomatic channels.[34]

The next British communication, handed on 19 January to the envoys of both countries in London, was harsh. Ignoring for the time being the question of sending regular troops to Finland, the note complained that no answer had been received from Stockholm to the request for the transit of British volunteers going to Finland.* Permission was actually granted one day later, Prytz assuring the Foreign Office that the delay was due to a misunderstanding. This was at least formally true, since Foreign Minister Günther feared that even the volunteers in fact were aimed at the Swedish ore fields.†[35]

To Halifax's great disappointment, the hopes of the Swedes joining the Finns came to nothing. As a Swedish authority on the subject, Krister Wahlbäck, has shown, the Swedes had made up their minds at the beginning of February, mainly for the following reasons: (1) the Soviet Union by its peace proposal of 29 January had demonstrated that its objectives were merely territorial and limited to Finland; (2) Daladier had transmitted to Stockholm, through the mediation of the Swedish Consul-General in Paris, a document—allegedly a secret protocol of the Molotov-Ribbentrop pact (a false one, as it later turned out)—according to which the Germans would have had the right, in the event of the Russians extending their territorial expansion beyond Viipuri, to establish themselves in Western Finland; (3) the Germans had implied that they would take an unfavourable view of more active Swedish intervention in the Finnish war. These three arguments, including the "document" transmitted by Daladier, apparently against his own interest, convinced Stockholm that it was better to abstain from intervention—"with a heavy heart" as King Gustav observed.[37]

Even if hopes of Swedish intervention were now given up in London and Paris, the expectations that Stockholm would finally

---

* See. p.

† It may be mentioned that Günther at this time still entertained hopes of an Allied landing at Petsamo instead of at Narvik. His predecessor Sandler, who was in favour of more active assistance to Finland, had warned Ryti and Tanner in mid-January of the Allies' plans for intervention in the Arctic. Günther himself saw these plans in an entirely different light, as a chance to avoid the obligation of consenting to Allied transit.[36]

agree to Allied transit persisted to the end. This was partly due to certain Swedish representatives, who, obviously trying to be diplomatic, let it be understood that their "no" actually meant "perhaps". Prytz in London seems to have gone farthest in his veiled promises.[38]

As far as Norway was concerned, Allied patience was nearing breaking-point by the third week of February, when a British destroyer, violating Norwegian territorial waters, found 300 captured British sailors on a German auxiliary vessel, the *Altmark*. Daladier proposed to make use of this incident to send troops to Norway and to occupy Narvik and Trondheim. The War Cabinet, however, rejected the idea: the agitation caused by the *Altmark* incident in Norway was so great that even Churchill admitted that an attempt to occupy the coastal bases would certainly have provoked armed resistance.

The incident in no way aided the third and last Allied attempt to persuade the Scandinavians to agree to transit to Finland before it was too late.[39] On the contrary, it affected the development of the Scandinavian situation in another decisive way: Hitler had had grounds for expecting an eventual Allied landing on the Norwegian west coast. The seizure of the *Altmark*, as we know, gave him a final motive for occupying Norway and Denmark.

Without going into the details of the German preparations for Operation *Weserübung*, we may note that the Allies had known about them as early as the turn of the year. Halifax had indeed informed the War Cabinet on 6 January that the Germans had not even gone to the trouble of hiding their activities in the harbours and air bases on the German Baltic coast. Maybe it was their intention, he had reflected, merely to frighten the Scandinavians. The concentration of 400 transport planes on the airfields of North-eastern Germany implied a massive air transport operation; but was this directed against the Swedish ore fields? The Chief of Air Staff, who had attended the meeting, had calmed the ministers by explaining that, merely because of the overwhelming supply problems, such a military operation was unlikely.[40]

The Allied supreme command grossly underestimated German capacity for managing large-scale troop movements by air and sea. Ironside, for instance, described to the War Cabinet how hazardous it would be for the enemy to attempt the invasion of Stavanger from the air: Stavanger was a town of some 40,000 inhabitants, many of whom were trained as volunteers, the General explained, less than three months before the *Weserübung* began; "even very small forces could successfully resist an air-borne invasion of this nature." At the Admiralty the sentiments were even more self-confident: "If they did invade Norway, I would be glad", Churchill said. "They would become involved in a serious commitment."[41]

A German attack on Narvik from the sea was unimaginable, whereas a landing at the northern end of the Gulf of Bothnia or on its eastern coast, in the Finnish rear, was considered a possibility to be seriously reckoned with. The question of Finnish defence was actually proving itself the Achilles heel of the larger operation plan, as the Chiefs-of-Staff concluded:

The fate of Finland is certainly a most important factor. If Finland showed signs of collapse and the Swedes, alarmed at the prospect of a Russian invasion, called for the protection of Germany, our last hope of obtaining Swedish co-operation would have disappeared, and with it any possibility of stopping the export of iron-ore from Sweden to Germany.[42]

In Helsinki the hope persisted almost throughout the entire war that the Germans would ultimately not leave the Finns in the lurch but would support them, at least by letting the Swedes come to their assistance. Such speculations were almost entirely based on the intimations given by Goering, who had bitterly opposed Ribbentrop's eastern policy, to his Swedish and Finnish visitors. As late as 25 February, Tanner had a cable from Professor Kivimäki, a former Prime Minister of Finland, now on his way back from Berlin, that Goering had no objections to Swedish assistance, if only the Western Powers kept out.[43]

In London and Paris it was understood that a Swedish intervention was no longer possible simply because of German animosity. "Indeed we know from Roger Maugras'* telegram", Daladier reported to his Ambassador in London 21 February, "that the Reich has made it known to the Swedish Government that it considers all official assistance given by Sweden to Finland as an act justifying war, a *casus belli*...."[44] Although Hitler might not necessarily have gone so far in reality, the conclusion was correct: in order to prevent the prolongation of the conflict, which the Allies could exploit, and to demonstrate their benevolent neutrality to the Russians, Hitler had discouraged the Swedes from increasing their assistance to Finland.

4

At the beginning of March 1940 an unexpected justification presented itself to the Swedish Government for the refusal of Allied transit, which was now requested for the third and last time:

---

* French envoy in Stockholm.

Stockholm was informed that the proposed Allied intervention in Finland was in fact part of a larger offensive plan against the Soviet Union, which would be connected in the south with operations against the Caucasus, in particular Baku. Strangely enough, the information was included in a personal message brought to King Gustav from the French Premier by the Swedish Consul-General in Paris. It was the second time that Daladier happened to reveal to the Swedes facts that affected their attitude in a manner contrary to apparent French and Allied aspirations.*

Paul Stehlin, then a captain, and later an army general and Chief-of-Staff of the French air force, who was sent to Finland in the winter of 1940 as a member of the French military delegation, recollected how before leaving France he was taken in front of a large secret map at air force headquarters. On its surface he saw two big arrows, one starting from Syria and the other from Finland, meeting east of Moscow. General Bergeret, assistant to the Chief-of-Staff, had explained the plan as follows:

"Russia is now allied to Germany. Accordingly, by attacking it we will deprive Hitler's Germany of its essential resources and also remove the war further from our borders. General Weygand is in command of our troops in Syria and the Lebanon, which will march in the direction of Baku in order to put an end to the oil production there; from there *they will proceed towards the north in order to join the armies that will march from Scandinavia and Finland on Moscow.*"[46]

The plan in question seems to have been the one requested from Gamelin and Darlan in mid-January, when the possibility of attacking the Soviet Union from the north, from the Arctic Ocean, had attracted serious attention in France. It is doubtful whether Daladier had considered the operation in earnest. According to French general staff documents published in 1941 by the Germans, the objectives seem to have been limited to the paralysing of Soviet oil production and export. In Daladier's original instructions there were three alternatives: to cut off German oil deliveries in the Black Sea, to instigate the Soviet Muslims in the Caucasus to revolt and to occupy the oilfields, or to intervene directly in the area. More than a month later (20 February 1940) the military authorities, referring to Turkey's opposition and the danger of their own vessels being exposed to enemy air attacks, rejected the idea of a sea blockade as being ineffective and impractical. Two alternatives remained, both implying interference with Soviet internal affairs and the likelihood of open hostilities with Moscow.[47]

---

* See above, p. 106.

The commander of the Levant army, General Weygand, had only two divisions at his disposal at this time. Not more than two additional divisions could be detached from home. It seems incredible that the French could have planned the capture of Moscow with 150,000 men. Even Napoleon had twice that number! The plan revealed to Stehlin must of course have involved a far more massive concentration of forces, and have represented a serious outline of the possibilities involved if the planned course of events led to an all-out conflict between the Allies and the Soviet Union.[48]

In his post-war critical biography of de Gaulle, Henri de Kérillis maintained that in the winter of 1940 his subject drew up a plan for a "mechanized expedition, which would have come to Finland through Norway and quickly pushed back the dispersed Russian hordes, and marched on Leningrad". Considering actual conditions in Finland, this has its ridiculous aspect—as indeed may have been the intention of the author, known for his aversion to de Gaulle*.[49] Nevertheless the idea of experimenting with a *blitzkrieg* in Finland may not have been so strange to de Gaulle, remembering his ideas on mechanized warfare and his burning ambitions.* On the other hand, the composition of the French expeditionary corps earmarked for Finland, its small armoured equipment, as well as the personal testimonies given to the present writer by Generals Béthouart, Ganeval and Stehlin who were all closely associated with the intervention preparations, seem to prove that the sending of French troops to Finland with such a task was never planned. Whether de Gaulle in fact made his proposal is indeed an academic question, since the plan was never put into effect.[50]

The centre of Soviet oil production, Baku, was situated far behind the mountains on the Caspian Sea, and its seizure and destruction by land forces was considered impracticable. It was therefore proposed that the operation should be carried out by air. The R.A.F. commander in the Middle East agreed that the attack had most chance of success if carried out from the French air bases in North-eastern Syria. It was estimated that at least three squadrons of heavy bombers would be required, which the French did not possess and the British did not dare to detach from Europe for fear of a German spring offensive. In the course of the following weeks the Turks, who even in March had seemed inclined to agree to the passage of the bomber squadrons, and perhaps even to a joint ground

---

* As a proof the author refers to the later statement by Paul Reynaud, Daladier's successor and de Gaulle's personal friend, according to which the plan had influential supporters in the Government. In his memoirs Reynaud denies having given any such statement. Still he quotes de Kérillis extensively, giving the impression that the alleged plan might not have been entirely fictitious.

operation, changed their minds as the result of the fall of Finland. After the German attack on Scandinavia had drawn Allied attention and forces elsewhere, the Baku project was given up finally at the end of April 1940.[51]

In spite of their limited scope the offensives planned for the Caucasus were politically, and even strategically, connected with the Finnish situation up to 13 March. In Paris a military campaign against the Soviet Union had probably been discussed as an eventuality even earlier, at least around Christmas, as can be deduced from the memorandum of Paasonen already quoted.* The fact that the Red Army had finally failed to take Viipuri was believed to have made an impression on the reluctant Turks. It was expected that an attack on Baku—while the Soviet forces still had over 1 million men, 3,000 tanks and 2,000 aircraft engaged against Finland—would at one blow have stopped the oil exports to Germany and at the same time seriously limited Soviet consumption: the effects, it was believed, would extend to the entire Soviet economy, especially the country's recently mechanized agriculture. It is in this light that we should look at the guiding principle given to Gamelin at about this time by the almost fanatically anti-Soviet Weygand: "I for my part consider it of the utmost importance to break the back of the Soviet Union in Finland . . . and elsewhere."[52]

The plan, even if it remained in draft only, reflects the unbelievably provocative attitude of Daladier towards the Soviet Union in the winter of 1939-40. As the promises for assisting Finland were delayed, he tried to appease his critics by intensifying the persecution of the French Communists as well as the Soviet representatives in Paris. The restriction of their activities might in fact be considered justifiable, since the peace propaganda directed from Moscow threatened the French war effort. Still, the connection between the Finnish question and governmental police activities seems obvious. This found its most glaring expression on 8 and 9 February when Daladier, preparing for a secret discussion on foreign policy in the Chamber of Deputies and anticipating right-wing criticism of his passivity in regard to Finland, let his police occupy the Soviet commercial delegation and expel all Communist representatives from the Chamber.[53]

Daladier's instructions to Naggiar reveal that these unprecedented forms of pressure, which in March culminated in the non-renewal of the expired French-Soviet trade agreement and the expulsion of the Soviet Ambassador, Souritz, were calculated to provoke the Kremlin to freeze relations with France. This, however, did not

* See above, pp. 88-9.

happen.[54] Despite his gambling, Daladier avoided an open break
with the Soviet Union for as long as he held office, although he was
constantly assuring the Finnish envoy that he was prepared to take
that step if London were ready to follow suit.

5

Chamberlain was in a somewhat different position *vis-à-vis* the
Soviet Union, since, unlike his French counterpart, he did not have
a strong and vehement anti-Soviet pressure group against him in
parliament. The opposition in the House of Commons, at least its
responsible leadership, in fact became worried, as the Finnish War
was prolonged, lest British assistance might lead to conflict with the
Soviet Union. It was actually the Prime Minister's own party that
contained most of the activists supporting the Finnish cause at any
price. In restraining their fervour and in defending the Government's
eastern relations, however, he was greatly assisted by Winston
Churchill, otherwise his unquestioned rival.

In the Cabinet, the situation throughout the whole Finnish War
was somewhat paradoxical, since the Prime Minister, pressed by the
First Lord of the Admiralty, gradually yielded to seemingly anti-
Soviet intervention proposals, while at the same time, with the First
Lord's support, he guarded relations with Moscow with the utmost
care and discretion. Apart from calling home His Majesty's
Ambassador in Moscow—who personally favoured breaking off
relations with the Kremlin—and the interruption of trade negotiations, the Cabinet did nothing to jeopardize the remaining links
and an easy normalization of relations should the occasion demand
it. Butler had once admitted to the Swedish envoy that the Allies
and the Soviet Union might one day find themselves at one. When
Prytz reminded him of this at the end of the fatal year 1939, Butler
replied: "History is never built on logic."[55]

At the time, however, the thaw was still far away. The Soviet
Ambassador, during the first weeks of the war, had personally
experienced the hostility prevailing in London:

...An icy void came into existence around our Embassy...at many diplomatic
receptions people avoided my wife and myself as they would the plague...
Grippenberg [*sic*]...became the hero of the hour: he was photographed,
interviewed, invited to all kinds of receptions and in general given every
possible assurance of sympathy and support.[56]

Still Maisky took note of the basically correct attitude of the
Government and realised that this provided a starting-point for a
change of policy. An opportunity came to resume the dialogue

before it was too late with the visit to Moscow of Sir Stafford Cripps. The Labour politician, with a much younger companion, Harold Wilson, had left for a tour of Asia on his own initiative, but on Maisky's recommendation. After his arrival in China he was invited to Moscow, but did not go there until 15 February. The discussion he had with Molotov the following day was, according to his diary, purely informative.[57] Cripps' report to Halifax was not dispatched until after his return to Chungking on 3 March, too tardily in any event to have any effect on policy, since the Finns would by then already have made the appeal for aid which the Allies had proposed.

Meanwhile Maisky had summoned up enough courage to go to the Foreign Office and call on Butler, in accordance with the wish frequently repeated by Under-Secretary of State that "we should see each other and talk more often." This confidential discussion, on the afternoon of 30 January, was evidently their first since the outbreak of the Finnish War. After a few soothing words on Soviet-German relations, which he asserted were built on common interest rather than on sentiment,* Maisky recalled the successful co-operation between himself and Eden during the Spanish Civil War. Eden had proposed limiting the conflict within the Spanish borders, the Ambassador continued; could not the same tactics be applied to Finland? Butler took the hint but ended the discussion with something like, "Eden would be the first to tell you how the Finnish situation differs from the Spanish one!"[58]

This is what Halifax reported to the Cabinet on the discussion. There is nothing to support Clark's conclusion that after leaving Butler, Maisky was convinced that the Allies did not take their intervention idea seriously, and even if they did, it would be too late for them to save the Finns. The Soviet offensive on the Isthmus, which had been long and thoroughly prepared, could have been— and indeed was—carried through irrespective of what Maisky may have read in Butler's mind during a single conversation.[59]

It is of more interest that on 16 February, on the same day that Cripps ended his short visit to Moscow, the contact was continued. Maisky had invited Butler to his embassy for an intimate lunch. According to the host, the table talk revolved around the Finnish question:

I replied that...we had no claims at all on Sweden and Norway, all we wanted was that they should remain neutral in the Soviet-Finnish war. We had no intention of annexing Finland, but we could not put up with the

---

* The Soviet Union and Germany were at the moment drafting a trade agreement which was signed on 11 February 1940.

fact that the rulers of that country were ready to serve every enemy of the USSR. My words had had the effect of calming Butler. Evidently growing bolder, he put to me the direct question: *"Can't the Soviet-Finnish war be ended by mediation?"*[60]

Six days later Maisky had the chance to present Butler with the reply cabled from Moscow, that the Soviet Union followed its own foreign policy independently of Germany and had no aspirations in the Scandinavian countries. Moreover, the message made it clear that the Kremlin was ready to finish its war in Finland as soon as possible. For this purpose it even presented the Soviet peace terms, requesting that the British Government forward them to the Finns.[61]

After receiving instructions from the Foreign Secretary, with the Prime Minister's approval, Butler rejected Maisky's proposal the next day, arguing that the peace terms now being offered were harder than ever before.* The Soviet government had better present them directly to Finland, Butler explained, and he continued: *"I said that a continuance of the war must have unforeseen results for Anglo-Soviet relations, and it would be impossible to see what the consequences would be if the Soviet insisted in their attack* and were not able to end the war on terms which the Finnish Government could accept."[62]

This obvious threat annoyed Maisky: Britain lost a good opportunity for improving relations between the two countries, he observed with bitterness. Butler nevertheless remained unperturbed and stated that his government could not be requested to back "the terms which yielded the whole line of the fortifications which the Finns had so manfully defended, with all the physical and psychological consequences which might flow from such a surrender". This was too high a price to pay for a British-Soviet rapprochement, he proudly pointed out—the Ambassador should put things into their proper perspective.[63]

Halifax understood that Maisky had only wanted to demonstrate London's unwillingness to do anything to end the conflict. In order to avoid this accusation, he informed Helsinki of the terms delivered by Maisky, stressing that the British, because of the severity of the terms, had refused to mediate.†[64] Butler is reported as having been unhappy (according to Cadogan, even "very disgusted") because of the cold shoulder the Cabinet had given to the Soviet approach.

---

* For the first time the Russians now asked for the cession of Viipuri, Käkisalmi and Sortavala, including the entire Mannerheim Line, and demanded the signing of a defence treaty, covering all of the Gulf of Finland, between Estonia, the Soviet Union and Finland. The demand for a defence pact was later dropped.

† This episode in fact remained without practical significance: by now the Swedes had indeed undertaken to mediate between Helsinki and Moscow and on the day when His Majesty's government refused their good offices in London, conveyed the same peace terms to Erkko.

It seems clear indeed that Maisky made what seemed to him a serious impression when giving his assurance that unless attacked by Britain or France, his country would not depart from its policy of neutrality toward the Allies. Maisky's attempts at a rapprochement or, as a Soviet official history of diplomacy tells us, at "neutralizing the activity of the British Government which aimed at prolonging the Finnish-Soviet military conflict", were in the end—like the efforts made by Sir Stafford Cripps—unnecessary as they were unproductive of result: the War Cabinet had in fact decided to concentrate all forces, as soon as winter was over, against Germany which, in London even more than in Paris, was considered enemy number one. Intervention in the Finnish War had never been regarded as an end in itself, but only as a means. Suddenly, after the Soviet peace offers, the continuation of the conflict was considered unnecessary and even unwelcome: "If, however, the Finnish government made terms with the USSR," Halifax observed when commenting on Cripps' report," it might be worth while exploring the possibility of detaching the latter from Germany."[65]

It was characteristic of the Allies' policy then that while they themselves were somewhat inadequately informed on the situation in Finland, it was relatively easy for the Germans to follow Allied intentions in the north. Towards the end of the Finnish War this balance of information improved, after the envoys from both Britain and France were changed and the supply of news from Finland was made easier. However, the leaking of Allied intervention plans continued till the end. One cannot exclude the possibility that it was because of the rumours of Allied intervention that the Soviet Union decided after all to start peace talks with Finland instead of undertaking a military conquest of the country.

During the autumn of 1939, as we know, the British Minister Snow had become almost *persona non grata* in Finland. Although, after the offensive of the Red Army had come to a halt, Snow had become calmer, the Foreign Office were tired of his mammoth-size cables and memoranda, which in fact were less reports than advice to His Majesty's Government. Ling's first visit to Finland had revealed to what extent, after all, London lacked information on the Finnish situation. In order to rouse the elderly military attaché, Colonel Goodden, in Helsinki, the energetic Major Magill, who knew Finnish, was appointed as his assistant. (A few weeks later Goodden was replaced by Colonel King-Salter.) At the same time the Foreign Office started looking for a suitable diplomat to replace Snow. The choice fell on Gordon Vereker, a former counsellor at the British embassy in Moscow, who now arrived in Helsinki during the last week of February.[66]

At the French Legation things were even worse. Ganeval, who was appointed as Gamelin's liaison officer at the end of December, had evidently done a better job than even Ling, a much older man than himself. Ganeval, however, had to return twice to France for negotiations, losing much time on these trips which, for reasons of security, he undertook using a false civilian passport. Also his efficacy was limited by what Holma called "morbid caution" as well as by the fact that he was completely his master's (Gamelin's) apprentice.[67]

The French Minister in Helsinki, Magny, is said to have "disappeared morally and physically" after the outbreak of war. The second-in-command at the French Legation, M. Coulet, later recalled that he had received a telephone call from Daladier one night in February, and had had to tell the Premier that he had no idea of his chief's whereabouts. A leading French press commentator on foreign affairs, Pertinax (André Géraud), maintained in a book written in America during the war that Magny had fallen into disfavour after disclosing to the Finns that the actual purpose of the intervention was to cut off ore exports to Germany.[68]

Because no corresponding evidence is to be found in the Finnish sources, Pertinax's story should be treated with scepticism. On the other hand, the following conversation, throwing a grim light on the state of affairs at the French Legation in Helsinki, shows the basic reason for Magny's dismissal. At a secret meeting of the Chamber of Deputies on 19 March 1940, M. Tixier-Vignancourt* alleged that Magny had been forced to stay in Helsinki for almost the entire period of the war, to the end of February, without receiving any cabled instructions. The following dialogue then ensued between him and the Premier-Foreign Minister:

Daladier: It is not true.
Tixier: And since this matter has been brought up, let me tell you: it was impossible to send him instructions, because he had lost the cypher.
Daladier: That's not true, *the cypher was not lost, Monsieur Magny had burnt it contrary to instructions—*
Tixier: If Magny had burnt the cypher, a Quai d'Orsay official should have been sent to Helsinki.
(Violent applause, from the right and centre numerous voices: "Léger, Leger!", from the left: "It's a scandal!")[69]

Though in reality things were not as bad as this implied, and Magny did not lack all means of communication, Daladier was no

---

* A lawyer who became well-known during the political trials of the 1960s and was de Gaulle's right-wing opponent in two presidential elections.

doubt rather poorly informed on the situation in Finland. While he was able to follow the development of the war through the messages which Ganeval and the other members of the military delegation sent by their own cyphers to the French high command, he was in no position to obtain much first-hand political information from Helsinki. It remains a mystery why Daladier or the widely-criticized Léger failed to send a new envoy or even a new cypher to Helsinki earlier. According to Holma, Léger became interested in assisting Finland only when it was obviously too late. Was Daladier for his part so interested in Finland that he wanted to listen only to the opinions of the Finnish envoy? The replacement of Magny as late as early March with a diplomat who had already been assigned to Havana and received his new assignment to Helsinki with only forty-eight hours' warning, came too late to be of any decisive help.[70]

In making its final decision to send over 100,000 men across the North Sea, the Supreme War Council understood that the first prerequisite of success was surprise. If the enemy learnt of the preparations, it would do its utmost to be there first. At worst it would intercept the army bound for Scandinavia at sea. But as Ironside had feared, there were too many cooks at work, and the preparations could not be kept secret. Within less than a week, news of the Vincennes decision had reached diplomatic circles and then the press.

In retrospect the soldiers' attempt at concealing their preparations seem droll. Béthouart's troops, for example, were distributed with mosquito nets and map rolls with open ends, in which one could make out the Caucasus. Ironside decided to move his ski training centre from Aldershot to Chamonix in France, less for the snow than for reasons of discretion. "Everybody knows that we are preparing", the General sighed, "but I am hoping that it is being put down to Finland, and that the method of our approach is not known."

His hopes, alas, were in vain: on 22 February, five days after making this entry in his diary, Ironside heard that the French Legation in Stockholm was spreading news of an expected Allied landing at Narvik. The camouflage measures were still continued on a wide scale. They went as far as planning the removal of an air squadron from Aden to Palestine and giving the British officials in the Middle East false orders whereby they had to be prepared to receive additional troops from Britain at the beginning of April.[71]

Meanwhile the War Cabinet was greatly vexed when one of its former members, Hore-Belisha, who had ceased to be Minister of

War six weeks earlier and was well acquainted with the intervention plan, suddenly wrote an article about it for the *News of the World*. The preventive censorship removed twenty-four lines from his first instalment which, according to Halifax, was "of the most objectionable character possible". However, Hore-Belisha obstinately continued in the following Sunday's issue, comparing Norway in Napoleonic terms "to a pistol which is pointed to the heart of Britain and warned that it might be charged...."[72]

The first article, published on 18 February, referred to the security of the ore fields in Northern Sweden and stressed the importance for British interests of the defence of Finland. It seems to have impressed Churchill, who held the author in high esteem. At the Cabinet meeting the same Sunday, when it became known that Sweden had now officially turned its back on Finnish appeals, he unexpectedly called for Allied troops to be sent to Finland without delay:

The First Lord of the Admiralty emphasized the importance of our having some troops in Finland as early as possible. Even if the Finns were driven back and our troops with them, there would be a reasonable chance that, in the course of their retirement, they might after all secure possession of the Gälivare ore fields and thus deny them to Germany.[73]

Churchill had thus once more ended up at the ore fields— although the order had changed: earlier he had always paid attention to Narvik and the ore fields in the first instance, whereas now he was also acknowledging the importance of Finland, if only as an indirect factor. It remained undefined by which route the special unit suggested by Churchill would finally have reached Finland.

The proposal was based on the fear, by now expressed by the Chiefs-of-Staff, that the Finns would present their appeal for help before the Allies had completed their preparations. Fearing the same, the French general staff had studied Churchill's idea further and, at the end of February, brought up the possibility immediately sending a British-French representative unit of one or two companies to Finland by air. Following Ironside's suggestion, the Chiefs-of-Staff rejected the proposal, chiefly because of the lack of resources for transporting by air a unit of this size. As it turned out, even taking into account all the available civilian aircraft, the Air Ministry was unable to find in the whole of Britain enough heavy transport planes to fly more than forty men and their equipment to Finland. It was also feared that the sudden appearance of British soldiers in Finland would alarm the Germans. Thus the sending of a token force would have done more harm than good.

The commanders of the Scandinavian operation were not appointed until the Finnish War was over. The man appointed for the task was the Assistant C.I.G.S., Lieutenant-General H.R.S. Massy, who in fact took command during the Norwegian campaign of April-June 1940. Major-General P.J. Mackesy was appointed commander of the Northern force in late February. The French General Audet, commander of the French troops in the expeditionary force, would probably have been the officer responsible for the expedition to Finland. Neither Mackesy, who was in charge of the Narvik operation, nor Audet, who at the time was senior French officer at the Namsos bridgehead, later achieved any special distinction as a front line commander.

Audet, in his diary notes published later, has given detailed accounts of his discussions with the British General Staff in London on 19-21 February. The General was able to inform his British hosts that the French troops earmarked for the operation would be ready to leave three days before schedule, i.e. as early as 3 March. But it appeared that the British were more than ten days behind in their preparations.* Audet viewed the slowness and vagueness of the discussions with dismay, and noted with obvious amazement the continuing divergence of British and French objectives:

In the French General Staff the only talk about Finland; in the British General Staff Finland was mentioned only casually, but the importance of taking over the Swedish mines was emphasised....

The matter of the timetable, Audet concluded, caused a good deal of disagreement; the British wanted to prepare the expedition slowly but carefully whereas the French wanted to hurry, because Finland was running out of resources. Back at Vincennes, Audet noticed that, whereas Gamelin accepted the British delays without objections, many of his staff officers angrily pointed out that the entire enterprise would miscarry if it were not carried out quickly and with sufficient forces. In his official capacity, Audet had to defend the British general staff and emphasise to his brother-officers the need to consider certain facts such as the lack of forces and tonnage, as well as the limited capacity of the northern harbours and railways. Nevertheless, as he observed, the enthusiasm among his fellow-countrymen for saving Finland seemed rather unrealistic compared with the British goals — the mines.[75]

Daladier seemed not to share the generals' pessimism over the

---

* As the French archives seen by the present writer reveal, Darlan had even tried to propose that the French troops of the 'Avonmouth' force should be despatched to Narvik, separately from the British, as early as 12 March.

feasibility of the plan. Notwithstanding his performance at the decisive meeting on 5 February, which had been somewhat passive, he interpreted the Supreme War Council decision to intervene as a great personal victory for himself. The thought of the far-reaching effects, military risks and political complications involved, however, caused his voice to tremble as he rose to speak at a secret session of the Chamber four days after the Vincennes meeting. "Come what may, God is our judge!" he proclaimed amid applause, referring to the confidential intervention resolution, presumably familiar by then to everyone present. "As I have now, a few days ago, attained my goal, have I perhaps made a mistake? The future will show!"[76]

In February the Supreme War Council decision, the *Altmark* incident and the collapse of the main Finnish defence line on the Isthmus decided the future development of the Finnish War, which was at the cross-roads. Not only the parties directly concerned but all the powers interested in the conflict were faced with far-reaching choices: the Allies in their relations with the Soviet Union and their attitude towards the insistence of the Scandinavian countries on their neutrality; Germany gambling on whether to strike west or north; the Soviet Union with the alternatives before it of either using its present military success to force Finland to its knees or accepting a compromise before foreign powers intervened. The hard-pressed Scandinavian countries for their part, in the hope of saving themselves from being invaded, seemed to have chosen the road of isolating the conflict and leaving Finland to the mercy of the Soviet Union.

Out of the three alternatives which at the beginning of the month seemed open to Finland—Allied intervention, continuation of the war with Swedish assistance or peace—only the last remained at the final bitter settlement in March. Even this was restricted: to avoid a dictated peace, the Finnish Government decided to exploit the threat of Allied assistance as its last card, well aware that in the end it would not have been effective enough to stop the Red Army, but, on the contrary, would have entangled both Finland and the Soviet Union in a world war.

VII

ENDING THE AGONY

February-March 1940

As General Ling, together with the new British envoy Gordon Vereker, was finally about to introduce the intervention plan to the Finnish Government on 24 February, Soviet troops had already penetrated the outer port of Viipuri, ten miles from the city. Since the Finns had also been forced to leave the fortified islands of Koivisto (Björkö), at the western flank of the Isthmus, the Soviet Seventh Army was able to cross the Bay of Viipuri, firmly frozen due to the exceptional severity of the winter, and to threaten the southern coast of the Finnish mainland, which for the time being was undefended. The movement was effected without delay, with the result that ten days later the Army had six of its divisions with armoured and air support attacking the opposite shore of the bay.

On the same day that Koivisto was evacuated, Tanner had had the unhappy task of informing the Cabinet that the Kremlin would not be satisfied with less than Peter the Great's borders,* in addition to which the Russians were demanding that Finland sign a defence treaty with the Soviet Union and Estonia.[1] While confirming these terms to the Swedish Minister in Moscow, Molotov had added that, if the Finns were to reject them, the Red Army would march on and the Soviet Government would raise its peace terms. "It has been asked here", Assarsson reported Molotov as saying, "whether it would not have been better to negotiate with Kuusinen's 'people's government' than to wait for an answer from the present Finnish Cabinet." *As far as the assistance promised to Finland by the Western Powers was concerned,* Molotov continued, *the Soviet Government did not believe this would be realised.*[2]

Moscow had thus wanted to prevent the Finns from using the Allied intervention offer as a bargaining counter. Mannerheim had actually recommended such a policy, and recently urged Walden that "the government should exploit the rumours of the intervention". [3] Apart from the Premier no other member of the Cabinet at first favoured such a line of action. The Allied proposal was most strongly criticised by Paasikivi, who perceived quite clearly that intervention would in fact be aimed at Germany.[4] It was at

---

* In 1721 after a twenty-year-long war with Sweden, the Tsar had annexed to his empire an area of Finnish Karelia roughly corresponding to the South-western territory ceded to Russia in March 1940.

his suggestion that the Cabinet's reply to the Russians had been delayed, on 23 February, until Professor Kivimäki returned from Berlin to report on how the problem was seen there.* But first of all the Cabinet preferred to find out what was the final word of London, Paris and of Stockholm: could Allied aid at last get through to Finland and how quickly?[5]

After presenting his credentials to the President of the Republic (the ceremony took place in a basement shelter of the presidential palace), Vereker, accompanied by Ling, paid a visit to the Foreign Minister. He had been authorised to tell the latter that the Allies planned to send an expeditionary force of 22,000 men to Finland, with twice the normal firing capacity. The troops could leave Britain on 15 March, be in Finland a month later and take charge of defensive operations, at least in the north of Finland as far south as the altitude of the town of Kemi, or *maybe even farther south if Mannerheim so wished.*[6]

This was in fact contrary to what Ling had been instructed to say, in other words that *the use of the troops south of Kemi was out of the question.* Even the size of the force was exaggerated. According to what had been decided and told to Ling in London, the strength of the troops to be sent to Finland would have amounted not to more than 20,000 but to 9,000 in the first instance and a maximum of 15,000 men later.

In addition, Vereker transmitted to the Finnish Government the request to back up Allied diplomacy by asking the Scandinavians, by 5 March at the latest, to consent to the transit of the reinforcements. The Finns would have to notify their neighbours that if consent was refused, the appeal would be made public, and they were advised to propose that the Alied troops might go through Scandinavia in private groups.

To Tanner's remark that the Finns too were thus in danger of being drawn into the great war, Ling gave the familiar answer—evading the main question, which concerned the likelihood of German intervention: "But Finland is not *at war* with the Soviet Union. Neither would Britain be *at war* with the Soviet Union. The British troops at the Finnish fronts would make war on their own." Instead, neither Vereker nor Ling was so far able to answer two further difficult but vital questions: would the Allies guarantee Finland's independence and frontiers at the final post-war settlement, and would they take charge of the Finnish defence expenses if the war were prolonged?[7]

Because of the situation, the Cabinet had been convened for the

---

* See above, p. 108.

following Sunday afternoon, the 25th. An hour before the meeting, Tanner, together with the Premier, met the British representatives once again, remarking that their answers to the questions posed by the Finns were still "vague, and diverged from earlier information". Ryti, however, seems to have been rather satisfied: he later reported to the Cabinet that by now Vereker and Ling had promised that the Allied troops for Finland would be ready to leave on 5 March,* with a strength of 24,000 men and with a fire-power such that "a battalion would be equal to a regiment". In another context the Premier went further and said that the British were "ready to finance us further and commit themselves to guaranteeing our frontiers at the peace settlement".† The British would have had nothing against Finland making peace either, he added surprisingly; in fact *"they seemed not to be too interested in continuing the war."*[8] All this went beyond what Vereker and Ling had offered the Foreign Minister the previous day.

At the same meeting Tanner reported that the Swedes had now consented to allow the transit of volunteers "in groups". It might be possible, he concluded, to infiltrate regular troops into Finland in this way, as Ling had suggested. This, however, might inevitably lead to involvement in the general war: Kivimäki had indeed cabled from Berlin that although Goering had not opposed Swedish aid to Finland, he had threatened German intervention if regular Allied troops were to arrive in Scandinavia. Tanner considered hopes of an internal collapse in Russia or of Turkey entering the war as "speculations on which we cannot build our policy". Personally he urged that the decision be taken immediately.[9]

After Paasikivi and Walden had again pronounced in favour of making peace, the Premier joined them but on the definite condition that *the treaty of mutual assistance proposed by the Soviet Government should be avoided: "It would lead us into war against Germany, since German-Soviet friendship would not last."* Instead, the President of the Republic, Kyösti Kallio, who was present at the meeting, seems to have changed his mind again and spoken for the continuation of the war. At his suggestion the Foreign Minister was once again asked to leave for Stockholm *to study all three alternatives:* to get milder peace terms from the Soviet Union, to have more expedient and efficient assistance from Sweden, or to make sure that the Allied transit to Finland would finally be permitted.[10]

However, Tanner's visit to Stockholm on 27 February proved ineffective. The attempt to obtain more lenient peace terms only

---

* This may have been the result of a confusion: the date for the official Finnish appeal, as we know, had been fixed as 5 March.
† Cf. following page.

resulted in a Soviet ultimatum to Helsinki the following day, giving the Finns two days to decide whether they would start negotiations or not. The Swedish Premier, for his part, rejected the requests presented to him and, according to Tanner, exclaimed: "If the Western Powers were to attempt passage without permission, Sweden would find herself at war with Finland on the side of the Russians." The only positive results Tanner obtained from the Swedes were the promises to help Finland's reconstruction and to consider the signing of a mutual defence pact between the two countries once the Finnish-Soviet conflict was over.[11]

Meanwhile the War Office had learnt of what Vereker and Ling had promised to the Finns and realized that the figures they had given were exaggerated. The envoy was instructed to correct his statement and to inform the Finnish Government that only 12,000 to 13,000 men could be expected and then not until the latter part of April.*[12] Vereker acted as ordered and thus, on 28 February, only a couple of hours before the Soviet peace ultimatum was received in Helsinki, gave Tanner an unpleasant surprise. The depressing effect of the statement was hardly alleviated by the fact that Tanner was still dissatisfied with Vereker's replies to the questions of whether the Allies would guarantee the independence and borders of Finland at the peace settlement and for how long the Allied troops were to stay in Finland.†[14]

After consulting the Commander-in-Chief in Mikkeli, Ryti reported at the Cabinet session of the afternoon of 29 February that the former also considered that peace had to be made immediately. Consequently an answer to Moscow was drafted, on be despatched that very same evening.[15] During this long afternoon both British and French envoys tried to apply pressure on Tanner, but failed to change the course of events. Magny (instructed by Daladier to make a strong effort to convince the Finns to proceed without waiting for the Scandinavian transit permit) again exasperated Tanner by giving divergent information on the size of the expeditionary force and by threatening the Finns. If the Finns accepted peace, the envoy told Tanner, they would have to answer for their own fate: the offer of assistance would not be

---

* The figures corresponded to the numbers suggested by the Allied High Command in late February.

† Vereker's instructions as to the answers he should give Tanner were drafted on similar lines to the proposal for the assurance given to Belgium six weeks earlier: "..whereas it was impossible to guarantee anything, the Finnish Government could be sure that, if our two countries were both in the war as allies, we should do everything in our power to maintain the integrity of Finland, and that the whole resources of the British Empire would be exerted in the common struggle."[13]

repeated, sympathy toward Finland would cool, and the country would be considered as having moved over to the German side....[16]

The Parliamentary Foreign Affairs Committee had meanwhile discussed the peace question at two meetings held on the same day, and approved the procedure of the Cabinet with only one member (Kekkonen*) opposing. The Cabinet then brought this historic 29 February to an end by giving, an hour or two before midnight, the final touch to the reply to be sent to Moscow. During the very same night the text was cabled to the *Chargé d'affaires* in Stockholm—with the instructions that it be forwarded later, on the appropriate order being given. At any rate the decisive roulette seemed to have been set spinning, leaving the Finns as passive spectators.[18]

2

After Tanner had left for Stockholm for the third time on the evening of 26 February, the General Headquarters in Mikkeli informed the Foreign Ministry that the proposed timetable of the Allied expeditionary force was unsatisfactory. The Chief of the Political Department consequently suggested to Premier Ryti that the Finnish representatives in London and Paris be requested to find out whether the promised help could be obtainable at an earlier date. Ryti agreed and even phoned Holma in Paris confirming the cable instructions. "I guessed what the reactions of the two envoys would be," Pakaslahti writes in his memoirs. "They, so to say, quickened their pace."[19]

Pakaslahti (who, in his capacity as the responsible senior official, later attached his personal protest to the Cabinet decision to accept the peace terms) makes no secret of the fact that he himself had tried on several occasions to persuade the Foreign Minister to turn to the Allies; Tanner's attitude to the intervention offer, he writes, "was not altogether negative." According to him, even the most authoritative member of the peace triumvirate, Premier Ryti, had been "very active" in this respect.[20] This might indeed be true. It has to be stressed, however, that Tanner's earlier interest in Allied

---

* Dr. Urho Kekkonen, now President of the Republic, has later explained his position by pointing out that he — like many other Finns in leading positions, with the possible exception of the military leadership—did not know the situation was so desperate: "Since I had opposed the Soviet proposals before the war, it was logical not to accept even worse terms during the war....I was naturally unaware of the real state of affairs.... I had good reason to suppose that our fight could continue successfully, due to the information I had received from a good friend of mine who was placed in the midst of things at the general headquarters".[17]

military assistance had faded towards the end of the war; and as for Ryti, he might from time to time have been "active" in support of Allied intervention, but never "very active"; had it been otherwise, the peace of Moscow would probably never have been signed.

Tanner's absence, however, had given Pakaslahti the opportunity to appeal to Ryti directly.[21] Holma for his part asked for and obtained an appointment to see Daladier on the evening of the 27th. The official French report maintained that the envoy had "said that he had received instructions by telephone from the Finnish Prime Minister *to express the gratification of the Finnish Government at learning that the British and French Governments were prepared to send troops to Finland, and their hope that it might be possible for this aid to be accelerated.*" According to what Holma reported to Helsinki, Daladier had said that the Allied force (which, during another conversation with Holma the following morning, he declared to be "at least three divisions at once") would reach Finland by the end of March, or even earlier if the British were prepared for it.*[22]

Holma's first reports on Daladier's promises, though received in Helsinki on the last day of February, failed to affect the government's decision to give Moscow an affirmative answer. Tanner said outright to the French envoy that the new deadline, the end of March, was technically "impossible". But then Holma's further cables and his phone call to Ryti at midnight the next day, as well as a telegram from London—in which Gripenberg warned that the peace contacts might endanger the Allied arms deliveries and lead to a complete isolation of Finland—suddenly changed the course of events.

When it met the following morning, the Finnish Cabinet decided to suspend its affirmative reply to the Kremlin (which, it may be recalled, had already been despatched to the Finnish Legation in Stockholm). Instead, so as not to interrupt the peace contacts altogether, a request for clarification of the Soviet terms was sent via Stockholm. In the meantime, London and Paris were approached again to inquire whether the Allies could supply Finland immediately with a considerable number of bomber aircraft and troops.†[23]

---

* In fact, Daladier had informed Holma in the presence of three leading officials of the Quai d' Orsay that the former number of 12,000 men meant Chasseurs Alpins only, and that by the end of March there would be arriving in Finland, not 20,000 as promised by the French Minister to Tanner the previous evening, but *50,000 men*—"*volunteers*", *with special equipment*. Further, he expressed his belief that the Scandinavians would in the end consent to transit, and promised that the Allies would arrange the matter directly with them.

† See below, p. 128.

At this stage, however, no additional promises were forthcoming from London. On the contrary, Gripenberg's question as to whether the promised help could be made attainable earlier irritated the Chiefs-of-Staff. Ironside considered the question "inopportune" and thought it might be due "to the ill-judged and irresponsible pressure of the French circles in Helsinki which, with no knowledge of the facts, were always suggesting that matters might be hurried." The British were even more vexed since the French had managed to keep their lead in delivering war material to Finland and were trying to set the pace of the intervention preparations.* Two days later, in the midst of the Cabinet meeting in fact, another report arrived according to which Daladier had responded affirmatively to all the Finnish requests and consequently promised to raise the numbers of the expeditionary force, speed up the timetable and take care of the transit question. "The French action was a bad example of lack of co-operation," the Cabinet members commented:

The French were apparently prepared to bluff, knowing that they could throw on to us the whole blame for the failure to redeem their promises as they had undertaken the direction of the enterprise.[24]

Daladier instructed the French Ambassador in London to suggest to the Foreign Office in the morning of 29 February, that Holma's démarche should be considered "as a kind of appeal, if not the actual appeal which figured in our plan". The Allies ought shortly to take measures to procure the necessary permission from Norway and Sweden. By so doing they would at least have covered themselves against accusations of passivity, even if the Finns were forced to make peace. The responsibility for the eventual collapse of Finland would in that case fall upon those to whom it really belonged, the Premier concluded, namely the Scandinavians.[25]

Halifax showed obvious interest in Daladier's proposal. The Cabinet, however, decided to find out first whether Holma's démarche was really meant as an appeal and, if so, whether the necessary measures should at once be taken in Oslo and Stockholm. Meanwhile Vereker was instructed to make clear to the Finns that, unless the expected appeal took place, the Allies might

---

* The French had recently responded to Finnish armament requests in a spectacular way by promising them new artillery and aircraft: the British having been unable to help Mannerheim, who in the middle of February had urgently demanded from them almost 100 field-guns with ammunition, the French had immediately decided to deliver to Finland two additional batteries of 75-mm. guns, a total of thirty-six. At about the same time they had promised to send to Finland over 100 fighter planes of an old model (Cf. below, p. 142).

announce publicly that they at least had been prepared to take action to assist Finland.[26]

In contrast to the spectacular and consistent activity of the French, the policy of the British Government proved, even as the crucial moment approached, vague if not incoherent. Its basic motive was timidity, and unconscious awareness of the fact that the resources available were not adequate for the task ahead. When the French Ambassador, Corbin, complained to Chamberlain that Daladier might lose his position if Finland were not assisted effectively, the Prime Minister replied that since Finland did not appeal for help, the Allies were not answerable. Corbin pointed out that the Finns might, after all, never appeal *"because they knew that we [the Allies] were not willing or able to send them effective help".*[27] These verbal flashes give deep insight into the motives of the British and French leaders on this question. It is likely that both Chamberlain and Daladier were basically afraid of sending their troops to Finland, and therefore hoped to blame the Scandinavians for failure. The difference between their approaches to the problem was one of means rather than purpose. In this respect the Munich politicians and the strategists of the "phoney war" proved to be kindred spirits.

3

On the morning of 1 March the Foreign Secretary heard from Gripenberg that the Finnish Government had to decide that same day whether or not to enter into peace negotiations. The Finns might do so, the envoy added, because they doubted the efficacy and timeliness of Allied assistance. After the War Cabinet meeting a little later—at which Halifax demanded that Oslo and Stockholm be immediately prepared for an eventual request for transit—Gripenberg again called on Halifax (during this busy day he saw the Foreign Secretary five times in all) and inquired whether the Allies could deliver 100 bombers to Finland immediately and 50,000 men by the end of March.[28]

As we know, the decision to ask for increased assistance had been made in Helsinki the very same morning when the Finnish Government, an hour and a half before the deadline set by Moscow, decided to postpone the choice between peace and war. It was in fact induced at the last moment by the personal intervention of Marshal Mannerheim.[29] As Vereker reported three days later, the Finns tried to make the best of the situation. The War Cabinet, indeed, did not know whether the military position in Finland had really deteriorated to the point of catastrophe and, if so, why this had happened so unexpectedly. As late as 28 February Mannerheim had told a French officer* that Finland did not need troops from abroad —so why this sudden request for 50,000 men ?[30]

The information crisis of the War Cabinet was not greatly improved by the replacement of the permanent British representatives in Finland. Communications, as always, were slow and uncertain. At the beginning of March, for instance, an important cable sent to London by the new military attaché, Colonel E. J. King-Salter, following his first visit to the Finnish general headquarters took no less than three days to arrive. On the other hand, trustworthy first-hand reports from Finland were not entirely lacking,† if only the Cabinet had dared to face up to the perplexing realities. It is rather difficult to avoid the fact that, at the peak of the crisis, there were in London signs of slackening not to say exhaustion of interest in the requirements of the Finnish situation.[31]

The War Cabinet records of 27 February offer a clear illustration of this uncertainty. Gripenberg had called on Lord Chatfield, the Minister of Defence, the day before — when the morning papers reported that the Finns had been forced to evacuate Koivisto with its coastal artillery—and again repeated the demand for additional heavy artillery. When reporting the interview to the War Cabinet, Chatfield commented rather sarcastically:

He had spoken as if this were his last request and as if the Finnish resistance must collapse if it were not granted.

He said that the Finns had already been sent 114-mm. howitzers in January and 84-mm. field-guns in February, as well as a promise of a dozen heavy mobile coastal guns to come. But he failed to mention that they had for the past month constantly been asking for long-range artillery for dispersing enemy troop concentrations and that these requests had come not only through Finnish representatives in London but also through Ling, as well as influential politicians like Philip Noel-Baker and Harold Macmillan, who had visited Finland. In the Cabinet, however, "it was generally agreed that this was another example of the great difficulty of dealing with uncoordinated requests from Finland, not placed in any clear order of priority." To crown it all, it was decided to postpone the matter in order to have, once more, the opinion of the military attaché in Helsinki—who then naturally answered that the guns should be delivered.[32]

---

* Evidently Colonel Ganeval.
† Cf. below, pp. 168 and 170.

The Cabinet's irritation may well have been the result of its feelings of impotence. As the Secretary for War reported, there were in Britain at that moment no shells for 155-mm. heavy howitzers—these had to be taken from the Western Front. As for the lighter 114-mm. howitzers, the reserve divisions then being trained in Britain had only half the necessary number at their disposal, and not one single piece could be spared. "The willingness of the Finns to continue the struggle seemed to depend on our acceptance of a demand for assistance," the Cabinet concluded three days later in unusually clear terms, "*which it was not within our power to provide.*"[33]

It is evident that the decisive breakdown of plans for assistance to Finland took place during the latter half of February. After lingering unnecessarily for two weeks, the Allies proposed intervention just as the Finns, having been beaten on the Karelian Isthmus, were resigning themselves to an enforced peace. The first condition for Finnish acceptance of the offer would have been its immediate fulfilment, but neither the British nor the French were prepared for this.

General Airo, the Finnish Chief of Operations during the war, informed the present writer that the most important reason for not accepting the offer was the inability of the two powers to present it by a joint *demarche*. A second reason was the completely divergent information they provided on the extent and timing of the assistance. It appears from official French archives that Magny was instructed on 5 March to co-ordinate his activities with his British colleague. But this was too late. The fighting spirit of the army, which had lost its allegedly unbreakable main line of defence, was not greatly enhanced by promises that, after at least six more long weeks, it might be assisted by a few foreign soldiers, whose presence in Finland, moreover, might invite an attack from a new and more formidable enemy, Germany. In seeking a better position for negotiations with the Russians, Ryti had gone along with the additional offers from London and Paris on the last day of February, which resulted in the postponement of the peace negotiations. The only outcome of the delay was that the war, which was growing increasingly bloody as it approached its end, had to be continued for another ten days or so.

4

In the British War Cabinet, the principal dilemma over assisting Finland—transit through Scandinavia—was now a fixed item on the daily agenda. At the morning meeting of 1 March Halifax again demanded that a preliminary announcement on Allied intentions should be made immediately to Oslo and Stockholm. Churchill disagreed, and once more tried to propose that discussions with the Scandinavians should not be started until the first echelon had arrived at Narvik. If, he argued, the Norwegians, in spite of everything, were to resort to arms, the expeditionary force could re-embark, but he added that "*at this stage he would not entirely exclude the use of some force in order to make our way through.*"[34]

The Cabinet however thought differently: the British envoys in Oslo and Stockholm, jointly with their French colleagues, were instructed to inform the respective governments on 2 March that the Allies were planning to send reinforcements to Finland, whose military position was "becoming desperate", and would therefore ask Norway and Sweden for transit permission in due time. Both countries were again offered military assistance against eventual German countermeasures and proposed detailed preparatory discussions between their and Allied general staffs.[35]

The decision was in fact made without illusions. The question of what was to be done if the Scandinavians remained intransigent was left unanswered except for Churchill's comforting remark that the Allies would in any case have demonstrated that they had done their best: "We had done all we could, had behaved honourably." Unless the Scandinavians consented, a military representative reminded the Cabinet, the operation would in any case have to be completely reorganised. Despite this, Halifax considered himself in a position to assure the Finnish envoy a few hours later that even a negative answer from Oslo and Stockholm would not hinder the two powers from carrying out the plan.[36]

After the Scandinavians, less than two days later, had rejected the proposal, the Allied governments were for a while in a state of confusion. In London the War Cabinet even wondered whether the Scandinavians should be asked what they would do if the Allies carried out their intervention plan regardless.[37] But before the Scandinavians could be approached again, it was necessary to get the Finns at long last to give the green light to intervention. The Finnish refusal to appeal for intervention unless the Scandinavians consented to the transit beforehand turned the problem, as Daladier bitterly remarked, upside down and compromised the intervention plan. During the following days the discussions were centred on the dilemma of how to persuade Helsinki to act immediately. Finland's armament shortage was one factor which could be used to this end.

The Finnish inquiry presented by Gripenberg on 1 March* had

---

* In addition to a request for 100 manned bombers and 50,000 men, the inquiry included the question whether the Allies would allow their troops to be placed

caused a fairly heated discussion to take place in the War Cabinet, especially as Daladier, without consulting the British, had just given in completely to the Finnish demands. The representative of the Chiefs-of-Staff argued that it would take at least a month to send to Finland the crews, field personnel and ground equipment for the number of planes involved. Even the sending of a small number would, according to the military view, weaken the British air forces* *without holding down the forces of the main enemy, Germany, and without having a decisive effect on the outcome of the Finnish war.* As for the troops requested—nearly four divisions—they would have outnumbered the land forces needed for the first echelon of the Scandinavian expedition. The representative concluded that the timetable which had been prepared was the fastest possible, but *because of transportation difficulties it was not possible to transport more than 12,000–13,000 men to the Norwegian harbours before the end of March.*[38]

Gripenberg for his part made it clear that the arrival of even a limited number of bombers in Finland would have a powerful moral effect.[39] He received support from the French Ambassador who, after talking to him on 3 March, went straight on to see Cadogan. Corbin's intervention conformed to the active line adopted by the French government. After deciding on his own to deliver twelve new Potez-63 bombers to Finland, Daladier had ordered them to be made ready for delivery at once. Applications for transit visas through the Scandinavian countries were made for the 200 volunteers who were to accompany the planes. At the end of the war the planes were on their way to Finland, but were returned in accordance with Daladier's instructions.[39]

In London the discussion of the matter was prolonged by another fatal week. Halifax, referring to political grounds, tried to have at least a smaller amount of planes despatched, but the reluctant Minister of Aviation, backed by Chamberlain and Churchill, persistently opposed him. On 5 March, the deadline set for the Finnish appeal, Lord Chatfield suddenly called for the immediate delivery of 100 bombers. He said that a smaller number was not enough; unless a sufficient amount of armed assistance could be detached for Finland, there would be no object in sending anything at all. Chatfield was told that no material assistance could be considered until it was known whether the Finns would make their appeal

---

* In the case of heavy bombers, 100 planes represented two-thirds of the British home forces.

---

under Mannerheim's command and eventually to be used on other fronts than that of Northern Finland. The fourth point of the inquiry, concerning transit, had already been answered by Halifax when he had told Gripenberg that the expeditionary force would get through to Finland in any case.

or not. He was then charged with the task of explaining this to the Finnish envoy, whom he was to see the same afternoon.[40]

Gripenberg, in his diary, describes his conversation with Chatfield as somewhat dramatic. The Minister of Defence had spoken of a "new front" to be formed in Finland with Allied support, naturally accompanied by the supply of war materials. But if the Finns made a sudden peace, these materials would be lost, and that was the reason why nothing could be delivered until the objectives of Helsinki were known. "Things are now moving in a circle", Gripenberg answered, "the Allies will not send war material if Finland does not continue to fight, and Finland cannot continue to fight if it does not receive war material." Chatfield agreed, and then added: "Only Finland can break this circle."[41]

5

By now the Finnish Government had decided to break out of this vicious circle, but in the opposite direction to that which the Allies had wished—in other words, towards peace. The British War Cabinet, however, failed to understand why the Finns considered the situation so infinitely hopeless. A number of remarkable comments were made. In general, the members of the Finnish Government, Tanner most of all, were distrusted, whereas the Commander-in-Chief enjoyed unbounded confidence. It was even maintained that the Allied offers of assistance had been purposely concealed from Mannerheim by the Finnish Government. But once the new military attaché in Helsinki had been to the General Headquarters and reported to London that "the Field-Marshal had all his telegrams before him and is certainly fully in picture", the War Cabinet was utterly confused. Mannerheim was under pressure, it was explained; he had been instructed by his ministers to exaggerate the seriousness of the situation. The Finnish Government was trying to get more arms by acting in this way![42]

Ling, who had once more returned to London, described the Finnish situation in much more optimistic terms than Mannerheim had done to King-Salter: he was of the opinion that *the Finns, despite the difficulties, would be able to hold out until the spring thaw and, having succeeded thus far, would continue with their resistance until the following July at the earliest.** In Paris, on the contrary, the Finnish situation was regarded with alarm since Ganeval, obviously better

---

* General Enckell was also informed from home on 5 March that the military situation was seen as unchanged for two days, even if the Russians tried to besiege positions from the side of the Gulf of Finland: the fighting capacity of the Finns remained unbroken, but their physical fitness was under severe strain.

acquainted than his British colleague with what was happening at
the front, had sent Paris a pessimistic review of the situation. "The
Finns", he reported after the peace was concluded, "*were no longer
in a position to hold out until the thaw*"! Thus Daladier's demands that
the Finnish Government should present its appeal immediately,
which he repeated from the beginning of March with growing
impatience, were no doubt justified. It is of course another matter
whether the French Premier imagined that a Finnish appeal would
have had any result other than to put the Scandinavians in a
difficult situation.[43]

In Helsinki feelings had changed from hope to despair. On the
morning of 3 March, Vereker had once more called on Tanner and
told him that the total of Allied troops arriving in Finland by the
middle of April would be only 6,000 men. This information, un-
equalled in its frankness, was presumably based on the minimum
figures given by the Chiefs-of-Staff. (Vereker may also have meant,
as he specified a few hours later, that *Britain alone* would be sending
6,000 men with the expeditionary force.[44]) He, as well as Magny,
had recently called on the Foreign Minister, and had failed to
explain how the Allied troops could have reached Finland in spite of
Scandinavian opposition. Utterly disappointed, Tanner now had a
good case show for demonstrating to the Cabinet that "the end of the
rope had been reached".[45]

At the Cabinet meeting the same evening, all the members without exception had come round to Tanner's view. Paasikivi once more
suggested that German diplomatic support should be sought, but
Tanner objected rigorously. As long as the negotiations with the
Allies continued, he said, it would be "disgusting double dealing" to
approach Germany. By now, however, the Cabinet was unable to do
anything but await the Russian "clarification of terms" which it had
demanded in order to gain time—it did not know that this demand
had never even been forwarded to Moscow, because the inter-
mediary agents in Stockholm, Günther and Kollontay, had found
it unsatisfactory.[46]

Meanwhile the situation at the front deteriorated rapidly. On the
morning of 5 March, Mannerheim was suffering from influenza and
was tired and feverish. Talking to Walden on the telephone, he
described the situation as very critical: the Russians had dug into
the west coast of Viipuri Bay and were developing their offensive
westwards along the ice of the Gulf of Finland in the direction of the
towns of Hamina and Kotka. North of the Isthmus, the industrial
district of Vuoksenlaakso was about to be overrun by the Red Army:
the factories had to be evacuated at once, the Marshal said, "the
last minutes are at hand". At a 10 o'clock Cabinet meeting, a few

hours before the deadline set by the Allies, Tanner openly expressed his dissatisfaction that the Soviet peace offer had not been given a clear and affirmative reply four days earlier. The Allies would not arrive until the Finns were pushed all the way to the shores of Bothnia, he concluded. Their assistance should be left as the last resource in case Moscow refused to negotiate.[47]

On the Premier's proposal the Cabinet then approved what in fact had been Mannerheim's suggestion, namely that *the representatives of the Western Powers be informed of the Government's intention to seek peace negotiations, but at the same time to keep the intervention preparations in being against an emergency.* The decision may seem naive; however, its motives were understandable: the Allies' interest in intervention was so obvious that they were hardly likely to compromise their preparations, despite the Finnish peace negotiations. This, at least, was the impression that the Finns themselves received. The President of the Republic had also finally accepted the necessity for peace negotiations on 5 March: President Kallio had previously talked with Ganeval and gained the impression that at least France would have no objections to the Finns making peace—if they considered themselves capable of doing so.[48]

Meanwhile in London too the opinion was gaining ground that the ending of hostilities might be an acceptable, even a welcome alternative. After establishing, at the Cabinet meeting of 6 March, that the Finnish appeal had not arrived by the set deadline and would probably not come later either, the Prime Minister dismissed the whole problem. "The Finnish government is perfectly free to take what action they think best," he said, "They can either ask us to send an expedition or, if they do not desire this, they can ask us to send heavy bombers, guns and other material. On the other hand, *if they wish, they can make the best terms obtainable with the U.S.S.R.*"

By now Chamberlain was no doubt prepared to drop the entire intervention plan. To this end he even proposed that a time-limit of twenty-four hours be set for the Finns to decide whether they wanted reinforcements or not. If no answer were received from Helsinki, the intervention plan would be given up, but assistance to the Finns would still be continued, provided that they continued to fight, in which case they could also have the bombers they had asked for.[49]

Chamberlain's change of attitude was partly due to Halifax's energetic pressure, partly to the reports of Ling, King-Salter and Magill, who considered it indispensable to deliver the bombers in order to repel Soviet attacks on the Southern coast of Finland. The Secretary of War was an unexpected convert, acting strongly in favour of giving the Finns the bombers; he too saw an opportunity to induce the Cabinet to give up the plan to send an expeditionary force, which was far more inconvenient from Whitehall's point of view than sending a few dozen aircraft to Finland. After the majority had adopted the Prime Minister's position—the Minister of Aviation alone dissenting—the delivery of fifty Blenheims (eight long-nosed and forty-two short-nosed) was decided on 7 March.[50]

In Finland the decision was favourably received. Possibly, together with other promises of assistance transmitted by Colonel Paasonen to Headquarters at the same time, it induced Mannerheim to consider momentarily making an appeal to the Allies. Tanner in his instructions to London dramatically emphasized the urgency of getting the bombers at once: "The distress is great—try to get them on the way immediately," he cabled to Gripenberg on 8 March. "Russian troops are pouring over the ice...."

At this time the War Cabinet was also aware of the seriousness of the situation, having had fresh and seemingly reliable first-hand information from Finland:

Major Magill's assessment of the present situation had been as follows. The Finns, by character, had immense powers of endurance, but once they cracked they would break altogether. There were signs of physical failing, due to the tremendous strain to which the rank and file had been put, but the fighting troops would not be likely to give in unless the Finnish High Command began to weaken. *The fear, therefore, was that the rot would set in at the top, particularly as the result of the constant defeatist pressure which Sweden never ceased to exert.*

Magill, who had returned from Finland by air on 4 March, had informed the War Minister that he had met Mannerheim on several occasions, but "had never seen him so depressed". His conclusions may seem exaggerated, but they are more or less confirmed by the French military delegates, who had arrived at the headquarters about the same time and talked with the Field-Marshal. According to them, too, the end was near.[51]

Meanwhile the Finnish Government had indeed accepted the renewed Soviet offer for negotiations and sent a peace delegation to Moscow, led by Premier Ryti. On the evening of 8 March, twenty-four hours after the delegation had arrived, it learned through a lengthy telegram from Helsinki that the Commander-in-Chief had changed his mind. Mannerheim, it was reported, favoured making the appeal to the Allies if no modifications were obtained in Moscow's peace terms.[52]

The change was due to the specific information which Mannerheim had received from Colonel Paasonen, freshly back from Paris. Returning home by way of London, Paasonen reported that the C.I.G.S., General Ironside, had broadly confirmed to General Enckell what Paasonen had cabled from Paris three days earlier: an Allied expeditionary force, with the strength of four divisions, was ready to leave Britain on 12 March. Moreover, according to Paasonen, the British and French believed that the Swedes would consent. He was even told that the Allies were still preparing the Petsamo expedition and would start their operations in the south, towards Turkey, on 15 April. The source of his arguments remains unknown.[53]

Paasonen's arrival in Helsinki just before the start of the peace negotiations in Moscow made a favourable impression on Pakaslahti. Tanner, on the other hand, did not hide his dissatisfaction with the Colonel for having spoken "quite fanatically in favour of the Western Powers". He was appalled by the thought that Paasonen, in his capacity as A.D.C. to the President of the Republic, would influence Kallio, who viewed the peace negotiations with constraint. So he resorted to a stratagem: "I told him to take his information to Headquarters at once in order to get him out of Helsinki."[54]

Pakaslahti had helped the Colonel in Helsinki to work out the memorandum which he presented to Mannerheim on 8 March. According to this document Ironside had announced to the Finnish officers in London that the first echelon of the expeditionary force would be ready to leave for Norway on 15 March (i.e. three days later than Paasonen had reported from Paris). Allegedly it would have comprised a 15,500-strong front division, comprising:

2½	brigades Chasseurs Alpins	8,500
2	Foreign Legion battalions	2,000
1	Polish battalion	1,000
1	British Guards brigade	3,500
1	British ski battalion	500

Total 15,500*

The second echelon was to comprise three British divisions of 14,000 combatants. Paasonen's statement that "*the total of combatants of the expeditionary force is thus 57,000*", appeared to be in accordance with the previous information from Paris. It no longer seemed necessary for Mannerheim to doubt the authenticity of what had been cabled by Holma and even by General Enckell. But who had authorized Ironside to announce that all the forces reserved for the Scandinavian

---

* In addition, the first echelon was to include "supply and maintenance troops" to be shipped to the Norwegian harbours.

operation would gradually be sent to Finland, is another question.*[55]

At the War Cabinet meeting on the morning of 4 March, Ironside had promised to "make clear to General Enckell why it would not be practicable for the Allied troops to operate south of the waistline [of Finland]". In his report to Mannerheim, Enckell did not touch on this, but Paasonen maintained that the C.I.G.S. had spoken to the Finns in quite different terms from those he had used with the British government: *"General Ironside expressly commented that Field-Marshal Mannerheim was at liberty to use the expeditionary force on any front in Finland."* Ironside's promises were received not only by Paasonen but by Enckell, a man who enjoyed the Field-Marshal's confidence and who personally had reservations concerning the Allied plans. Thus Paasonen's report was not entirely devoid of credibility, although his information on the preparations for the Caucasus and Petsamo operations seems doubtful and makes one suspect that he was not over-discriminating.[56]

For Mannerheim it was probably most alarming to realize, as Paasonen had warned, that the Allies were prepared to cancel all assistance if Finland sought peace. The end of the fighting, the memorandum went on, might in these circumstances mean national suicide: it would give the enemy the opportunity to choose its own moment for the decisive battle. Finland would be left alone, without the support of her Nordic neighbours, the Allies, or even "the sympathy of the entire civilized world". Moreover, Paasonen maintained, the French intelligence service had announced that the Soviet Union would ask, at a suitable moment, for the handing over of all war material supplied to Finland by the Allies.[57]

Paasonen's interference could be passed over in one sentence, had it not revealed that Mannerheim in fact was far from having made up his mind to accept an enforced peace. In the afternoon of the same day, the 8th, the Field-Marshal had studied the memorandum and indeed had let his chief of intelligence phone the Foreign Ministry in Helsinki to say that in order to secure the success of the peace negotiations and at the same time a favourable outcome to the request for bombers, it was advisable to make the appeal asked for by the Allies without delay. In the course of the evening Mannerheim repeated this opinion twice when phoning personally to Tanner, and finally confirmed it in an official letter. The next day, having heard that the promised British bombers would not arrive

---

* According to the archives of the French Embassy in London, Ironside had indeed proposed to Enckell that the troops prepared for Finland would in the first instance comprise four divisions.

immediately,* and convinced that, even if appealed for, the Allied expeditionary force would not join the battle until it was too late, the Field-Marshal reverted to the policy of peace.[58]

This episode is omitted in the memoirs of Mannerheim as well as in those of Heinrichs, who otherwise gives a fairly detailed account of the March 1940 crisis. The head of the delegation in Moscow, however, reported later that Mannerheim's advice had had so unsettling an effect on the Finnish negotiators that some of them had been prepared to go back home after the first contact with the Soviet representatives.†

6

While seeking peace, the Finns had tried to adhere to the difficult principle of making their real wishes known to both enemy and friend. Still, for some reasons—less linguistic than psychological—they frequently failed to appreciate correctly what was demanded of them. This is particularly true of the negotiations with the Soviet Union in autumn 1939 and in January-February 1940. As regards the Allies, the Finns seem to have acted in March on the presumption that because Allied representatives had been informed of Finnish objectives in good time and had expressed their understanding of the country's difficult position, all was well.[59] Hence it was particularly galling for Helsinki to learn of the reactions of the Allied governments as the moment of truth approached.

Immediately he heard that a Finnish peace delegation was bound for Moscow, Daladier called Holma to see him. After deploring the political difficulties he was in because of the Finnish peace overtures, he dictated a message to Holma to be sent to Helsinki. According to his own account, Holma succeeded in effecting a couple of minor corrections in the text but failed to remove the last sentence, which was somewhat menacing. Daladier explained to him that his intention was to make it clear that, contrary to what had been said in Sweden, the territories eventually surrendered by the Finns to the U.S.S.R. might not be returned after the war.‡[61]

---

* See below, pp. 141-2.

† According to Ryti's version, Paasikivi and Voionmää demanded that the negotiations be interrupted in order that the delegation could go back to Finland to submit the matter to Parliament and thus have the opportunity of finding out whether the new offers of assistance had influenced the policy of peace. Ryti reports that, together with Walden, he had opposed the proposal and announced that the vote of the chairman was decisive.[60]

‡ According to the Finnish translation presented to the Cabinet by Tanner on 9 March 1940, the complete text was the following: "For several days we have only been waiting for an appeal from Finland in order to come to her assistance

The following day Daladier tried to renew his plea, this time directly to Ryti and his fellow-delegates in Moscow, warning them against making a "shameful peace" and encouraging Finland to continue the fight with the "unlimited" support of the Allies. In spite of his efforts, the French *Chargé d'affaires* in Moscow did not succeed in forwarding the message to the effectively isolated Finnish delegation. Other means of pressure also failed, such as the hint given to Holma at the Quai d'Orsay that the French had captured a Soviet radio message according to which Kuusinen was to settle in Viipuri![62]

"The French were desperately afraid that the Finns would make peace," Churchill reported on 11 March after returning from negotiations in Paris. Although visiting France primarily for other reasons, he had discussed the question of Finland with Daladier, Léger and Reynaud. The French had openly expressed their bitterness at the slowness and hyper-caution shown by the British in the matter; in their opinion, he told the War Cabinet, "the loss of Finland would be equivalent to the loss of a great campaign."[63]

In order to forestall criticism of his government, Daladier had hurried to make public the extent of assistance to Finland. He repeated these figures when answering a question on 12 March in the Chamber of Deputies, and maintained that France had delivered, among other things, 175 planes to Finland. As pointed out by Léon Blum at a secret meeting four days later, this figure corresponded only with the planes promised to Finland; up to that moment, only the thirty Morane fighters and a dozen Potez-63 bombers had left France for Finland (the bombers only the day before) and "a few" of the Caudron and Kolhoven planes, which had been repaired at the depots, had received export licences.[64] Defending his policy on this last day of the Finnish war, Daladier once more tried to warn Helsinki against taking the crucial step. Evidently he no longer seriously believed in the continuation of Finnish resistance and therefore paid more attention to publicizing his own efforts. After

---

with all the means at our disposal. It is difficult for us to understand why this appeal is still not forthcoming. *We know the pressure that is being put on you by Sweden in favour of peace, which would leave you at the mercy of Russia. We know that Russia is afraid that you will make an appeal to the Allies because she fears their intervention would cause a catastrophe for her. In order to avoid this, she is ready to negotiate in order to destroy you later.* I assure you once more that we are ready to come to your assistance immediately. The aeroplanes are ready, the expeditionary force is ready to start. *If Finland will not now make an appeal to the Western Powers, it is evident that these cannot take any responsibility at the end of the war for the final arrangement of Finnish territory.* I therefore ask your government to make their decision quickly." The sentences put in italics by the present writer were, according to the *Journal Officiel* (13 March 1940), omitted by Daladier when he read the text of this message during the open session of the Chamber of Deputies on 12 March 1940.

emphasizing the importance (without mentioning figures) of the Potez bombers, "which have certainly reached the Finnish front in time",* he disclosed that the French expeditionary force had been ready to depart as early as 26 February. The reason why it had failed to set off was that not only the Scandinavians but also the Finns had been unwilling to welcome it: "I do not wish my country to tear up the rules of international law even in war," he boasted. "It is not possible to go to the assistance of Finland with a land expedition without an appeal from Finland herself, for assistance."[65]

In London the pressure put on Finland took a more painful form: the delivery of the sorely-needed bombers was postponed and, ultimately, never took place. A day after the Foreign Office had learnt of the Finnish-Soviet peace negotiations, on 8 March, Gripenberg called on Halifax informing him, on the lines of instructions received from Helsinki, that his government was waiting for the final terms, but hoped that the Allies would continue their intervention preparations and allow Finland extra time for making the appeal until 12 March.†[66]

Chamberlain, strangely enough, concluded from Gripenberg's statement that "their situation was not so desperate as to demand an immediate answer to their request for bombers." On these grounds he forthwith proposed a revision of the decision made two days earlier whereby Finland was to have some of the Blenheims she had asked for. In spite of the protests of Halifax, Hoare and Simon that, for political reasons, the bombers should be delivered unconditionally and without delay, the Prime Minister had his way. As suggested by the Chiefs-of-Staff, the Finns were not to get the bombers unless they first made a public appeal for assistance. Gripenberg's disappointment was now without limits. "I said [to Halifax] that I regretted the decision deeply; it would be a mistake, a great mistake," he wrote in his diary, and concluded: "As a matter of fact, the policy of the British Government is most cynical...."‡[67]

It was Vereker's sad duty to forward the War Cabinet decision

---

* They in fact never reached Finland, and were returned to France from the half-way point in their journey at the conclusion of the peace in Moscow.

† Gripenberg did not mention that the peace delegation had gone to Moscow, and was unaware of it when visiting the Foreign Office. The latter was informed through the British envoy in Stockholm.

‡ At the same meeting the War Cabinet dealt with the proposal made by a certain foreigner—according to Gripenberg's diary the Swedish Count von Rosen—that the Allies carry out, from their home bases, a massive attack with heavy bombers against Soviet concentrations on the Karelian Isthmus, but—not merely for technical reasons—this plan was considered impracticable.

to Helsinki. On Saturday evening 9 March he arrived with the cable at the Bank of Finland in the midst of a Cabinet meeting and there drew up (with Pakaslahti's assistance!) a memorandum addressed to the Finnish peace delegation in Moscow and to Field-Marshal Mannerheim. The Finns were reminded that the offer of assistance could not be held open if they failed to make their appeal publicly. But once this took place the British would deliver, within four days, eight Blenheim bombers and, within another ten days, forty-two of the same aircraft, and would put effective pressure on the Norwegian and Swedish governments in order to secure free passage for the Allied expeditionary force to go to Finland. Nevertheless, if the appeal was not made before the 12th, the expeditionary force would have to be dissolved.[68]

Pakaslahti interpreted the message as meaning that the Allies had now decided to pass through Scandinavia, whatever the means. Tanner disagreed with him, and as proved by Chamberlain's original draft, his interpretation was the correct one.*

The Finnish Cabinet was thus definitely ready to authorize the delegation in Moscow to accept the peace terms.

The French strongly criticized the form and content of the message forwarded by Vcreker, predicting that the Finns would find it discouraging. Daladier's last comments on the conflict, however, reveal that he also no longer considered the sending of the expeditionary force to Finland feasible. Still, he was prepared to do anything to make the Finns continue their fight and urged the necessity of sending them bombers. Corbin was again instructed to bring this to the notice of the British authorities, which he subsequently did in close co-operation with the Finnish envoy. The efforts of both diplomats proved fruitful in that, two days before the end of the conflict, the Cabinet resumed the matter on Halifax's initiative, and decided to deliver the first eight Blenheims at once, without waiting for the Finnish appeal.[70]

Gripenberg had proposed to Helsinki that the British government should now be asked to make a public statement as to its readiness to help Finland by all available means, if the latter asked for assistance. It was argued that this might help the delegation in Moscow to obtain better peace terms. Tanner viewed the proposal without enthusiasm, but since Mannerheim favoured it, he had it approved

---

* The last sentence read: "If they [Norway and Sweden] would oppose...*even by passive resistance*, the transit of our troops may appear to be impossible and His Majesty's Government will put pressure on the two countries by all possible means in order to get their co-operation [italics by present writer].' Chamberlain's original draft used the following wording: "We will do our best to shame them into allowing our troops to pass through."[69]

by the Cabinet. Gripenberg could thus on Sunday evening, 10 March, present the request to Chamberlain. After a night's reflection, the latter accepted it and made the requested statement by the fixed time, before noon on Monday the 11th, in answer to a question in the House of Commons by the Opposition leader Attlee.*[71]

The Chiefs-of-Staff Committee, according to their records, took the statement seriously. It was understood that the Prime Minister had promised to help Finland "with the whole strength of the British Empire". Up to now, it was observed at their meeting on 11 March, *the possible defeat of Finland had been considered a political loss to the Allies; from now on it was identical to a military loss.* In the end the conclusions of the Chiefs-of-Staff were even more strange: "The despatch of a force to-support Sweden might not now be required and in this event we could send a large force to assist Finland."

The events of the following day, the 12th, decisively upset the situation, so that the Prime Minister's statement remained a dead letter and the generals were never asked to explain their mysterious comment. Because of slow telegraphic connections, the text of the statement did not reach Helsinki and Moscow until the peace terms had been finally decided. Its only significance, as seen by Paasikivi in his memoirs, was to encourage the Finns at the moment of an enforced peace to imagine that they had not after all been left alone. In this respect the statement fulfilled its purpose, in Chamberlain's own words of giving the Finns moral assistance.[72]

At the eleventh hour London even agreed to another request made by the Finns, namely to ask Norway and Sweden for the third and the last time whether they would allow the Allies transit to Finland or not. Tanner reveals that this last request was made on 11 March in order to give the Western Powers solid evidence of the impossibility of the transit. The French were cautious, considering that the measure would not become urgent until Finland had presented her official appeal. Corbin was sent to Halifax to explain that the request was "Mr. Tanner's intrigue, and the Allies had better not comply with it". Halifax, who had already given his envoys in Oslo and Stockholm instructions in accordance with Tanner's request, later tried to revoke them as desired by Corbin, but without success; both ministers had already acted and again received negative answers, as expected.[73] Thus the outcome was

---

* "The House will be aware that both the French and British Governments have sent and are continuing to send material assistance to Finland. This has been of considerable value to the Finnish forces. As His Majesty's Government have already informed the Finnish Government, they are prepared, in response to an appeal from them for further aid, to proceed immediately and jointly, to the help of Finland, *using all available resources at their disposal.*"

not what Daladier might have had reason to fear: that Norway and Sweden would have consented to Allied transit at the last minute. The final and absolute refusal of the Scandinavians in fact strengthened the propaganda against them which the French Premier, fighting for his position, resorted to as his last resort.[74]

The Finnish delegates signed the peace treaty in Moscow on 12 March at a meeting starting at 10 p.m., on the mandate granted by their government the same morning. The conditions were even more severe than expected. Finland was to cede to the Soviet Union one of her richest provinces, Karelia, with the towns of Viipuri, Käkisalmi and Sortavala; eastern parts of the regions of Kuusamo and Salla; and the western coast of the island of Kalastajasaarento in the Arctic Ocean—in all a tenth of her former territory.* The inhabitants of the regions concerned, 12 per cent of the total population of the country, had to leave their homes and settle down elsewhere in Finland. In the North of Finland the Russians demanded the construction of a line to link the Finnish and Soviet railway networks at Salla—a condition which worried the Scandinavians, since the new railway was seen as a means of mounting offensive action towards Northern Sweden. In the South, the forced lease of Hanko as a Soviet base was regarded as a serious threat to the security of the Finnish mainland. Still, the treaty did not include any clauses demanding the demobilisation, disarmament or limitation of the fortifications of the Finnish forces, nor did it, in principle, interfere with the country's sovereignty. Thus the Finns had by no means fought in vain.

One hour earlier Vereker went to see Tanner at his home to report that the Allies had decided *to send troops to Finland at her request even if Norway and Sweden refused their transit*. This last attempt, which to the Finns seemed more than anything like a conjuring trick, was made too late or at least to the wrong person: the Foreign Minister seems not to have informed anyone about it until the peace had been signed. The proposed "great political change of front", to use Tanner's expression in his diary on the last day of the war, was, after all, of no interest to the Finns.[75]

Allied Scandinavian strategy was based on the presumption that Finnish resistance would last at least until mid-April, when the expeditionary force, on the pretext of assisting Finland, would have penetrated into Norway and Sweden and occupied the ore fields before the Germans or the Russians. The Finnish military situation

---

* As to Petsamo proper, it was returned to Finland and annexed to the Soviet Union only as a result of the armistice treaty of 1944.

however, grew more and more precarious from the end of February onwards, and offered no possibilities for continued resistance. It is clear from the statements given to the present writer by experts who themselves took part in the Finnish Winter War—above all General Stehlin—that not even the 100 bombers asked for by the Finns could have checked the Soviet westward offensive along the coast of the Gulf of Finland, or eastwards towards Käkisalmi: Allied bombing technique during the first year of the war was in fact rather primitive and there was still a lack of operational experience of co-operation between air and land forces.

The sending of a few dozen bombers, if they had been delivered immediately after 1 March, might of course have made the Finns hesitate longer before going to Moscow. By promising only twenty planes instead of 100, however, and even these belatedly, the Allies gave insufficient proof of their willingness to help. The assistance measures of the British Government during the two last weeks of the war, even more than those of the French, proved ineffective, not to say negative. Many incidents indicate that both Premiers, Chamberlain and Daladier, had lost interest in the matter and were hesitating—basically appalled at the possibility that they might have to answer for their promises to rescue Finland. The loss of prestige, however, would have been much greater if the Finnish war had continued and intervention, once started, had ended in a crushing military defeat.

VIII

SEQUEL

1

When, on the evening of 12 March, the BBC correspondent in Helsinki reported the first news of the signing of the peace treaty in Moscow,* the officers responsible for the force bound for Norway three days later were being briefed at the Prime Minister's house, 10 Downing Street. They were now told that, according to the instructions approved by the Cabinet the same day, the "Avonmouth" force was *to penetrate as far as Narvik, even if the Norwegians were to offer light resistance.* In principle the opening of fire was prohibited, but the commanders were entitled to resort to force "as an ultimate measure of self-defence should their forces be in jeopardy". This is what was implied in Vereker's message to Tanner the same evening, according to which the transit would be carried out in spite of Norwegian and Swedish opposition.[1]

In practice the naval commander, Admiral Evans, was instructed to sail past the 4-inch coastal guns guarding Narvik Fjord, "disregarding warning shots". Once in Narvik he and the commander of ground forces, General Mackesy, were to go ashore and persuade the local military and civilian authorities to accept the *fait accompli.* In the War Cabinet the instructions had been interpreted as meaning that the disembarkation troops were to be prepared to suffer losses without defending themselves, should the defending forces fire on them: "Only the commander on the spot...could decide whether opposition was serious enough to compromise the success of the operation," the Chiefs-of-Staff had observed. For this situation there were two alternatives: (1) to carry on the operation while using any force necessary to gain the end in view, or (2) to retreat. These principles were to be observed also in the case of Soviet naval forces trying to interfere. The instructions reveal that Finland was seen as a secondary target: *it was finally up to the commander of the ground forces, General Mackesy, to decide whether the planned expeditionary force could be sent to Finland or not....*[2]

Halifax had objected to the instructions, maintaining that if the expeditionary force had to resort to force, it would never get further than Narvik. On the other hand, on the evidence of discussions

---

* This information was still in fact groundless.

within the Norwegian Cabinet at the time, Norway would not have put up any organized resistance. Similarly, Sweden would possibly have offered little resistance, despite what Hansson and Günther had told the Finns.[3] This does not rule out the possibility of incidents during the disembarkation and transit, which eventually could have delayed the arrival of the troops in Finland. It is also unlikely that in the end Mackesy would have been allowed to send his troops further east than Gällivare, since the Germans might have exploited the fatal break between the Narvik-Trondheim operation and the occupation of Bergen and Stavanger and invaded Southern Norway the same week. Hitler's orders of 4 March indeed envisaged such an emergency operation, under the code name *"Minimalfall"*, with the precise instructions that after 10 March the troops reserved for it were to be in a state of alert for four days.*

Meanwhile, on the other side of the Channel the impressive French transport fleet was ready to sail: thirteen warships, nine cruisers and carriers, a hospital ship, seven freighters and six large passenger vessels. The shipment of the heavy equipment of the French "mountain brigade" had been completed at Brest. The next day, in the midst of the enthusiasm for departure, the news broke that the peace had been signed in Moscow.[5]

Towards the end of the 13th, it was learnt from reliable sources that fighting had indeed stopped on all the fronts in Finland. Chatfield asked the Prime Minister what was to be done about the departure of the expeditionary force which was to take place in two days' time. Chamberlain seemed to have forgotten—at least, according to Ironside—that the long-prepared departure was now really at hand, and ordered the Minister of Defence to stop the preparations until the Cabinet had discussed the matter the following day. According to the War Cabinet minutes:

He had in mind that there was a possibility of the peace treaty not being ratified by Finland, or even of a *coup d'état* which would turn out the present Finnish Government...

Where had the Prime Minister got this idea? Could it have been inspired by that day's *Evening Standard*, which carried a banner headline proclaiming: 'Finland may turn out Government and

---

* Hubatsch observes that the *Minimalfall* plan was not kept up with the preparations of the *Weserübung* plan carried out one month later. However, this does not exclude the possibility that Hitler, for example after the Allies had turned up in Narvik, might have demanded the carrying out of the orders he had given ten days earlier—and been successful in this.[4]

fight'?* The next day Chamberlain was ready to admit that no miraculous change would occur after all. At his suggestion, and rejecting Ironside's dissenting views, the Cabinet now decided to disperse the troops assembled for the Scandinavian expedition as soon as it became clear that the peace would be lasting. The War Office carried out the decision just a few days later.[6]

The delivery of war material to Finland was forbidden immediately after the conclusion of peace. Gripenberg was informed by the Foreign Office that not only the goods already embarked but still at anchor in Leith but also all that had already been sent to Finland were to be returned. The Cabinet turned a deaf ear to the envoy's objections that the goods had been purchased and now legally belonged to the Finnish Government. But then the envoy referred to political considerations and pointed out that Finland might at any moment fall victim to renewed aggression; if she now had to return all the arms she had received from the Allies, Norway and Sweden would conclude that she had been left to her own resources.[7]

This argument had the desired effect on most members of the Cabinet. But it was opposed by Churchill, who argued in rather characteristic terms:

The First Lord of the Admiralty thought that the Finns, having now lost their strategic advantages, would not be able to resume the struggle. We should try to secure the return of all war material (especially the aircraft and guns) which we had sent to Finland at so great sacrifice to ourselves.[8]

Once it was learnt that the French had tried to get back from Finland only a few of the most important consignments such as the bombers, the Cabinet's attitude began to soften. Nevertheless, at least three ships carrying British material and one with French goods for Finland were unloaded in British ports. Finally, after the Norwegian expedition had started in April, it was decided to release no more deliveries for Finland: 'Although it was undesirable to hurt the feelings of Finland, it would be foolish to supply her with any further equipment, even if it were physically possible for it to be delivered,' the resolution read. 'We should be receiving heavy demands from Norway, which we should rather meet.'[9]

In the light of the distressing state of Britain's own resources, it is understandable that the deliveries were limited to her closest allies such as Norway, hitherto virtually unarmed. Still, as far as

---

* According to French diplomatic archives Colonel Ganeval too believed that the Finnish troops could resume their fight, provided that the Allies immediately made a decisive *geste*—for example by declaring war on the U.S.S.R. ...

Finland was concerned, the policy of the War Cabinet speeded up the process which forced Finland into the arms of Germany in the course of the same year. The main responsibility lies with Churchill, who had quickly made up his mind regarding the effects of the peace of Moscow on the overall situation. Even earlier, the viewpoint that the end of the Finnish War would not necessarily be contrary to Allied interests had been heard in Cabinet meetings. Indeed, it was observed that, now that the conflict was over, Germany might have lost any pretext for advancing along its eastern ore route to the Gulf of Bothnia, since this might annoy the Soviet Union.[10]

As Churchill had noted ten days before the conclusion of peace, Finland was in any case lost as far as the Allies were concerned and could no longer be used as a stepping-stone in the Baltic. This being so, the Allies had to get a tenable hold of Norway and Sweden. The fear aroused in Scandinavia by the peace of Moscow, particularly the transit permission granted to the Soviet Union in Northern Finland, provided an opportunity, as Churchill pointed out to the War Cabinet on 14 March, which the Allies should take advantage of by renewing their offer of assistance to Norway and Sweden. Thus, he calmly continued, the plans for the occupation of Narvik should be kept alive:

Our real objective was, of course, to secure possession of the Gällivare ore fields.... Up till now we had had assistance to Finland as a 'lever' for such a move on our part, but we had now lost this justification for intervention in Scandinavia. The only chance seemed to be to take the line that our national interests were directly threatened by the possibility of Russia making her way through Scandinavia to the Atlantic.[11]

At first Churchill's propositions met with no response, since the whole Cabinet seemed of the opinion that the Soviet menace would no longer be taken seriously in Norway and Sweden. The more tangible danger, it was thought, was that of Germany, and for this reason the Scandinavians would hardly be more inclined to co-operate than before. Halifax, the most caustic critic of Churchill's views, belittled the importance of the railway link to be built from the Soviet border to Haparanda, and maintained that Norway and Sweden could be secured in a less aggressive way than that proposed by the First Lord of the Admiralty. This time, however, Churchill remained adamant and, encouraged by the French, continued his efforts for bringing about an intervention in Scandinavia. Two weeks later, on 27 March, he succeeded in getting the Cabinet's blessing for his initial plan of mining Norwegian waters—too late in the event.[12]

The importance of Finland in British policy thus suddenly shrank to pre-war proportions. *Finland seemed no longer to play any part in the strategic schemes of the Chiefs-of-Staff*—not even within the framework of the Nordic defence alliance, which was discussed between Finland, Norway and Sweden immediately after the peace of Moscow: this project was regarded in London, even before it was finally halted by Russian objections, as still-born from the start. In the Cabinet Halifax persisted in his idea that the most important task for the Allies now was to "do everything possible to recreate morale in Finland and to prevent the Finns from losing heart". As a means towards this end, among other things, Finland was promised financial help towards reconstruction.[13]

But if the Cabinet imagined that it could thus wash its hands in public, it was mistaken. The general discussion on Finland in the House of Commons on 19 March was opened by the Prime Minister in conceited terms. The armed assistance given to Finland was considerably overestimated. In the end Chamberlain's self-praise proved a Pyrrhic victory for the government. For the first time his war policy became the object of relentless attacks, not so much from the opposition but from his own Conservative backbenchers. The most outstanding critic was Harold Macmillan. He presented authoritative evidence from Finland that throughout the whole war, the material sent by Britain had been either too little or too late. The Prime Minister's reference to transportation difficulties, he said, was only a pretext. The talk of British generosity was exaggerated, considering that Finland had paid for all its orders except for a few donations. Finland's troubles had not been her own fault, even if she had not presented an official appeal for assistance; nor were they the fault of the Scandinavians, who did not want to expose themselves to German counter-measures. The fault, Macmillan concluded, lay nearer home in "the delay, the vacillation, the changes of front" of the British Cabinet; it was, to use Burke's expression, "a proof of the irresistable operation of feeble council."[14]

2

In France, as in Britain, the reactions to the peace of Moscow were similar to those of an audience expecting to see a sensational play but learning that it has been cancelled. The Scandinavians, mainly the Swedes, bore the brunt of this indignation—Sweden has hardly ever received rougher treatment from the French press than in March 1940. The Paris headlines express the prevailing mood: "The Cowardice of Sweden", "The Contemptible Betrayal by

Sweden", "Sweden in the Pillory", "The Infamous Servility of Sweden before Germany"...[15]

The purpose of this anti-Swedish campaign is revealed by a French note to the Foreign Office three days after the signing of the peace of Moscow. The French asked whether Norway and Sweden, after giving way to German pressure at the end of the Finnish war, had proved "as neutral as the Allies were entitled to expect"; had they even done everything within their power to save Finland, victim to Soviet aggression? No, was the reply: the Allies should draw the appropriate conclusions and reconsider the proposal for assuring the control of the Scandinavian territorial waters, possibly even of certain Norwegian harbours.[16]

In fact, the French, like Churchill, were suggesting that the recent Finnish-Soviet conflict should be exploited as a possible pretext for penetration into Scandinavia. They stressed that the Allies should not let the end of the war in Finland affect their decision to cut off German ore supplies from the north. At any rate the Allies had to find speedy means for eliminating the loss of prestige they had suffered with the peace of Moscow, which the Germans exploited to the full. Referring to this, the French proposed that *"it would be necessary to assume the initiative vigorously in Norway in order to put an end to the alarming consequences that might result from a Finnish surrender for the moral and diplomatic position of the Allies."*[17]

In London Corbin's initiative at first met with reservations. The War Cabinet had in fact uttered a sigh of relief when the peace of Moscow offered a plausible excuse for giving up the preparations for intervention, since these had caused the ministers and officers concerned more and more mixed feelings as the moment of departure had drawn nearer. Still, the Scandinavian plans were reanimated by Churchill's renewed efforts. Halifax told the French Ambassador on 21 March that his government was in principle ready to accept the initiative. At the sixth meeting of the Allied Supreme War Council one week later, it was decided to bring up the intervention plan again, primarily referring to the pretexts proposed by the French.*[18]

In other ways Daladier's attitude towards Finland, even after the peace of Moscow, was not comparable with Churchill's coldly calculating approach. Holma noted with satisfaction that when the message given to him on 7 March and repeated by Daladier at the

---

* "The Allied governments cannot acquiesce in any further attack on Finland," the consequent *aide-mémoire* addressed to Oslo and Stockholm began. "If such an attack should take place and the Norwegian and Swedish Governments should refuse to facilitate the Allied efforts in helping Finland, they were cautioned that Britain and France would consider it to be contrary to their overriding national interests."

session of the Chamber of Deputies five days later, was published in the official journal, it omitted the irksome threat that in the peace settlement following the European war France would not answer for the return of the Finnish territories surrendered to the Soviet Union.* In the light of later events, this gesture had no practical importance; from the point of view of Daladier's new policy towards Finland, however, as planned after the peace of Moscow, it must be considered prognostic.[19]

In contrast to Chamberlain as well as Churchill, Daladier also showed understanding towards the Finnish desire not to return the *matériel* delivered to them during the war. Likewise the French instructors sent to Finland were allowed to remain there for the time being (most of them returned home shortly after the German attack on Norway). When Holma and Paasonen called on Daladier on 15 March, the day after his successful performance in the Senate, the Premier had promised to continue the assistance, assuring the two Finns that he still considered Finland as belonging within the French sphere of interest.[20]

Daladier's sympathy towards Finland failed to save him in the end from the revenge of the Right. At a secret meeting of the Chamber convened to deal with the Finnish problem, only four days after his initial victory the Senate, the Premier was harassed from almost every bench. Léon Blum criticized him from the Left, forcing him to admit that the figures concerning aircraft sent to Finland were far from realistic. The decisive attack, however, was made by some of the future men of Vichy, led by Louis Marin, who now paradoxically clamoured for a more active war policy.[21] The Premier's defence was touching but resigned, as demonstrated by his comment on the importance for the Allies of the peace of Moscow:

Gentlemen, don't look at things out of proportion! Charleroi† is not in question. Nevertheless, the Peace of Moscow is a tragic and painful event. It means a great victory for Russia, does it not? It certainly means a political gain for Germany. . . .[22]‡

The former Minister of Finance, Paul Reynaud, assumed the leadership of the new government. On the question of intervention in Scandinavia his views did not differ from those of Daladier,

---

* See above, pp. 189-40.

† Reference to the decisive initial victory of the Germans in the First World War.

‡ The vote of confidence on 20 March was won by 230 votes to 1, but with 300 abstentions. Realising that he had lost his majority, Daladier immediately resigned.

however much he may have criticized the latter in his memoirs. The decision, advocated by the French delegation at the sixth session of the Supreme War Council, to carry out the intervention in Norway was a natural consequence of the policy initiated by Daladier at the fourth meeting of the council a week before Christmas. Nor did the French attitude towards Finland undergo any drastic changes after Daladier's fall, as had been feared by the Finns, especially Holma. In Paris the renewal of the Finnish-Soviet conflict was in fact considered inevitable.[23] French interest in Finland, uninterrupted even after the middle of March, remained alive up to the moment when the developments in Norway on 9 April and on the Western Front exactly one month after that destroyed all Allied illusions.

3

Twenty-five days after the conclusion of the peace of Moscow, on the morning of 8 April, the Royal Navy was laying mines in the coastal waters of Norway, in accordance with the new plan decided on by the Supreme War Council. In the Clyde, Admiral Evans' fleet had been working for twenty-four hours to prepare the "Avonmouth" force once more to sail for Narvik. The troops destined for Trondheim, Stavanger and Bergen were waiting with their equipment in transport vessels. At this moment the Admiralty received news that large German naval units had been observed moving into the North Sea in the direction of the Norwegian coast. The British flotilla laying mines at the tip of the Lofoten Islands was instructed to sail out into open sea under the protection of heavier vessels. Evans's ships which had been waiting for final orders for departure, were cleared of troops and sent to pursue the enemy. These two preventive measures meant that the British—not the Germans, as Chamberlain boasted in the House of Commons the following day—"missed the bus": Narvik, as well as three of the ports assigned for the disembarkation of the "Stratford" force, was occupied during the next two days under the very noses of the Royal Navy.[24]

The Allies were thus obliged to launch their Norwegian expedition under far less advantageous circumstances than those envisaged in the plans drawn up during the winter. The troops detachable for a counter-offensive were largely the same as those which had been ready to depart on their vessels on 8 April, as has been mentioned, but had been moved ashore again. In the general confusion, several units had left their equipment on the ships, which had then steamed off to chase the Germans on the northern seas;

consequently, these units now had to borrow new equipment from various quarters. The French troops embarked at Brest were caught in a similar situation: their heavy armour and even part of their personal equipment, were loaded on to different vessels from themselves, with the result that, for instance, many of the Chasseurs Alpins later had to make do without their transport and even without skis and sunglasses.[25]

Of the British troops sent to Norway only the 24th Brigade had been included in the force planned for Finland one month earlier. The French troops for their part consisted entirely of Béthouart's original "mountain brigade", the expeditionary corps later enlarged into a light division which, from the middle of March, had been garrisoned in reserve. In addition to the Chasseure Alpins, this corps comprised two Foreign Legion battalions and four Polish ones. Apart from the ski battalion which had been part of the British Guards brigade and was by now dissolved, the forces sent to Norway thus consisted mainly of the same troops that had been suggested for Finland a month before. Since their equipment and even their command were the same as earlier, the Norwegian expedition offers an interesting demonstration of the effectiveness of the assistance Finland might have received from the Allies if she had continued fighting.

The official war historian T. K. Derry observes that the 24th Brigade, unlike the British battalions earmarked for theatres of war further south, was made up of enlisted troops. Still, its inadequate equipment did not in itself differ greatly from that which was normally used by the British army, and it had not been trained for northern conditions (except for the disbanded ski unit). The standard of the reserve battalions originally destined for Southern Norway left even more to be desired. They could hardly be expected to offer serious resistance to the élite troops of the German army.[26]

Of the Allied troops sent to Norway, the first to engage the enemy were the Chasseurs Alpins who arrived on 18 April at Namsos, north of Trondheim, together with a landing force commanded by a British general. The Namsos force had to operate without its own air support, and even without anti-aircraft equipment, and it was thus little wonder that the *Luftwaffe*, operating from the air bases it had occupied farther south, immediately succeeded in securing control over the bridgehead. By unscrupulously bombing the unprotected port, the Germans paralysed the disembarkation activities of the detachment, so that for two weeks after occupying the town it could do nothing but wait for an opportunity to re-embark. The errors in loading which had been committed on embarkation in the home ports now made themselves seriously

felt: many vessels carrying equipment had to return because of
air attacks—thus the only troops at Namsos able to ski, the Chasseurs
Alpins, had to manage without their skis.

In his memoirs Stehlin, who happened to pass by Namsos on his
way back from Finland, describes this stage as having been extremely
depressing. He had arrived on foot in the town, which was completely destroyed by air raids. No one had even asked him for his
papers, although he wore civilian clothes and his appearance and
language were clearly not those of a local. The first Frenchmen he
met, an unloading party of about fifty men, had just got hold of a
barrel of wine on the quay and were happily getting drunk. The
port was littered with equipment thrown out of the ships, including
a lot of skis without straps. After arriving at the French headquarters, Stehlin found that both the commanders and the troops
had been terrorized by the German bombers. A few days later,
anti-aircraft guns did in fact arrive, but the men assigned to use
them were untrained. The first shell fired in a low-firing position
hit a young second-lieutenant, the head of the section, in the
chest.[27]

At this juncture, the British and French commanders of the
Namsos force began planning their departure, in spite of the protests
of the local Norwegian commander. The welcome news of the
decision to evacuate was received ten days before the last troops
managed to reach their ships and escape out to sea with German
planes harassing them. At the embarkation point some units
were forced to retreat from the port three or four times to escape
enemy air raids and to wade back through soft snow to their bases
in the forests outside the town. Large amounts of the heavy equipment, dragged with great effort to the port, had to be destroyed.
Withdrawal along the roads leading north was given up for fear of
bad road conditions. A few days later the Allies had occasion to
observe that the Germans were able to advance along roads which
they had considered unserviceable, in some cases making use of the
Peugeot equipment left behind by the French.[28]

In his memoirs General Béthouart has claimed that Stehlin's
report from Namsos was too critical. At any rate his reasons for
doing so are not personal, since Stehlin thought very highly of
Béthouart, whom he met at Namsos, as a front commander. Derry
also dealt with Béthouart's role in the operations leading to the
reconquest of Narvik on 29 May, and pictures him as an intelligent,
energetic and brave officer. It has to be borne in mind, however,
that if the expedition to Finland as originally planned had been
realized, Béthouart would have operated under General Mackesy,
the commander whose excessive caution, not to say slowness, was

probably the reason why Narvik was not taken earlier. The only tangible result of the Narvik operation, undertaken too late and called off too soon, was thus the destruction of the ore port. The importance even of this measure proved exaggerated, as the Germans had repaired the port into serviceable condition by the beginning of the following year.[29]

The experiences gained from the Narvik operation confirm the earlier warning by the Allied military attachés in Helsinki that western troops could not be used in the climatic conditions prevailing in the north of Europe before June. Mackesy's army would scarcely have been of any help in the Finnish war even if it had joined the fighting in time. Its soldiers would simply have been unable to cope in the snow and the freezing cold. Mackesy himself stated this as an axiom in his official report in London:

Blizzards, heavy snowstorms, bitter winds and very low night temperatures were normal—even those magnificent mountain soldiers, the French Chasseurs Alpins, suffered severely from frostbite and snow-blindness. Troops who were not equipped with and skilled in the use of skis or snowshoes were absolutely incapable of operating tactically at all...Shelter from the weather was of vital importance.

The official historian adds that the French sent to Narvik had no more than seventy skiers to each battalion, and that they too were unaccustomed to camping in deep snow. The British troops for their part were equipped, besides normal summer and winter clothing, with special Arctic outfits for the Finnish expedition, thirty-five articles of clothing per man, but with no means of transportation at the start; the Guards joked that they were "mechanized to immobility". In addition to the lack of transport material the troops suffered from a shortage of signalling equipment, maps and even interpreters. The language problem might have proved serious if the expeditionary force had continued its journey to Sweden and Finland—with three different nationalities involved, not to mention the Foreign Legionaries.[30]

War historians writing about the Narvik operation have admitted that the Allied troops concentrated there were numerically superior to their opponents and could easily have gained a victory if only they had been commanded with greater determination; at the final stage when the snow was no longer an obstacle, all the troops, including the Poles, proved their competence. In one respect the situation there was the same as at Namsos: once the Allied troops started arriving in mid-April they were immediately subjected to German air attacks. Anti-aircraft equipment arrived only at the end of the month and heavy guns even later at about the time when, on

6 May, the Scots Guards observed that even Skua fighters were to be seen flying in the area—"the first British aircraft that had been seen since our arrival in Norway—a very welcome sight".[31]

This should prove that, if the Germans had acquired an air base at the operational radius of their heavy bombers—that is 600 miles or less from Narvik—they could have seriously impeded the operations of the "Avonmouth" force or at least prevented its advance to Finland. This purpose would have been served even by Oslo airport, from which the *Luftwaffe* could have reached at least the middle of the Lofoten Islands, if not Narvik itself, as well as Gällivare and Luleå. In the light of German preparedness and of what happened a month later, there can be no doubt that the Germans at this point would have been able to occupy Oslo or even other bases nearer Narvik.*

The campaign in Norway revealed some serious deficiencies in Allied military fitness, which makes it difficult to believe that their assistance to Finland would ultimately have been of any decisive value. First of all, as the official historian points out, there was the weakness of their intelligence, especially regarding German intentions in Scandinavia. We may add here the inability to understand the requirements of modern warfare in general and the Finnish Winter War in particular.

The second drawback was the unsuitability of the field forces earmarked for use in the intervention operation. The troops sent to Narvik in mid-April largely corresponded, as we know, with the original "Avonmouth" force, whose commander was to use his own discretion in assembling and sending an expeditionary corps to Finland. The Allies had no other troops reserved for the Finnish War. The helplessness later displayed by the same commander at Narvik and the quality of his troops, not to mention the inadequacy of their equipment and above all that of their air cover, arouse serious doubts as to whether this force could ever have reached even its main target, the Gällivare mining area. In any case the Finnish war effort would hardly have been made easier by the arrival of these troops.

The final outcome of the developments in Norway in May-June 1940 does not provide grounds for establishing whether the decision made by the Finns in March was right or wrong. The peace of Moscow, of course, was made in the light of the information available and the prospects at that moment. For all that, the German invasion of Norway is inextricably connected with the Finnish War and the subsequent period of transition in Allied war policy.

---

* See above, p. 147.

As far as Finland was concerned, it led to her isolation between Germany and the Soviet Union, and thus in a way predestined her fate, whereas a different outcome—even the permanent Allied occupation of Northern Norway—might have given another turn to the country's future. For the Allies it meant the end of the first phase of the war and the end of the belief that it might be possible to defeat Germany by depriving her of raw materials and food, as in the First World War. While carrying out the operation originally planned under the pretext of assisting Finland, the Allies for the first time had to face the realities of the Second World War. They displayed insufficient imagination, organization and strength to pass the test with any credit. Instead of gaining a foothold in Norway and blockading Germany from the north with a big enough navy, a modern air force and a properly equipped field army, they had to leave the Norwegians to their own devices—being unable to provide them with more than a thousand rifles![32]

4

"Many friends of Russia thought she should have waited to get the readjustments she wanted without copying the Nazi methods of aggression," Sir Stafford Cripps told the Soviet Ambassador in Chungking in February 1940.[33] This sincere statement reflects the moral defeat which the Soviet Union had suffered in the eyes of public opinion because of the Finnish War and from which she was not to recover until she herself became the victim of aggression in June 1941. The ultimate reason for this desperate act—if we may call it so—remains unexplained, at least as long as the relevant Kremlin archives remain closed. It is another question whether the Soviet Union would have had time to wait, as Cripps somewhat naively suggested, until Helsinki was ready to make concessions. According to the official *History of the Soviet Communist Party*, there was no time: after the conquest of Poland Hitler might have immediately turned on the Soviet Union—as the Allies hoped.[34]

Ignoring the issues of the bases demanded from Finland by the U.S.S.R. the strategic importance of which proved rather limited in the light of the events of 1941, we may consider that Moscow was mistaken in its belief that Finland would lend a hand to any power threatening the Soviet Union. Still the Finns could only promise but could not demonstrate that they would keep their promises. This, probably more than anything else, was the reason why they were driven into war. "Frankly speaking, there is a good deal of mistrust between you and us," Stalin had told Paasikivi in October when demanding Hanko in order to bar the Gulf of Finland from the North as well as from the South. "Consequently, the fire control must be concentrated in the same hands."[35]

Even so, it is clear that the peace made in Moscow in March could only be a truce with a new battle lying ahead. The Soviet government, first of all, saw no need to handle Finland with kid gloves after having mangled it with a mailed fist. But the idea of revenge was born at the very moment of the enforced peace. One does not need to read Clausewitz to understand that even a small country, which in a defensive war has lost territory but not its army, naturally awaits its opportunity to regain its former frontiers—by fair means or foul.

The unscrupulous pressure put on the Finnish delegation at the peace negotiations with a view to speeding up the settlement, such as Molotov's use of the threat of the "alternative" Kuusinen government, had increased the suspicions which even the most moderate Finns harboured concerning the Kremlin's intentions. Since the idea of a Nordic defence alliance had failed, the leaders of Finland began looking for support from where they had refused it at any price one year earlier. Before the fatal month of March 1940 had come to an end, Ryti and Mannerheim, both of them anything but pro-German, had provided the country with a new government and a new Foreign Minister with the task of giving a new line to Finnish foreign policy, or, as Ryti made known on 23 March to a ministerial candidate, "a certain rapprochement with Germany".[36]

This development, which—we should not forget—started before Hitler's aggression on the Nordic countries, is the most evident proof of the Allies' failure to retain their influence in the northern Baltic, regardless of the Molotov-Ribbentrop pact. If Soviet armed sanctions on Finland have to be regarded as a policy of desperation, the same description applies to the attempts of the Allies, above all Britain, to strengthen Finnish resistance in the autumn of 1939. Even the Polish crisis a few months earlier was handled with more discretion: Poland was given guarantees without encouragement to fight, while Finland was encouraged but given no guarantees—nor even supplied with armaments.

The only extenuating circumstance in this short-sighted policy was the fact that neither London nor Paris dared to imagine that the Soviet Union would go as far as it did. When the attack finally took place, the defender's chances were at first considered so slight that the only way of giving support considered worthwhile was by statements to satisfy public opinion and by mostly symbolic deliveries of equipment. Thus, during the first month of the war Finland was left virtually on her own, with the result that during the following month, when the conflict was to be used to further Allied objectives, the Finns had lost their illusions and lacked the confidence to invite reinforcements from abroad.

The Finnish war affords an unflattering picture of Allied war policy during Chamberlain's and Daladier's period of office. While supporting Finland against the Soviet Union, Britain and France weakened the military position of their would-be ally on her crucial north-eastern border and, indirectly, worked in favour of their main enemy, Germany. The reactions of public opinion, energetically exploited by anti-Soviet forces everywhere, closely influenced the vacillating policies of the Allies. Orthodox Conservative pressure handicapped the work of those who represented a different kind of thinking, including Churchill, the architect of the great alliance with the Soviet Union. It was largely thanks to him that the Finnish war was ultimately used to frustrate the strategic interests of Germany rather than those of the Soviet Union, and that the episode in the end did not seriously harm British relations with Moscow.

Even today the idea still persists that the Allies would have risked war with the Soviet Union if they had responded to the Finnish appeal for assistance. The possibility cannot be denied: anyone who plays with fire has to reckon with the possibility of a conflagration. But if we jump to the conclusion that intervention would automatically have led to armed conflict with the Soviet Union, we would certainly be off the mark.

After all, the Allies, especially the British, acted with their eyes open. At the League of Nations they voted for the expulsion of the Soviet Union but rejected the sanctions which might have driven the Soviet Union definitively into the German camp. They refrained from the Petsamo operation, since it could have led to confrontation with the Soviet Union. They were certainly ready to detach for Finland a minor part of their expeditionary force destined for Narvik, but would hardly have allowed it to operate anywhere other than on the northern front —in a manner similar to the Swedish volunteer corps in Salla; the participation of the volunteers in the fighting would probably not have affected Allied relations with the Soviet Union. British precaution culminated in the fact that, despite repeated requests by the Finns, they were not prepared to send their pilots to Finland until the very end of the war, although Finland was given dozens of planes made in England.

Even if the Allied high command, after the Soviet reverses in the first month of the Finnish War, had revised its earlier view that an armed conflict with the Soviet Union would have imperilled the Allied strategic positions, the political leadership deemed it wiser to concentrate against the enemy *par excellence*, Germany. As from January assistance to Finland was considered necessary, but never important enough to justify a war with the Soviet Union, however weak the Russian forces were estimated to be at the moment.

The concepts of intervention and war are always liable to broad interpretations but were unusually so during this conflict: the Soviet Union had not declared war on Finland, even if she was ready to sign a peace treaty with the country; Britain disapproved of the Soviet sea blockade of Finland, since there was no formal state of war between the two countries; the French were of the opinion that Petsamo, at the request of the League of Nations and with the consent of Finland, could be cleared of Soviet forces, arguing that these forces had no legitimate right, not even that of a state of war, to penetrate into the territory.

The Soviet Union, expelled from the international community and isolated in company with Germany, would in fact have found no support in jurisprudence, not even in the event of the Allies putting their extreme intentions into effect and starting to destroy the Soviet oil industry. War would probably not have profited the Russians at all: it might have given them a temporary opportunity for conquests in the Middle East but would at the same time have increased their economic dependence on Germany and weakened their defensive preparedness in Europe. It was in the Soviet interest to keep itself detached from the great war at any price.*

On several occasions during the Moscow negotiations Molotov assured the Finns that his country was not concerned about the possibility of intervention. But, as Ryti observes in his draft memoirs, his very manner of constantly coming back to this assertion proved that the Allied intervention haunted the minds of the Soviet leaders. For Ryti this was naturally a justification of his own policy: to use the threat of intervention for obtaining better peace terms.[38] Without going into the hypothetical question whether or not the Finns might have been able to extort more favourable terms—for example by using the previously mentioned method of delay—it is evident that the information reaching Moscow about the Allied intervention plans, maybe even about German counter-preparations, affected the willingness of the Soviet Union to end the war as soon as possible. Marshal Meretskov, who broke ɩhe Mannerheim

---

* An illustration of the Soviet Union's policy of neutrality is provided by its attitude to German sea operations from the base of Sapadnyaya-Litsa in Motovsky Bay near Murmansk, which had been leased to the Germans since the autumn of 1939. After the Germans had sent the supply vessel *Jan Wellem* from this base on 6 April 1940 to transport supplies to their landing unit at Narvik, the Russians did not allow the ship to return.[37]

line, states it plainly in his memoirs: "Any delay in bringing the war to a victorious conclusion would have enabled the French and the Swedes [*sic*] to send in reinforcements, and instead of a war with one state we would have had to fight against a coalition."[39]

This argument, admittedly based on flimsy evidence, is the only one available. In this respect, too, the political history of the Finnish war remains locked in the Soviet archives. As may be recalled, Molotov alleged at the negotiations that the military command disagreed on the need to make peace: the Red Army wanted to march on. Then why was it not allowed to do so at least until the thaw which was then still a long way off? It is possible that Moscow was afraid of a German intervention, being aware of the importance of the Gulf of Bothnia for German ore transport.The image of Finland at the bar of world history was already outlined in President Ryti's defence speech at his war-guilt trial in 1945. In fact the Finnish Government never sought such an impressive role, though it is evident that certain Finnish circles still dreamt of a joint German-Allied crusade against the Soviet Union. Nothing more but also nothing less than the very existence of Finland was at stake: the question was whether to isolate the conflict with Russia or let it spread and become merged with the world war. The country seemed doomed to destruction and would possibly have been destroyed if two or three foreign armies had intervened at the end of the conflict. Ryti, himself unreservedly in favour of peace in Moscow, indeed gave proof of his statemanship: he did not want to "change the course of world history", but he accomplished more— he overcame himself and saved his people.

For the Allies, especially for Britain, the peace of Moscow meant a final farewell to the Baltic. Churchill, who seemed to imagine that Finland might still offer her hospitality to his fleet, admitted this to the War Cabinet on 4 March: "It would be no use hoping that we should be able to use Finland as a means of access to the Baltic."[40] The times when the Union Jack could fly freely east of the Danish Straits were now gone for ever.

As for Finland's military position, the settlement implied an equally drastic change. Ever since the 1920s, the country's defence plans had been based on the assumption that an aggressor could be delayed until it could be defeated with outside assistance. In this war game the Soviet Union was the traditional enemy, and Britain and France the ones giving assistance. These illusions were destroyed by the disappointments of the Finnish war. During the short peace of 1940-1 there were in fact similar schemes with Germany in mind, but the far-reaching political changes in the Baltic sphere resulting from the Second World War have put a

definite end to this way of thinking. At the same time the realities
of the situation have modified the attitude of the Western Powers
toward Finland. The treaty of friendship, co-operation and mutual
assistance signed between Finland and the Soviet Union in 1948 is
in harmony with the new situation and has, for its part, contributed
to banishing the grounds for speculation caused by the mistrust
between the two countries in earlier days.

IX

THERMOPYLAE EVERY DAY

Allied Public Opinion and Unofficial Assistance during the Finnish War

1

The title of this chapter is a quotation from Harold Macmillan's historic speech in the House of Commons on 19 March 1940, when he described the Finnish war as probably most of his countrymen had experienced it: it was not only a Thermopylae but a "Thermopylae every day". The press and radio, otherwise suffering from a lack of war news, had launched a spontaneous pro-Finnish campaign, which in the winter 1939-40 made Finland a headline topic of discussion, especially since by now newspapers were being read and the radio listened to more than in normal times.

It would nevertheless be a mistake to assume that the sudden sympathy of the British people toward this isolated country, whose name had hardly been known a few months earlier, was merely the result of propaganda; inveterate sports fans as they are, the British incessantly followed the uneven battle in the North and, rather naturally, took sides with the courageous smaller party. Tired of the defeatism of the late 1930s, they were fascinated by the image of the vanguard of the free, fighting against the eastern hordes in the pass on the road to Athens—the battle with no survivors.

The Finns resembled the Poles who pitched their cavalry against the tanks, with the difference that they never had any illusions of victory. In Britain the attack on Finland aroused far stronger reactions than the German aggression against Poland. Was this because the Finns had asked for nothing from the British, whereas the Polish requests for guarantees had dragged them into war? Or was the sympathy the expression of a bad conscience, awareness of the fact that Britain had failed to do everything within her capacity to save the four European countries engulfed by the dictators during the recent year-and-a-half? At any rate, the reaction was more emotional than practical, and no attempt was made to explain the Soviet action, however logical this might have been from the point of view of the German menace.

"It was the Soviet attack on Finland on 30 November, far more than the Soviet-German pact of August, which marks Stalin's real breach with British opinion", W. N. Medlicott remarked in his analysis of the events of 1939.[1] The general indignation indeed made itself known against Stalin and his imperialism rather than against Communism as such. In this the British view clearly differed from French opinion, which was primarily dominated by the Government's information policy and the right-wing press. For all that, the British reaction was exceptionally unanimous. One of the few public figures who dared or deemed it appropriate to expose the reverse side of the coin was George Bernard Shaw, whose opinions, expressed in the *Daily Mail* three days after the outbreak of war, largely followed the official Soviet theses.[2]

Shaw's statement was followed by other even more blunt views. Such was the well-written piece of propaganda entitled *Must the War Spread?* by D. N. Pritt, as well as articles by W. P. and Zelda K. Coates and the pamphlets of the Russia Today Society.[3] These protests hardly spread outside the small circle of orthodox Communists and known friends of the Soviet Union: this vein of propaganda indeed found no response in Britain during the winter following the Molotov-Ribbentrop pact. The spontaneous and widespread protests against the Soviet attack on Finland compelled even the Conservatives who favoured the improvement of British-Soviet relations with a view to an eventual anti-Hitler alliance, to join in. Gripenberg observed with satisfaction that even Churchill and Eden, whose basic line of policy would not allow them to join the anti-Soviet chorus with such fellow-Conservatives as Amery, contributed their skis to the collection arranged for the benefit of Finland.[4]

The sympathy of the party in power was generally unreserved and facilitated the pro-Finnish lobbying within the Cabinet and elsewhere. The Finnish Minister's most effective channels to the inner circle of the Cabinet were Lord Balfour of Burleigh, Lord Phillimore and Colonel Harold Gibson in the secretariat of the War Ministry. The contacts of the then chairman of the Anglo-Finnish Society—the former D.M.I., General Sir George McDonough—proved helpful for Gripenberg.

The other party in power, the Liberals, also produced active protagonists of the Finnish cause. The untiring activity of the former Minister of War, Hore-Belisha, in favour of intervention, has been mentioned above. Another old Liberal, the coal magnate Lord Davies, was known for his initiative for the despatch of an "international police force" to Finland. A third influential Liberal, on whose support the Finnish envoy could count, was Lord Lytton, a former Viceroy of India.

The protests of the opposition as a whole against Soviet aggression were even louder than those of the Conservatives and Liberals. Hugh

Dalton condemned it on behalf of the Labour parliamentary group in the House of Commons on the day of the outbreak of war. In a statement a week later the National Council of Labour expressed itself in pronouncedly ideological terms: "The British Labour Movement regards with deep detestation the action of the Soviet Government because it has in the past professed to be the leader of the world's working-class movement."[5]

Douglas Clark has written that the reaction of the British Left, especially its previously pro-Soviet intelligentsia, was comparable to "the vengefulness of the flouted lover"; however, it must be noted that the "worshippers of Moscow" of the 1920s and 1930s represented an influential but rather limited minority within the Labour Party and its kindred movements. The actual strength of the anti-Soviet movement in the winter of 1939-40 came from elsewhere: from the partisans of the League of Nations who had kept their political camp in the Labour Party, from the professional anti-Communists of the Socialist International, and perhaps also from the tacticians of domestic policy. The opposition in general saw here, as it did in France, an opportunity to harass the government, nor did it hesitate to exploit the emotions aroused by the Finnish War and to wash its own dirty linen in public. A historic example of this is offered by the Bournemouth Party conference in March, at which D. N. Pritt, the author of *Must the War Spread?*, was expelled from the Executive Committee as well as from the Party as a whole.[6]

The views of the Labour leaders were characterized by political expediency. The Party chairman Clement Attlee, and the then and future vice-chairmen Arthur Greenwood and Herbert Morrison, all expressed strong public criticism of Soviet aggression. The Labour representatives, however, failed to participate even formally in the campaign for assistance to Finland, which consequently became pronouncedly non-Leftist. Attlee and Greenwood later expressed their fears to the Foreign Secretary that active assistance to Finland, perhaps amounting to intervention, might lead Britain into war with the Soviet Union. Hugh Dalton, Labour spokesman in the House of Commons on the evening of the first day of the Winter War, soon forgot his emotional words and, eleven weeks later at the meeting of the executive committee of the International in Brussels, delivered an extremely cautious statement on the Finnish question: according to him, neither Labour nor even the British Government had considered the possibility of Britain entering a war against the Soviet Union.[7] In his memoirs he dissociated himself from the interventionists and described their activities as "mid-winter madness".[8]

The differences between the two trends, the nationalistically realistic and the internationally idealistic, were clearly reflected by the press. The newspapers of Lord Beaverbrook, a close friend of Churchill, most of all the *Evening Standard*, followed a somewhat cautious policy on the conflict, regarding Finland as doomed from the start,* whereas the *News Chronicle* of Sir Walter Layton, supported by Leftist radicals and keeping the flag of the League of Nations flying, favoured the Finnish cause from beginning to end.[9]

In the end the Finnish question seemed a hot potato for the Labour Party leadership. When the Finnish Social Democratic Party and trade union movement invited the Labour Party and the British T.U.C. in early January to send their representatives to find out about the situation in Finland, there was indeed a slight panic at Transport House as to who should go. Finally, the Party committee nominated as its main representatives the League of Nations expert Philip Noel-Baker and Sir Walter Citrine, the General Secretary of the T.U.C.[10]

2

The most conspicuous result of the Labour delegation's fact-finding trip to Finland (21 January—8 February) was the travel diary published by Sir Walter Citrine, obviously published to counterbalance Pritt's scandalous *Must the War Spread?*, but which did not reach the public until after the Finnish war was over. In spite of its improvised nature, it is one of the best reports published on the Finnish war by a foreigner. Rich in detail, true to reality and critical in spite of its basically sympathetic pro-Finnish tendency, the work could well have served its purpose, had it been published before the end of the conflict.[11]

The programme arranged for the delegation shows that great expectations were held of it in Finland: regardless of their many pressing tasks, the Prime and Foreign Ministers met the visitors on several occasions; the commander of the Western Isthmus army corps spent an entire day with them and took them to Summa; Field-Marshal Mannerheim received them for lunch and even paid a courtesy call at their hotel in Mikkeli. Official documents reveal that among other things the Labour delegates brought with them to London the detailed specifications of Finnish armed assistance requirements.

Citrine and Noel-Baker returned home firmly convinced that the Finnish war effort was justified. Their anti-Soviet stand had gained

---

* See above, p. 42. However, cf. p. 195, note 3.

strength, and this attracted attention in London. "Both Sir Walter Citrine and Mr. Noel-Baker had throughout their interview with him evinced the strongest hostility against the Soviet Union," was the Foreign Secretary's impression of a meeting with the Labour delegates shortly after their return. Halifax said that he had noted a distinct difference in their views from those of Attlee and Greenwood, which he had recently had occasion to hear.[12]

Noel-Baker presented the War Cabinet with an extensive and detailed memorandum on the Finnish situation, dated as early as 14 February. Unlike the written impressions of the Conservative representative who later visited Finland, this paper was circulated early enough to reach the Cabinet before the final outcome of the conflict. The basic tendency of Noel-Baker's memorandum, however, was opposed to the policy adopted by the Cabinet, and little attention was evidently paid to it. In brief he stressed that it was necessary to send additional war material to Finland without delay, with special emphasis on the strengthening of artillery and air defence; on the other hand, *foreign soldiers were not needed in Finland*. In this matter Noel-Baker referred to the views of the Finnish political and military leaders he had met during his journey. The unwillingness of the Finns to invite foreign—especially Allied—troops, he wrote, was caused by fear of the Germans; Ryti for instance had said to him outright that he considered the arrival of the Poles undesirable just because it might provoke the Germans.*[13]

In Noel-Baker's opinion Finland had to be helped to carry on its resistance, but in such a way as not to involve the Allies in hostilities with the Soviet Union or to provoke a German attack on the Finnish rear. The only acceptable alternative for the future was still to seek a favourable peace. First, peace would save Finland; secondly, a happy outcome would encourage the Baltic states, and thirdly, the salvation of Finland would increase the chances of the Scandinavians being able to defend their independence. Noel-Baker concluded: "*If Stalin can be induced to make peace with Finland on reasonable terms, it would be of the utmost advantage to Great Britain.*"[14]

His point of view was bold but not entirely inconsistent with the line of thought now emerging in government circles, whereby the continuation of the conflict might serve German rather than Allied interests.† Even so, Noel-Baker's paper soon became outdated. The Red Army had finally broken through on the Summa front on the very same day as the author had dated his memorandum.

---

* Noel-Baker, however, recommended that an international volunteer brigade be assembled and sent to Finland.

† See above, p. 115.

Given that the Allies were reluctant to encourage Finland to make peace in the first place, the Russians suddenly eliminated even this slight hope by tightening their conditions. The ways in which the War Cabinet declined Maisky's request for mediation two weeks later shows that it was not interested in bringing the Finnish war to an end at that stage. If the British had accepted Maisky's proposal and promoted a dictated peace, they would of course have risked the prestige they had gained trying to help the Finns. The only tangible suggestion put forward in Noel-Baker's memorandum —the proposal for a joint Franco-British committee to co-ordinate and accelerate the material aid to be sent to Finland—also came to nothing: *it was considered that such a measure would have reduced the authority of the ministries*.[15]

Three weeks later Finland was visited by two other leading British politicians, Harold Macmillan and Lord Davies. Their departure — at the initiative of the Committee for Assistance to Finland but with the object of procuring first-hand information for the War Cabinet — took place five days after the decision of the Supreme War Council to intervene. The favourable impressions which the two visitors, above all Macmillan, brought from Finland might have influenced Cabinet decisions had they not reached London much too late. The only tangible result of this visit, an eye-witness report, was included in the retired Prime Minister's memoirs published a quarter-century later: this was clearly based on the notes he made during or shortly after the trip.

Macmillan and Davies arrived in Turku in the evening of 12 February, the former wearing a white fur cap he had bought in Stockholm, which nineteen years later was to attract attention in Moscow when 'Supermac' paid his first visit to the Soviet Union. In Helsinki they first met Premier Ryti, who expressed views completely at variance with those he had confided to Noel-Baker: Finland needed manpower from abroad immediately, not so much individual volunteers (on which Macmillan agreed) as *regular troops*. At the British legation, old Colonel Goodden saw the military situation as virtually hopeless. Snow for his part was of the opinion that the only way of saving the Finns was to send them about 100 bombers, or to make an attack on the Murmansk railway through Petsamo. He agreed that volunteers were of no avail in that country during winter.[16]

On the morning of 15 February the visitors went to the town of Porvoo which was still burning after a large-scale bombing raid; they then had lunch with Niukkanen, the Minister of Defence, and General Walden. On this occasion they received detailed information on the Finnish requests for armaments. The two hosts admitted that, with their manpower dwindling away, the Finns were fighting a losing battle, and repeated that immediate reinforcements of artillery and aircraft were necessary to adjust the balance of power.

Because of the critical situation on the Isthmus, Mannerheim could not receive the guests at his headquarters. But after lunch at the Savoy Hotel in Helsinki, they met Major Magill, just back from Mikkeli, and heard from him more details of the situation at the front, which had taken an alarming turn the previous day. Macmillan and Davies decided to convey the information to London, the former to Chamberlain and Churchill, the latter to Lloyd George and Archibald Sinclair as well as Harold Gibson. Their messages stressed the gravity of the situation and the necessity of delivering without delay the war material asked for by the Finnish. According to the War Cabinet minutes, Macmillan's cable was brought to the notice of the ministers two days later, but did not occasion further measures.[17]

Accompanied by Magill and a Finnish officer, Macmillan then visited the front positions at Suomussalmi and Kuhmo in the north of Finland. In his notes he expressed his unreserved admiration for the Finnish soldier, but did not fail to notice that the men at the front had no illusions about the final outcome of the war. Accordingly, after interviewing Major Kari, one of the heroes of the battle of Suomussalmi, he wrote in his diary:

Although he [Kari] had taken this amazing part in a wonderful victory, having in effect destroyed two Russian divisions with his handful of men, he had no easy contempt for his adversaries.

Although they [the Russians] did not seem to understand the forest life, they were beginning to learn.... They were also learning to ski, but were not yet expert. They were extremely brave and indifferent to death. And, of course there was no end to them. If you destroy one division, they bring up another."[18]

While travelling back to the south by railway, Macmillan personally experienced the air terror raging over Finland: his party was obliged to wait for hours at the stations during the alarms, sometimes running for shelter into the snow-covered forests and seeing the railway station in flames. At Riihimäki he tried to enter the men's room in the restaurant but was told to go outdoors instead: after a recent bombing raid there was still a bomb in the lavatory waiting to be defused.[19]

After returning to Stockholm with Lord Davies, Macmillan, on cabled instructions from Butler, once more tried to find out how the situation could be saved. Having met Crown Prince Gustav Adolf,

Günther and Boheman as well as Erkko, now the Finnish representative in Stockholm, he concluded that hope was fading. As he noted
in his diary on 24 February, Erkko heavily criticized the Swedish
Government for leaving Finland in a state of uncertainty; the
British did not escape his criticism either.[20]

Macmillan also visited Oslo, where everyone seemed on edge for
fear of the Germans. Then on 1 March he returned home in a state
of depression. It is evident that he at once gave an account of his
impressions at least to Butler, so that they were known by the inner
circle of the Cabinet before time had definitely run out for Finland.
For all that, they did not influence the course of events in any way.
Macmillan's moment did not come until almost three weeks later
when he made a sensational speech in the House of Commons and
made use of the whole arsenal he had collected in Finland in order
to criticize Chamberlain's war policy. It was largely thanks to this
speech that he started his rise from the back benches to the circle of
command which was now taking shape around Churchill.*[21]

In analysing the unofficial support received by Finland it is
impossible to overlook the large-scale assistance given by private
organizations and persons. The political as well as material importance of this activity should not be underestimated. Certain trends of
opinion took it up because of its clear ideological tendency; in official
circles it attracted sympathy since it increased Allied prestige in
Finland and in the neutral countries. From the Finnish point of view
the results of this activity were far from negligible — especially in
the medical field. In Britain this activity was co-ordinated at the
initiative of the Finnish Legation, but through organizations like
the Red Cross; later Finnish Aid and the Finnish Relief Fund
became involved, the former organization being in charge of military
and the latter mainly of humanitarian assistance.†

---

* To the "unofficial" British visitors during the Finnish war may be added Sir Paul
Dukes, well-known for his memoirs from Russia, *ST 25* and *The Red Dusk and
Morrow*. He visited Finland in February for the purpose of studying there the
possibilities of intensified anti-Soviet propaganda, especially among Russian
prisoners-of-war. He tried, amusingly enough, to make the Finns believe that
they could still capture Leningrad and bring the entire Soviet system to collapse,
somewhat as in 1919. Whoever was his employer, his aspirations were irrelevant
to real Finnish interests—a fact which was realized in time in Helsinki.[22]

† One of the most efficient agents in this work deserves mention, the British-born
Mrs. Peggy Gripenberg, as indicated by a report received by Premier Ryti:
"If anyone is tireless here, it is Mrs. Gripenberg. She has performed great work
for the Red Cross. She is at home at the War Office and pushes almost everything through".
  The reference is evidently to Mrs. Gripenberg's discussions at the War Office
which resulted in the delivery to Finland of forty ambulances. During the early
part of the war another noteworthy organizer was the former British Consul in
Helsinki, Henry Bell, with whose co-operation funds were raised to send the
three Silver Star motor ambulance planes to Finland.[23]

3

Daladier's policy towards Finland was facilitated by the fact that all French political parties, with the exception of the Communist Party which had been forced underground, actively or at least unprotestingly approved of his anti-Soviet measures. In two large-scale debates on the Finnish War he was not once criticized for having undertaken to assist Finland — on the contrary, the aid was found insufficient. On the possibility of intervention proper, sceptical voices did make themselves heard in the press despite government control. Such at least were Émile Buré of *L'Ordre* and Pertinax (alias André Geraud) and Henri de Kérillis of *L'Époque*, all of them more or less anti-Munich and subsequently anti-Vichy.[24]

The division of opinion was not as clear politically as might be concluded from the above. Along with the extreme Right, the Finnish cause found supporters among the non-Communist Left, even among those socialists who after the collapse of France resisted Vichy and the Germans — after June 1941, in company with the Communists. Compared with the clear internal set-up produced by the Spanish civil war, the Finnish question divided the forces in a somewhat unexpected way: Léon Blum and his Popular Front found themselves, for a change, on the same side as his arch-enemy, Colonel de La Rocque and the latter's followers in the former Croix de Feu organization, with activists of Action Française and members of other groups of the extreme Right,[25] which are known to history largely as supporters of Pétain and collaborators with Hitler.

At the Brussels meeting Hugh Dalton took special note of the uncompromising attitude of Blum, who even went so far as to declare, in the name of his parliament and public opinion, that the French were ready to take up arms against the Soviet Union.[26]

The almost unreserved support of the parties and the press in general did not effectively help the rescue campaign for Finland, which produced less impressive material results in France than on the other side of the Channel. Despite this, the political influence of the pro-Finnish press, especially in providing the rearguard for the intervention-minded government, is deserving of special study in itself. The Finnish cause also offered a popular motive for beating off the Communist peace agitation: Daladier found a favourable occasion to demonstrate that Bolshevism differed from Nazism "as much as the plague from cholera".[27]

The future men of Vichy were indeed amazingly united in their attitude towards the Finnish war. It seems almost natural that their future head of state, Pétain, then Ambassador in Madrid, planned a trip to Finland during the winter. In spite of Mannerheim's cable of welcome, the journey came to nothing, however, since the old Marshal preferred to postpone his departure till the spring. Instead, another old soldier, François de La Rocque, the man who in the 1930s presented himself as the future leader of France, visited Finland in early March.[28]

Most of the Frenchmen who visited or stayed in Finland during the Winter War were military people. In addition to Colonel Ganeval, who was sent there on 15 December, the Finnish general headquarters received in the middle of February the previously mentioned four officers, representing the French air force, the armoured troops and the artillery as well as the Quai d'Orsay — the last-mentioned under a fictitious name, according to Stehlin, in order not to get the French Government involved! The French admiralty, too, had a liaison officer in Helsinki. Moreover, a number of French armament experts were sent to Finland. The largest group, comprising almost sixty officers and N.C.O.s, arrived just after the end of the war with the task of training the Finns, mainly in the use of older artillery equipment.[29]

The best-known and highest-ranking French officer who volunteered for the Finnish war was General Clément-Grancourt, past seventy and, "Protestant, royalist and deaf", as Coulet describes him. In his old-fashioned uniform he was sometimes the butt of the jokes of his junior compatriots: among other things it was said that he had asked for the command of the defence of the Viipuri area, an assertion which found no confirmation in the Finnish headquarters, not even as a joke. Mannerheim himself finally seems to have taken such a liking to the old soldier that he intended to give him the command of all the foreign volunteers arriving in Finland.[30]

Apart from the elderly general and a privately-sponsored mobile field hospital, few French volunteers arrived in Finland. From the outset Daladier viewed the enlistment reluctantly. France was waging a war and, unlike in Britain, the main part of her conscripts were fighting in the country's own army. Besides, as the French Premier used to point out, the sending of volunteers was unnecessary, since the Government was ready to send regular troops, who better represented the Tricolor. In spite of Holma's numerous efforts he kept to this position until the end of the war.[31]

On the other hand, Daladier favoured the enlistment of the thousands of foreigners staying in France into an international volunteer unit, the so-called Garibaldi Legion, the idea for which had been afoot since autumn. According to Paasonen this possibility had been included in Daladier's plan for an expeditionary corps in

mid-January. Ultimately the idea was dropped, partly because of
the unwillingness of the French who preferred to use regular troops,
partly because of the aversion of the Finnish Government to call in
foreign refugees mostly men who had fought on the Republican
side in Spain.[32]

4

From the first day of the war, the Finnish Legations in London and
elsewhere had received a flow of offers from volunteers willing
to go to Finland. Besides Britons and Irishmen, the Legation was
approached by candidates of various nationalities such as Austrians,
Czechs, Poles and White Russian émigrés, whose acceptance was
often out of the question. Minister Gripenberg also received a
number of individuals who wanted to start large-scale enlistment
and organizing of troops; among these was Lord Davies, who
brought up his favourite idea of assembling an international police
force against the aggressor.*

In Britain the volunteer activities found a more realistic footing
when Colonel Harold Gibson started looking for official support for
them in early January. At this time Gibson worked in the secretariat
of the War Cabinet but evidently got going on his own initiative,
though with the support of Anthony Eden, with whom he had
co-operated in organizing the International Board for Non-intervention during the Spanish civil war. It was Eden himself who
on 2 January presented Halifax with Gibson's proposal that Britain,
in accordance with the declaration given to the Secretary-General
of the League of Nations, should send a volunteer force to Finland.
Eden's predecessor as Foreign Secretary, Sir Samuel Hoare,

---

* On Lord Davies, see above, pp. 165 and 169-70. According to Gripenberg's
diary (12 Dec. 1939) Prince Bieloselsky-Bielosersky, mentioned as a good friend
of Mannerheim, had proposed to him the enlistment of Russian prisoners-of-war.
The British radical socialist Kerrow had on the same day suggested the
inviting of Trotsky to Europe to arrange radio propaganda against Stalin.
Likewise the son of the former Russian Premier Alexander Kerensky volunteered
to go to Finland to carry on anti-Bolshevik propaganda among the prisoners-of-
war (5 Jan. 1940). General Skoropadsky called at the Finnish Legation in
London with his friends to tell the envoy that he wanted to enlist Ukrainian
volunteers from the U.S.A. and Canada (8 Jan.), etc. Similar proposals were
made especially to the Legation in Paris. Besides, Helsinki was visited by the
delegation of the E.I.A. (Entente Internationale Anti-communiste—the
international anti-Communist league) which had its headquarters in Geneva
and was willing to offer its obscure services. In principle these proposals were
given a negative response, since the Finns were wisely prudent in not acting
in any way that might be interpreted as interfering with Soviet internal affairs.
According to the instructions given to the Finnish legations abroad it was, for
instance, forbidden to accept Russian volunteers.[33]

brought up the question in the War Cabinet, so that he too must have been aware of the proposal.[34]

According to Gibson, Lord Halifax had viewed the initiative favourably. First it was decided, as we know, that the matter should not be settled until the Scandinavian countries had announced whether they would approve of the transit of such a force.* Meanwhile the proposal met with resistance. Ling, among others, had expressed the opinion that a volunteer force could not be of great avail at this time of year and that it might instead be poor publicity for Britain. In the Cabinet it was feared that suitable candidates would be hard to find and that the volunteer movement would become an object of ridicule. It was warned that Finnish resistance would collapse and the British Government might have to answer for the security of its citizens enlisted and sent to Finland. One of the opponents was Ironside who had started assembling his own ski troop and was afraid that the few who knew how to ski would volunteer to go to Finland.[35]

By now Gripenberg for his part had begun actively supporting the initiative and had told the Foreign Office that Finland would be grateful for even a small British volunteer formation. In the back of his mind was the idea that the participation of volunteers might enhance the interest of the British public in the conflict and might incite the Cabinet to increase its military assistance to Finland.[36] At the decisive stage the initiative received influential support in Parliament, especially from L. S. Amery who started putting pressure on the Cabinet through Halifax.

Chamberlain took account of these opinions, and at his proposal the Cabinet decided on 26 January to accept the setting up of the volunteer office, formally non-official but secretly supervised and supported by the Government, provided (1) that its activities in connection with the Finnish Legation were carried on without publicity, (2) that the volunteers were not trained in Britain, and (3) that they were not to form a national detachment but "the British section of the international volunteer force for Finland". Thus the Cabinet, fully aware of the propaganda value of even a limited British auxiliary force, tried in advance to ward off Scandinavian and German negative reactions, and at the same time to rid themselves of responsibility if the plan were to miscarry or the volunteer force ran into serious trouble.[37]

In the middle of February, after the British had delivered or promised to deliver additional aircraft to Finland, the idea gained ground that even R.A.F. personnel might be sent to operate and

* See above, p. 106.

maintain the equipment. The opponents of the idea, especially the Prime Minister, drew attention to the risks involved, such as the increasing difficulty of obtaining transit permission and the danger of British pilots being captured by the Russians. Yet the advantages involved, above all the prestige (the faultless functioning of the British equipment sent to Finland), were found so considerable that R.A.F. personnel were finally allowed to leave for Finland in limited numbers. By the end of February only fifty had obtained the necessary permission, but since recruitment of flying and maintenance personnel for Finland started in early March, the number of R.A.F. men allowed to leave reached 300.[38]

The enlistment was facilitated when the volunteer movement was made public in Parliament.* At the end of February the Finnish Legation was receiving up to 300 applications every day. The Finnish Aid Bureau, an organization whose task was to recruit and select the volunteers as well as to coordinate and if necessary inform the authorities of Finland's needs and aid requests, was now fully employed. Gibson, who had been appointed director, managed the office with enthusiasm during its entire period of activity. At the wish of the Cabinet, the Finnish envoy was elected chairman of the volunteer committee, whose members were well known persons interested in the matter: apart from the old friends of Finland, Lord Balfour and Lord Davies, the committee included the King's physician, Lord Dawson of Penn, the Conservative representatives Amery and Macmillan, General McDonough, Lord Lytton and Lord Nuffield, the motor-car manufacturer.

There was, however, a considerable defect in the set-up of the committee; despite attempts at an opening to the Left, not one Labour representative joined it, not even Citrine or Noel-Baker. Likewise Lord Beaverbrook, who was close to Churchill and avoided all anti-Soviet activity, stayed off the committee, even though he, together with Nuffield, was one of its chief financial supporters.[40]

The Finnish Aid Bureau set as its initial objective the assembly of a 500-man volunteer force. The first detachments sent to Finland

---

* The earlier attempts to conceal recruitment were partly because of the so-called Foreign Enlistment Act of 1870, which did not allow British subjects to enlist in the service of a foreign power, was still in force. Since it had been applied recently in connection with the Spanish civil war, it was expected that those opposing the volunteer movement would refer to it. Indeed, on 14 February in the House of Commons, D. N. Pritt asked the Government for information on the question. The Foreign Secretary, who was prepared for the request, refuted it by pointing out that His Majesty's Government had promised the League of Nations to assist Finland which was subject to aggression; consequently, he maintained, the British volunteers leaving for Finland were in a way serving British interests.[39]

were selected from relatively few applicants, and the suitability of officers and other ranks was not properly tested before departure. Therefore, the British volunteers in general did not come up to the standards of the other nationalities coming to Finland from outside the Nordic countries, such as for example the Hungarians.[41]

Because of the dallying of the War Cabinet the results of the enlistment remained rather unimpressive. During its six weeks of activity the Finnish Aid Bureau shipped, by 15 March, a total of 225 men from Britain, and prepared 751 for departure; 1,207 men were ready but unequipped.* Moreover there were on 15 March 6,000 men waiting for pre-selection examination. The Bureau could thus look forward to reaching its initial numerical objective— at the final stage the target was raised to 1,000 men. In any case, the problem was not the quantity but the quality of the candidates.[42]

The volunteer committee had chosen as commander of the detachment Colonel Kermit Roosevelt, son of the former U.S. President Theodore Roosevelt (and cousin of President Franklin D. Roosevelt), who was serving as a volunteer in the British Army. The choice was vindicated by the fact that he was known as a First World War veteran, and his name had some international prestige. The Foreign Office at first maintained that the choice might offend the American sense of neutrality—though the real reason for reluctance was probably the wish to have a British officer in the post. When it was learnt that the White House had approved of Colonel Roosevelt's appointment, Halifax gave in. The new commander even gave the soldier's oath to the Finnish flag at the Legation, but in fact never had occasion to leave for Finland, nor did the main body of the British detachment, since the peace of Moscow was signed three days before the date fixed for embarkation.[43]

The first group of volunteers shipped to Finland was entrusted to a retired British General, Sir Ormonde Winter, who was also to take charge of the maintenance and training of the detachment in Finland.† On the way there, however, Winter fell seriously ill and had to hand over command to his subordinate Captain Chandor,

---

* The equipment of the volunteers—which included, apart from the normal personal equipment of the British army procured through the War Office, a number of specialities for Arctic conditions such as exceptionally warm winter clothing—and their arms (pistols, rifles, sub-machine-guns and light machine-guns) were sent to Finland separately.

† The men themselves travelled in civilian dress and were to have their uniforms only after arrival in Finland. The badges and buttons for these uniforms had originally been made for the International Non-intervention Committee in Spain, and were in the form of a chromium-plated rose engraved "NI", standing for "Non-intervention". Turned up the other way it became "IN" for "Inter-

actually appointed for maintenance duties only. The officer commanding the second detachment had to be dismissed and sent back immediately since he appeared completely indifferent to his duties. These incidents, as well as the unexpected change in the general war situation, marked the rather unhappy end of the story of the British volunteers in Finland.

After the peace of Moscow the Bureau interrupted the sending of volunteers to Finland but agreed, at a request from Helsinki, that those on their way to Finland or already there could stay in the country if they themselves so wished. Chandor's force was attached to a special detachment, *"Sisu,"* formed of foreign volunteers and stationed at Lapua for training. In April the British were attached as a formation of their own to the Finnish 3rd Division and transferred to the south-eastern border near Lappeenranta. But after the crushing success of the Germans in the Nordic countries and the West, it was suddenly found undesirable to keep British soldiers in the Finnish Army. By the end cf May the last of them had been transferred into civilian service and were for the time being stationed at a camp near Jyväskylä.[44]

The repatriation of the British volunteers proved to be a serious problem. Of those who had arrived in Finland, a quarter had tried to return home by the beginning of April. The vanguard of this group happened by chance to reach Oslo on the morning of 9 April, just as the Germans were approaching the city. Most of them succeeded, by abandoning their baggage, to sneak back to the last train leaving for Sweden and rejoin their comrades who had stayed in Stockholm. Eleven unlucky ones were taken prisoner.[45]

For those remaining in Finland and Sweden, plans were made to have them transferred to Northern Norway, but the Germans got there before them. The volunteers then had to wait half-interned on both sides of the Gulf of Bothnia for their repatriation, but they did so in vain. Although various plans for transporting them were suggested, all were given up, mainly because the Germans refused any guarantees and threatened to deal with those departing as citizens of an enemy country. Remarkably enough, the same scruples did not apply in the Soviet Union — where transit permission was granted to a few who tried to make their way home through Soviet territory.

There were, at the time, some insinuations in the press that the volunteers remaining in Finland suffered from the unfriendly attitude of the Finnish authorities. It is plausible that the constant

---

national", the Finnish Aid Bureau director reported, "and the rose, which had originally stood for the Tudor Rose of England, now became the White Rose of Finland".

bad news of Allied defeats and Axis successes, as well as the corresponding change in Finnish opinion from being pro-Allied to pro-German, were factors which embittered the minds of the volunteers. One should bear in mind that — according to Clark — at least 70 per cent of them had come to Finland out of sheer goodwill. Nonetheless, as far as the material aspect was concerned, the Finnish authorities had certainly, at Mannerheim's express wish, taken particular care of the subsistence of the volunteers. Authorized observers visiting the unit, especially Lord Balfour in May 1940 and Colonel Gibson in August, reported that the conditions of the British volunteers were as comfortable as could be asked for in military quarters in a country at war.[46]

The fact that the volunteers were not sent home in due course was partly due to the British authorities who, for example, seemed in no great hurry to gather them in Sweden. After the Germans, in September 1940, had started their troop transports through Finland to Norway and back, the keeping of a few dozen British in the country was of course worthwhile, if not only for reasons of intelligence. A considerable part of the volunteers were employed in various temporary jobs outside their main camp, dozens even in the capital. When Finland in June 1941 joined the war on the German side against the Soviet Union, the remnants of Chandor's force were finally hurried on to Sweden, but even then at the initiative of the Finnish and not the British Government. Despite the worsening of relations with Britain, there was still in Helsinki enough sense of responsibility to manage the matter without accidents: thus the story of the British volunteers ended without a single one being interned in Finland as a citizen of an enemy country.[47]

5

The first Allied troops considered for use in Finland were the Polish troops interned in the Baltic States and the Balkans and those being re-organized in France and Britain. The idea of enlisting these forces for use in Finland occurred almost simultaneously with the proposal for sending Polish naval units to Petsamo. As early as 11 December the British envoy in Latvia, Orde, had suggested that the 4,000 Poles who had escaped to Latvia and been interned there (frontier guards and one air force regiment, all belonging to the regular troops) should be transferred to Finland by way of Sweden.

It is characteristic of the situation in the Baltic States during the latter part of 1939 that such plans could be made and even put into practice in spite of the Soviet military presence: according to

Mannerheim, these countries had indeed agreed to the partial freeing of the interned Poles and their transportation to Sweden. The documents of the Polish refugee government reveal that some 300 of their disarmed soldiers had left Latvia via Stockholm during the month preceding 15 January 1940.*[48]

A week after Orde's proposal the British Minister in Bucarest, Sir R. Hoare, suggested to the Foreign Office that pilots who had escaped from Poland be enlisted for Finland and provided with British planes. Considering that some 100 Polish pilots were assembled, as was alleged, in Stockholm alone in late January 1940, the idea seemed attractive. Mainly because of the lack of equipment and also because the R.A.F. wanted to get hold of the Polish pilots for its own use, Hoare's initiative received a cool welcome in London. The Foreign Office gave it the cold shoulder, arguing that this was a matter concerning the Finnish and the Polish Governments.[49]

In Helsinki the question was still alive in February. Accordingly Noel-Baker, who had returned from Finland by way of France, brought it up at his discussions with C. M. Liberman, leader of the Polish Social Democratic Party. Noel-Baker reports that he had told Liberman of the Finnish wish to have eighty Polish pilots and asked him to forward the message to the latter's good friend General Sikorsky.[50] For certain political reasons even this initiative failed. At first Daladier seemed prepared to support the sending of Polish pilots to Finland, provided that the British gave them planes. But after it was decided to send an Allied expeditionary force to Finland, the idea of enlisting Polish volunteers was buried.

The transfer of those interned in the Baltic States to Finland via Sweden was in fact still under consideration — but with no result. According to Mannerheim, the plan failed because of Swedish opposition.[51] Polish documents, however, reveal other aspects. Sikorsky had sent a personal representative to Finland to give extra strength to the démarches of the Polish envoy in Helsinki. According to his own report, the representative, Lieutenant-Colonel Tadeusz Rudnicky, had encountered 'great difficulties' in his task: he had been told that the negotiations concerning assistance would be held in Paris, where Mannerheim had just sent General Enckell as his representative.

The Finns evidently did not want to have any talks with the Poles in Helsinki, since it was difficult to keep them secret there.

---

* In his memoirs Mannerheim mentions that a total of 20,000 Polish soldiers had been offered from Latvia and Lithuania. This figure does not appear in the documents the present writer has dealt with and is probably based on verbal information received by the Commander-in-Chief.

Regardless of the fact that the initiative came from the Finns, the Colonel wrote, "they seem in no hurry to start negotiations..." Before his departure on 16 February, Rudnicky had met Mannerheim's confidant, General Walden, and they had agreed that in the end the real obstacle to the arrival of the Poles was the Swedish reluctance to grant them passage.[52]

At this stage the Finns were advised by the French to avoid direct contacts with the Polish government-in-exile at Angers. They were asked to deal with questions concerning the Polish troops, which it was planned to send to Finland with the Allied expeditionary force, directly with Paris and London. This was contrary to the aspirations of Sikorsky, who had accepted the Finnish appeals for assistance in the hope that Finland would recognize the Angers government and accredit a representative to it. When Holma informed Helsinki of the Polish wishes he received no response whatever; the Finnish Government was now aware of the political risks involved and of the fact that, were it finally to resort to Allied intervention, this could be carried out without political preconditions.[53]

In his discussions with Daladier on 4 January, at the time when he still hoped to use Polish naval units in the waters of Petsamo,* Sikorsky had drawn attention to the possibilities offered to the Allies by the Finnish War. When the plans for an expeditionary force for Finland had gained ground, Sikorsky, on 25 January, had pushed through in his ministerial council the proposal that this force should include a Polish volunteer brigade. It was presumed in the proposal that the Poles would be equipped by the French quickly enough to have them trained and transported to Finland at the same time as the rest of the expeditionary force. Moreover, the realization of the plan was not to hamper the re-organization of the Polish Army now taking place in France.[54]

In informing the French Foreign Ministry of its decision, the provisional government had demanded that it be represented in the Allied Supreme War Council when the intervention in Finland was being discussed. The Quai d'Orsay had ignored this unexpected request: Champetier de Ribes explained to Holma that this depreciatory attitude was for security reasons. It is likely that the War Council was less worried about possible leakages than about the Poles finding out about the real motives of their allies in preparing for intervention in Finland.[55]

In his memorandum on the question, Sikorsky's chief of general staff, Colonel Kedzior, admitted that even for the Poles political objectives were decisive:

---

* See above, pp. 87-8.

(1) the Polish troops will be on Finnish soil as a living proof that Poland exists and is fighting on the Allied side;
(2) the fact that Poland takes part in joint Allied measures allows us to make clear...the question of Poland's relations with its two allies;
(3) both these points are so important that solely in order to realize them we are ready to make certain sacrifices...in detaching part of our armed forces to a theatre of war outside our immediate interests.

As revealed in the memorandum, the Finnish question was thought to be a precedent, after which the Poles could demand participation in the Allied Supreme War Council activities in the future. Politically the presence of the Polish troops, attached as a dependent unit to the expeditionary force, might have created an unfavourable impression both in their occupied homeland and elsewhere in the world. It would have brought them down practically to the level of the Foreign Legion. Kedzior concluded: "We must therefore push through the principle that we will be equal members of the Allied expedition."[56]

The "maximum effort", of the Poles to assist Finland, as clarified by Kedzior in his memorandum, would ultimately have been limited to the following measures:

(1) sending a formation of some 25–50 planes to Finland, which, it was promised, was to have taken place after a two weeks' intensified training course (from the moment when the Allies delivered the planes and other necessary equipment to the Polish pilots);
(2) the transfer to the Finns of the right to purchase the coastal artillery which Poland had ordered from Bofors before the war;
(3) participation in the expeditionary corps planned for Finland with a force of approximately one reinforced infantry brigade.[57]

According to the statement given to Daladier by the chairman of the French-Polish military commission, General Denain, the Polish brigade was to be ready for departure three weeks after the Supreme War Council decision, that is, on 29 February. The formation would then include two half-brigades, each comprising a staff company, two infantry battalions, one railway company, maintenance units, etc. Denain complained that the troops concerned were still rather inadequately equipped and trained. The assembling of the requested ski company (for reconnaissance) and anti-tank company was out of the question in such a short time. It was said that the men were mainly Poles who had come to France to work in the coal mines, and lacked even the basic military training and experience. For this reason the brigade would evidently have been used chiefly in the rear.[58]

The delays and deficiencies in the equipment and training of the Polish troops, not to speak of the fact that the orders to prepare had been given practically without the knowledge of the provisional government, irritated Sikorsky. As indicated in his letter to Gamelin on 19 February, it was not until that moment that he had learned that the Polish detachment was to comprise 1-2 battalions more than had been agreed on. Certainly the General was not made happier by the consequent comments on Radio Moscow, alleging that he had first learned of the sending of Polish troops to Finland from the British press, and compared his volunteers to coloured mercenaries.[59]

After deploring the standards of the suddenly enlarged Polish brigade, as well as the lack of training of the additional troops, Sikorsky questioned whether such a force was at all suitable to be sent to the North. He maintained that the brigade's rifles and mortars were utterly antiquated, that the men had no gas masks, haversacks and tools, and that the Poles had not yet received any equipment or transport. "How, after the experience of four months," the General asked, referring to the stay of his expatriate army in France, "could all these deficiencies be repaired in ten days?"[60]

Three days later, on 22 February, Sikorsky instructed his Foreign Minister to inform London and Paris that his government considered the date of departure for Finland (one week later) of the Polish troops, which were being assembled at Coëtquidan in Brittany, unrealistic, because of the lack of material and training; the brigade would not be ready for embarkation until six weeks after it had been fully equipped.[61] Finally, on 24 February Sikorsky sent a strongly worded letter to Daladier, describing General Denain's disregard of the Polish provisional government as contrary to the Polish-French co-operation agreement which had been made seven weeks earlier. In the concluding paragraph of the letter are expressions of wounded pride:

It seems to me that the allusion by the Chairman of the French-Polish military commission, according to which it would be an honour for Poland to fight in the Allied ranks to aid Finland, is based on a misunderstanding. Poland has fulfilled its duties toward the Allies to the full. It has suffered and goes on suffering enormous losses, the amount of which cannot be appreciated until the future.[62]

The tension between Angers and Paris, created by the plan for sending an expeditionary force to Finland, gradually abated when Finland finally gave up its appeal for assistance. The Polish brigade was still allowed to retain its former strength of four battalions. Some two months later it was put to the test—evidently after its equipment and training had been improved—in Northern Norway, where it had been sent with Béthouart's French brigade of Chasseurs Alpins to fight the Germans. It was thus in Narvik, at the beginning of June 1940, that the 'Army of Free Poland' ended the first of its many dramatic campaigns—the one which might have come to Finland's aid.

NOTES

Chapter I, pp. 1-17

1. Winston Churchill, *The Second World War, I: The Gathering Storm* London 1948, p. 434.
2. Ibid.
3. For more background information, see the few general studies on the Finnish war available in English. Besides Max Jakobson's *The Diplomacy of the Winter War; an account of the Russo-Finnish War 1939-40* (Cambridge, Mass., Harvard University Press, 1961), also Eino Jutikkala-Kauko Pirinen, *A History of Finland* (New York, Praeger. 1962) and the American interpretation by C. L. Lundin, *Finland in the Second World War* (Bloomington, Indiana University Press, 1957)
4. See Juhani Paasivirta, *The Victors in World War I and Finland: Finland's Relations with the British, French and the United States Governments in 1918-1919,* Helsinki 1965, Ch. VI, and the present writer's study of Finland and the Allied intervention in the North of Russia in 1918-19 (in Finnish only): *Muurmannin legioona,* Helsinki 1970.
5. Anthony Upton, *The Communist Parties of Scandinavia and Finland,* London 1973, p. 203. Cf. D.N.Pritt, *Must the War Spread?,* London 1940, pp.110-12 and 118-26, and Didier de Roussillon, *Vérités sur la Finlande,* Paris 1946, pp. 32-54.
6. Annual Report on Finland for 1938, para. 2; enclosure in the letter: T.M.Snow to FO, 28 Feb. 1939, letter no. 51, FO 371/23648/139, Public Record Office (=P.R.O.). Cf. minute, dated 15 July 1939, by Lawrence Collier, Chief of the Northern Department of the F.O.; FO ibid. 3310, and Wipert v. Blücher, *Gesandter zwischen Diktatur und Demokratie,* Wiesbaden 1951 (the memoirs of the German envoy in Finland 1935-44), pp. 91-2. See also Juhani Suomi, *Talvisodan tausta, Neurostoliitto Suomen uilkopolitiikassa 1937-39, I: Holstista Erkkoon,* Helsinki 1973, pp. 133-4.
7. General Kirke's preface, dated 9 May 1939, in J.O.Hannula's *Finland's War of Independence,* London 1939, p. 9. On Mannerheim's association with the Western Powers, see Erik Heinrichs, *Mannerheim Suomen kohtaloissa,* II, Helsinki 1959, pp. 25-6, 45-54, 57 and 65-7.
8. Cf. W.R.Mead, *Finland,* London 1968, pp.160-9.
9. Annual Report on Finland for 1938, paras. 12 and 37. *Finnish Foreign Trade Directory* 1950, Helsinki 1950. On planned British paper imports in 1939-40, see the War Council Paper WPG (40) 103: "The Economic Consequences to the Allies and to Germany respectively of the seizure by Germany of Denmark and Norway", p. 3; CAB 67/6, PRO.
10. *Documenty vneshnei politiki SSSR,* tome 16 (1939), Moscow 1971, nos. 299 and 333, Blücher, pp. 31 and 104-5, and *Annual Report on Finland on Finland for 1938,* para. 20.
    Since Canadian nickel production in the 1930s made up as much as 80-90 per cent of world production, the Canadian trust had secured the

concession in Petsamo only to forestall eventual competitors from getting more nickel, as a Foreign Office paper commented when estimating the company's losses in the area ceded to the U.S.S.R. in 1944. Before the outbreak of the Finnish War in 1939, the company claimed to have invested £1.5 million in Petsamo—a memorandum by Anthony Nutting, 27 Dec. 1943, and a letter by D.O.Evans, director of the Mond Nickel Company, to the Foreign Secretary, 15 Sept. 1944, FO 371/43175/132. Cf. Hans-Peter Krosby, *Finland, Germany and the Soviet Union 1940-1941. The Petsamo Dispute*, Madison, Wis., 1968, pp. 4-5.

11. Churchill, ibid., pp. 363-5, 434-5, and 550-2. For the naval agreement see the article by D.C.Watt, "Anglo-German Naval Agreement of 1935: an interim judgement", *Journal of Modern History*, June 1956.
12. See, e.g., W.N.Medlicott, *British Foreign Policy since Versailles*, London 1968 (=Medlicott 1968), pp. 138-40, 148-9, and 169-96, and Pierre Renouvin (ed.), *Histoire des rélations internationales*, VIII: "Les crises du XXe siècle (II) 1929-1945", Paris 1958, pp. 77-101 and 120-39; L.Woodward, *British Foreign Policy in the Second World War*, London 1970, pp.1-16. Especially on the Franco-Soviet treaty of 1935, see William L.Shirer, *The Collapse of the Third Republic*, London 1972, pp. 263-4.
13. See e.g. V.Potiemkine, *Histoire de la diplomatie* III (1919-1939), Paris, pp. 542-55, 559-60, 571-8, and 640-66. In a recent official Soviet history of diplomacy, *Istoriya diplomatii* (Vol. IV, Moscow 1975), on the Finnish attitude, see p. 26.
14. C.G.E.Mannerheim, *The Memoirs of Marshal Mannerheim*, London 1953, p. 287.
15. Jane Dégras (ed.), *Soviet Documents on Foreign Policy*, III, London 1953, p. 320.
16. Väinö Tanner, *The Winter War*, Stanford, Calif., 1957, pp. 3-12. On the Soviet claims of guarantees and bases in the years 1938-1939, see Tanner, pp. 12-16, Max Jakobson, *The Diplomacy of the Winter War*, Cambridge, Mass., 1961 pp, 62-5, and *Istoria diplomatii*, IV, pp. 24-6. Besides, there are two important studies on the subject in Finnish: the second part of the history of Finnish-Soviet pre-war relations by Professor Keijo Korhonen, *Turvallisuuden pettäessä*, Helsinki 1971, and the work already mentioned—a Ph.D. thesis—by Juhani Suomi.
17. *Annual Report on Finland for* 1938, paragraph 35. Cf. Suomi, pp. 244-5.
18. Same and Korhonen, pp. 165-72.
19. Keith Feiling, *The Life of Neville Chamberlain*, London 1947, p. 403.
20. On the development of the international situation in 1939 in general, see Medlicott 1968, pp. 201-11, Potiemkine, pp. 678-710, Renouvin, pp. 169-75, Woodward, pp. 1-16, and Henri Michel, *La drôle de guerre*, Paris 1971, pp. 84-9.
21. Seeds to F.O., 15 May 1939, tel.no.29; *Documents on British Foreign Policy*, 1919-1939 (=DBFP), 3rd Series, V—London 1952—no.148.
22. Aarne Wuorimaa, *Lähettiläänä Hitlerin Saksassa*, Keuruu 1967 (memoirs

of the Finnish envoy in Berlin 1936-40), pp. 100-6. Snow to FO, 10 May 1939, tel.no.46; *DBFP*, ibid., 449. Cf. Jakobson, pp. 72-3 and 79-80.

23. See Aaro Pakaslahti, *Talvisodan poliittinen näytelmä, UM:n poliittisen osaston päällikon päiviä ja öitä*, Porvoo 1970 (memoirs of chief of the political department, Finnish Foreign Ministry, during the war of 1939-40), pp. 58-9, and Korhonen pp. 183-91.

24. Snow to F.O., 22 March 1939, tel.no.15, and 31 March 1939, tel.no. 23; FO 371/23647/1580 and 1753.

25. Pakaslahti, p. 76. on the general question of the fortification of Åland, in general see Jakobson, pp. 35-46, 60-2 and 73-8; Pakaslahti, pp. 34-40, 53-4, 59-60 and 70-7, as well as Krister Wahlbäck, *Finlandsfragån i svensk politik 1937-40*, Stockholm 1964 (=Wahlbäck 1968), pp. 137-44 and 162-3. On British attitudes see especially Suomi, pp. 226-32.

26. Staffan Söderblom to H.Beck-Friis at the Swedish Foreign Ministry 24 May 1939, private letter; Archives of the Swedish Foreign Ministry (=SUD) HP 20 a LXXXVII. Holsti's report no.66, 31 May 1939; Archives of the Finnish Foreign Ministry (=UA) 109 A 10e.

27. For the general background see Lord Strang, *From Home and Abroad*. London 1956, pp. 156-90, and G.A.Gripenberg, *Finland and the Great Powers: Memoirs of a Diplomat*, Lincoln, Nebraska, 1965, pp. 22-7.

28. See Churchill's article on the question in the *Daily Telegraph*, 8 June 1939.

29. See Georges Bonnet, *Fin d'une Europe*, Paris 1948 (memoirs of French Foreign Minister of the time), pp. 187-8, and Shirer, op. cit.. pp. 496-500.

30. On the British Government decision see tel.no.142 from F.O. to Seeds 19 June 1939; *DBFP* 3-VI, no. 89, and tel. no. 151 from F.O. to Seeds 27 June 1939; *DBFP* 3-VI, no. 151. On Kirke's visit, see Jakobson, pp. 187-8.

31. Snow's report (=r.) no 135 to the Foreign Secretary, Lord Halifax, 20 June 1939, FO 419/33, and Kirke's r., 20 June 1939, FO 371/23648/3310.

32. Halifax to Hore-Belisha, Secretary of State for War, 26 May 1939; F.O., ibid., 2456.

33. Collier's minute, 15 July 1939, FO, ibid.

34. Gripenberg's r. no 59, 5 July 1939, UA: raportit, Lontoo. Cf. Halifax to Snow, 20 July 1939, tel. no. 154; CAB 419/33, and Gripenberg, pp. 38-41.

35. Gripenberg's r. nos. 63 and 71, 26 July 1939, idem.

36. Gripenberg, pp. 43-4 Cf. Wahlbäck, 1964, pp. 162-3.

37. F.O.'s tels. to Seeds (182 and 597) 25 July 1939; *DBFP* 3-VI nos. 432 and 444.

38. A.J.P.Taylor, *The Origins of the Second World War*, London 1961, p. 256,

39. General André Beaufre, *Le drame de 1940*. Paris 1965, p. 124. See Bonnet, op. cit., pp. 176-82, 186-200 and 209-15. Also Shirer, pp. 502-4.

40. See Snow's r. of 20 June 1939 and an authoritative history of Swedish foreign policy during the Second World War: Wilhelm M. Carlgren, *Svensk utrikespolitik 1939-1945*, Stockholm 1973, p. 18, note 12.

41. Minutes of Meeting of Anglo-Franco-Soviet Military Delegations held in Moscow on 15 Aug. 1939; *DBFP* 3-VII, p. 577. Admiral Drax's final r. 28 Aug. 1939, ibid., p. 609. Cf. Beaufre, op. cit., p. 148. In general, see Shirer, op. cit., pp. 508-18.
42. Snow's tel. no. 78 of 3 Aug. 1939 and Collier's comment on it; FO 371/23072/10978.

Chapter II, pp. 18-40

1. On the German conquest of Poland and the Allied reactions on the Western Front, see General Gamelin, *Servir*, III: *La Guerre (septembre 1939—mai 1940)*, Paris 1947, pp. 1, 49-50, 58-61 and 67; Michel, op. cit., pp. 103-20, and Shirer, op. cit., pp. 583-93.
2. Chiefs of Staff Subcommittee (=COS) Report 'Military Value of Russia'; CAB 24/285, PRO, and the Foreign Office Memorandum on the Anglo-Soviet Negotiations; *DBFP* 3-V, 645.
3. A French Communist member of parliament, F.Grenier, who had escaped to England, later reported that when, during the retreat in June 1940, the false rumour became current that the Soviet Union had joined the war on the Allied side, many French soldiers re-organized their units and once more turned to face the Germans. Fernand Grenier, *France, Britain and the Soviet Union* ('Russia Today' Pamphlets), London 1943, p. 4. More on the Leftist pacifists in Michel, pp. 53-4, 93-4 and 199-202, and in Shirer, p. 598.
4. W.N.Medlicott, *The Economic Blockade I* (History of the Second World War, United Kingdom Civil Series), London 1952 (=Medlicott 1952), p. 51.
5. See C.O.S. memorandum COS (39) 105: "Soviet Aggression against Finland and Other Scandinavian Countries" 31 Oct. 1939; CAB 80/5.
6. War Cabinet 17 Sep. 1939, War Council Minutes (=WM) 18 (39) 8; CAB 65/1. Snow's communication to Halifax 6 Nov. 1939; FO 371/23693/6667, PRO.
7. Churchill, op. cit., p. 352.
8. The Finnish Ministry for Foreign Affairs: *The Development of Finnish-Soviet Relations During the Autumn of 1939, in the Light of Official Documents*, Helsinki 1940 (=*Blue-White Book*), pp. 38 and 41-2. In addition to the declaration of neutrality given on account of the German-Polish war on 1 September 1939, Finland declared its neutrality on 3 and 15 September 1939 with regard to France and Great Britain as well as other countries taking part in the war.
9. Pakaslahti, op. cit., p. 95.—F.O. document in *DBFP* 3-VI, p. 765.
10. Blücher, op. cit., p. 151. On Snow's démarches see Minister Erkko's memoranda of 6 and 11 Sep. 1939 and the memorandum of Tapio Voionmaa, Secretary-General, Finnish Foreign Ministry, of 3 Oct. 1939; UA: Muistioita, syys-lokakuu 1939.
11. Memorandum on Erkko's discussions with Minister Snow on 6 Sept. 1939 and memorandum on Voionmaa's discussions with the British

commercial secretary on 5 Sep. 1939 and with the French envoy 18 Sep. 1939; UA, ibid. Snow's letter to Halifax (no.1) 11 Sep. 1939; FO 371/23648/3444. Cf. Blücher, p. 148, and Medlicott 1952, p. 139.

12. Chief of Bureau Tauno Jalanti's memorandum of 8 September 1939 and anonymous P.M. on the war material orders of 18 Sep. 1939; UA, idem. Cf. Gripenberg, op. cit., p. 75.

13. Cf. Pakaslahti, p. 97, and Blücher, pp. 127-8, as well as 'Leading Personalities in Finland' (13.), enclosure in Snow's letter no. 114 to Halifax 23 May 1939; FO 371/23649/2730.

14. See, e.g., the report of the naval attaché in Moscow, Captain Clanchy, enclosure in Ambassador Seeds's letter no. 163; 30 May 1939; FO 371/23696/2758. On the Soviet war preparations, see K. A. Meretskov, *Serving the people*, Moscow 1971, pp .99-116, and the new official war history, *Istoriya vtoroi mirovoi voiny 1939-45*, III, Moscow 1974, p. 359.

15. F.O. tel. no. 44, 7 Sep. 1939, to Minister Orde (Riga), FO, ibid, 23658. Memoranda on the discussions of the Foreign Minister on 11 Sep. 1939 and the Secretary General on 20 Sep. 1939 with the British envoy; UA, Muistioita, syys-lokakuu 1939. Cf. Gripenberg, pp. 52-3.

16. Gripenberg's report no 83, 27 Sep. 1939, idem. Cf. Gripenberg 1960, pp.74-5. Present author's italics.

17. Collier's minute 21 Sep. 1939 and a letter signed by same, 25 Sep. 1939, to Under-Secretary of State at the War Office; FO, ibid. 23643/4712. On the failure of the Petsamo railway project, see letter no. DGHP/BM 2933 by the Ministry of Supply to the F.O., 1 Nov. 1939; FO, ibid. 5891.

18. Churchill, p. 364. Gripenberg's r., 27 Sep. 1939.

19. Memorandum on Voionmaa's discussions with the British Minister, 16 Sep. 1939; UA 109 A 10 d. *Blue-White Book*, pp. 40-1. Cf. Pakaslahti, pp. 93-94.

20. Snow's r. no. 203, 19 Sep. 1939, to Halifax; FO, idem, 23692/4885. Finnish Foreign Ministry (=UM) tel. no. L 173 to London, 21 Sep. 1939; UA 109 A 1. Cf. Blücher's tel. no. 235, 23 Sep. 1939 (Auswärtiges Amt, Büro des Staatssekretärs, Finnland Bd. I, photostat, copy in the Finnish State Archives (=VA): Auswärtiges Amt, box 96).

21. Holma's r. no. 46 of 27 Aug. 1939; UA 109 A 1. The Secretary General's memoranda on his discussions with the French envoy 18 Sep. 1939 and on some discussions with foreign envoys 16-18 October 1939; UA Muistioita syys-lokakuu 1939.

22. Snow's r., 19 Sep. 1939.

23. Collier's minute 2 Oct. 1939; FO, idem, 4912. D.W. Lascelles's and Collier's minutes 29 Sep. 1939; FO 371/23692/4828.

24. Snow's tel. no. 116 of 30 Sep. 1939. Lascelles's minute 2 Oct. 1939; FO, idem, 4212. Author's italics.

25. See Collier's minute of 8 Oct. 1939 and Halifax's minute of 9 Oct. 1939; FO ibid.; comments by Lascelles, Collier et. al. FO 371/23692/5455.

26. Snow's tel. no. 76 of 3 Oct. 1939; FO idem, 5080.

27. See Gripenberg 1960, p. 75, and Erik Boheman, *På vakt, kabinett-sekreterare under andra världskriget*, Stockholm 1964, p. 84.

Snow's tels. nos. 119 and 120 of 6 Oct. 1939 and comments by Sir L. Oliphant, Deputy Under-Secretary of State, on these of 8 Oct. 1939; FO ibid,. 5025 and 5026.

29. Berlin legation telephone message (Waltimo-Sallas) 10 Oct. 1939 at 10.05 A.M. UA 109 A 1. Wuorimaa op. cit., pp. 114-15. Cf. A.A.'s tel. no. 318 to Legation in Helsinki on 7 Oct. 1939, (A.A. Büro des staatssekretärs, Finnland Bd. I; photostat copy in Finnish State Archives: Auswärtiges Amt, box 96). Cf. Blücher, pp. 147-8.

30. Oliphant's memorandum 9 Oct. 1939; FO 371/23696/5203, and Halifax's letter no. 210 to Snow on 10 Oct. 1939. Cf. Finnish documents in the groups UA A1 and C1, as well as Gripenberg, p. 73.

31. The following description of the negotiations is based on the memoirs of Paasikivi: J. K. Paasikivi, *Toimintani Moskovassa ja Suomessa 1939-41*, I, Porvoo 1959, pp. 40-76. Cf. *Istoriya diplomatii*, IV, pp. 26-8. For a concise description in English of the negotiations as a whole see. Anthony F. Upton, *Finland 1939-1940,*, London 1974, pp. 28-42.

32. Snow's tel. no. 124 of 8 Oct. 1939 to F.O. and Lascelles's comment of 9 Oct. 1939; FO 371/23692/5093.

33. Collier's minute 10 Oct. 1939; FO idem, 5093. Cf. Gripenberg, p. 90.

34. Feiling, op. cit., p. 428.

35. Lord Halifax, *The Fullness of Days*, London 1958.

36. Holma's r. no. 63 of 5 Oct. 1939; UA, raportit: Pariisi. On Gripenberg's visit to Halifax, see Gripenberg, p. 79.

37. Under-Secretary of State R. A. Butler's memorandum of 3 Oct. 1939, FO 371/23692/5260, and Halifax's letter no. 226 to Snow on 31 Oct. 1939, FO 419/33. Gripenberg's cables to the Finnish Foreign Ministry in group UA 109 C1, and Gripenberg, pp. 80-2.

38. Halifax's letter to Lord Chatfield 17 Oct. 1939; FO 371/23692/5190. Author's italics.

39. The request was presented at Washington on 6 October by the envoys of the three Scandinavian countries—Snow's tel. no. 145 of 13 Oct. 1939 and F.O.'s comments thereon; FO, ibid, 5263. R.A. Butler's memorandum on Gripenberg's visit 13 Oct. 1939; FO ibid. 5260.

40. Collier's minute 15 Oct. 1939; FO ibid, 5251.

41. F.O.'s letter to COS 19 Oct. 1939; FO ibid. 5903.

42. Snow's tel. no. 161 of 21 Oct. 1939 and tel. of 24 Oct. 1939 to F.O. and F.O.'s comments; FO, ibid. 5522, and WM 58 (39) 10, ibid.

43. Mentioned memorandum of 31 Oct. 1939 "Soviet Aggression against Finland and Other Scandinavian Countries." Author's italics.

44. WM 67 (39) 9.

45. Halifax's personal letter to Snow on 24 Nov. 1939; FO 371/23693/6667.

46. Gripenberg's tel. no. 435 of 25 Oct. 1939 to UM; UA 109 C1. Cf. WM 67 (39) 1. Memorandum on Voionmaa's and British envoy's discussions 30 Oct. 1939; UA 109 A1.

47. As it appears from British records in group FO 371/23643 and Finnish documents in groups UA raportteja: Lontoo and UA 109/A1, as well as from the memoirs of the Finnish Minister of Defence during the war of 1939-40: Juho Niukkanen: *Talvisodan puolustusministeri kertoo* (Porvoo

1951), p. 168; and from those of the envoy in London: Gripenberg, p. 75.

48. Halifax's statement to War Cabinet 4 Nov. 1939; WM 70 (39) 5. Halifax's letter no. 227 to Snow 31 Oct. 1939; FO 419/5631. Cf. tel. of Sir Percy Lorraine, British Ambassador in Rome, no. 336; FO 371/ 23692/5399, and Snow's tel. no. 175 of 4 Nov. 1939; FO 371/23693/ 5947. Cf. Lascelles's minute of 18 Oct. 1939; FO 371/23692/ 5399.

49. Comment by C. Barclay (Chief of department at F.O.) 15 Nov. 1939; FO, ibid. 6667.

50. Gripenberg's mentioned tels.; see UA 109 A1. On Collier's statement and the reactions caused by it, see Gripenberg's r. no 89 of 11 Nov. 1939; UA, raportit: Lontoo. Author's italics.

51. Colonel Hiisi, Finnish military attaché in Paris, to Colonel Melander, Chief of the Foreign Department of the Finnish General Staff, 2 Nov. 1939, r. no. 227/9sal/36; Finnish war archives (=SA), T 17522/ 9. Author's italics.

52. Cf. Hiisi, 16 Oct. and 19 Nov. 1939, rs. nos. 210 and 249/39; SA, idem, and Holma, 7 Nov. 1939, r. no. 75; UA, idem.

53. Cf. Lascelles, 28 Nov. 1939, memorandum on discussions with de Castellane, Counsellor at the French Embassy; FO 371/ 23693/6668.

54. Idem and Holma, 9 Nov. 1939, r. no. 76; UA 109 A 10e. Author's italics.

55. Snow to F.O., 21 Oct. 1939, tel. no. 161; FO, idem, 5522.

56. Memorandum, 30 Oct. 1939, on discussion between British envoy and Secretary General; UA 109 A1.

57. Cf. the same and Gripenberg to Erkko, 13 Nov. 1939, off. letter; UA 109 A 10e. On the German offer to supply Russian submarines, see *Documents on German Foreign Policy 1918-1945,* D VIII: *The War Years 1939-1940,* Washington 1954 (=D.G.F.P.) pp. 501 and 507.

58. Woodward, op. cit., p. 17.—Butler told the Finnish envoy of this discussion: Gripenberg, 23 Nov. 1939, r. no. 92, ibid.

59. Hugh Dalton, *The Fateful Years: Memoirs 1931-1945.* London 1957, p. 295.

60. Gripenberg, 23 Nov. 1939. r. no 92, UA, ibid. Author's italics.

61. Halifax to Snow, 1 Dec. 1939, letter no. 258; FO 419/33/7054. Cf. Halifax to Seeds, 27 Nov. 1939, letter no. 836; FO 371/23693/6717. Gripenberg, 28 Dec. 1939, tel. no. 570; UA 109 C1. For the Mainila incident, see also Upton, pp. 41-61.

62. Maisky, op., cit., 40.

63. C. J. Hambro to Norwegian UD, 6 Dec. 1939, memorandum; Archives of the Norwegian Foreign Ministry (=NUD) P 1 L/VII, 2/39.

Chapter III, pp. 41-61

1. There is still no satisfactory, detailed and objective military history of the Finnish War of 1939-1940. Of the two recent books in English, *The White Death, the Epic of the Soviet-Finnish Winter War* (Ann Arbor, Mich.

1939-1940 (London 1972) by Elvire Eagle and Lauri Paananen, the former to some extent fills the gap, though even this study, with its pro-Finnish tendency, is far from being impartial. For the time being, the reader is advised to consult the short but penetrating study by Anthony F. Upton, mentioned above (London 1974). A strongly biased contemporary pro-Soviet description of events is to be found in *The Soviet-Finnish Campaign, Military and Political* 1939-1940 (London 1942) by W.P. and Zelda K. Coates. A Soviet interpretation is to be found in *Istoriya Velikoi Otechestvennoi Voiy Sovetskogo Soyuza* 1941-1945 (Moscow 1960-5), II, p. 258 (published in German as *Die sowjetische Geschichte des grossen Vaterländischen Krieges* 1941-1945, Berlin 1961); the recent English version *The Great Patriotic War of the Soviet Union* is abbreviated and gives little space to the Winter War). Besides, a more detailed Soviet description is given in the official history of the Leningrad military district: *Istoriya Ordena Lenina Leningradskogo Voennogo Okruga*, Moscow 1974. pp. 151-65, and Meretskov, op. cit., pp. 180-7.

2. On the Soviet blockade of Finland, see the material in group FO 371/ 23694/7135, P.R.O. The text of the agreement of 2 Dec. 1939 between the presidium of the Supreme Soviet of the U.S.S.R. and "The Democratic Finnish Government", as it was at the time read by Radio Moscow and published by *The Moscow Times*, is to be found in Tanner, op. cit., pp. 101-3.

3. See Chew, pp. 31-139.

4. Halifax to Snow, 1 Dec. 1939, letter no. 258; FO 419/33/7054. Collier's minute of 2 Dec. and Lascelles's minute of 3 Dec. 1939; FO 371/23694/ 6809 and 6863.

5. Gripenberg, op. cit., p. 89. Material in group FO, ibid. 7135. On the beginnings of Kuusinen's role in the conflict, Meretskov, p. 104.

6. Snow to Halifax, 2 Dec. 1939, tel. no. 207;CAB 419/33, P.R.O. On the first reactions of British opinion, see Douglas Clark, *Three Days to Catastrophe* (London 1966), pp. 34-42.

7. WM 101 (39) 5; CAB 65/2. Author's italics.

8. WM 101 (39) 6. Gamelin, op. cit., p. 190. Cf. Steinhardt (US ambassador in Moscow) to the secretary of state, 1 Dec. 1939, tel. no. 991; *Foreign Relations of the United States, Diplomatic Papers (FRUS)*, 1939, I, Washington 1956, p. 1015. Author's italics.

9. Feiling, op. cit., p. 427.

10. WM 103 (39) 6 and 7, idem.—On Gripenberg's requests for fighter aircraft see Halifax to Snow. 4 Dec. 1939. letter no. 257; CAB 419/33 and Gripenberg, p. 89. Author's italics.

11. Jacques Minart, *P. C. Vincennes, Secteur 4*, Paris 1945. It appears from the official French archives seen by the present writer that Minart's study, at least the part dealing with Finland, is based on authentic documents, pp. 172-3.

12. Report no. 23 by Lt.-Col. Vale, 23 August 1939; FO 371/23649/4234. Cf. an authoritative Finnish impression of the same manoeuvres: Harald Öhqvist, *Talvisota minun näkökulmastani*, Porvoo 1949, p. 32.

13. Vale to Snow, 26 June 1939, letter no. 12, appendix 2; FO 419/33. Cf. the report by Col. R. B. Goodden, British military attaché in Helsinki, on the fortification works on the Isthmus, enclosure in Snow to FO, 14 Nov. 1939, letter no. 230; FO 371/23649/6537.

14. Ohqvist, pp. 46-7.

15. Cf. the minutes by Lascelles and Collier of 3 and 4 Nov. 1939; FO ibid., 5910.

16. Col. Hiisi to Col. Melander 4 Nov. 1939, r. no. 239/9 sal/39; SA T 17522/9.

17. The material concerning the Finnish air force in group FO 371/23643. On Finnish coastal defence, the same group, especially N 5798 and 6736. Memorandum by Collier, 10 Nov. 1939, on discussions with Gripenberg and the Swedish envoy, Björn Prytz; FO 371/23693/6196. Galliéni, British Minister in Tallinn, to F.O., 16 Oct. 1939, tel. no. 22; FO ibid. 23692/5478. Cf. F. Maclean's and Collier's comments, 29 Nov. 1939 and 2 Dec. 1939; FO ibid. 23693/6537.

18. On the weather conditions during the Finnish campaign 1939-40, see Chew, pp. 132-3. The force estimates in the reports by Wing-Commander Johnson, British air attaché in Stockholm, 16 Dec. 1939, and by Col. Goodden, 1 Jan. 1940; FO 419/34.

19. Monson, British Minister in Stockholm, to the F.O., 2 Dec. 1939, tel. no. 190; FO 371/23649/6876. Halifax's report to the War Cabinet, WM111 (39) 5; CAB ibid. The same to Snow, 11 Dec. 1939, letter no. 264; FO 419/33/7556. Gripenberg's diary, 9 and 19 Dec. 1939, VA. Author's italics.

20. Halifax to Amery, 11 Dec. 1939, private letter; FO 371/23695/7224.

21. F.O. letter signed by Collier to Ministry of Supply, 9 Jan. 1940; FO ibid., 23696/7892. War Cabinet Minutes (WM) 108 (39) 5, 109 (39) 5 and 120 (39) 8; CAB, idem. On the participation of the British planes in the fighting, see a detailed study on the air warfare during the Finnish campaign 1939-40; Risto Pajari, *Talvisota ilmassa*, Helsinki 1971, pp. 150-1 and 202-3.

22. See Gripenberg's diary, 13 Dec. 1939 and 4 Jan., 1940 VA, and Niukkanen, op. cit., p. 167.

23. See C.O.S. report "Assistance to Finland and the Scandinavian countries" with supplements; FO ibid., 7927, and Gripenberg 1960, p. 88.

24. COS (39) 27; CAB 80/5. See T. K. Derry, *The Campaign in Norway* (History of the Second World War, United Kingdom Military Series), London 1952, p. 9.

25. Collier's minute, 30 Nov. 1939; FO 371/23694/6776. Sargent's comment, 27 Dec. 1939; FO idem/23646/7782.

26. Wahlbäck, 1964 p. 212. F.O. to Monson, 30 Nov. 1939; tel. no. 180; FO idem, 6753.

27. Monson to F.O., 19 Dec. 1939, tel. no. 240; FO 371/23696/7639. Report of Dormer, British Minister in Oslo 31 March 1940, on political events of 1939 in Norway; FO 419/34. Cf. minute by Collier, 13 December 1939; FO 371/23695/7353. A lecture given by C.J. Hambro, 16 March 1940, at meeting of the society 'Nordens frihet' in Stockholm:

note by the press section of the Finnish Legation; UA 109 C.

28. Monson to F.O., 3 Dec. 1939, tel. no. 130 with comments; FO 371/23694/6876. Corresponding telegrams from Stockholm and Oslo to the F.O. in group FO 371/23695. See Woodward, op. cit., p. 21. Cf. however, Carlgren, op. cit., pp. 67-8.

29. Dormer to F.O. 12 Dec. 1939, tel. no. 346; FO ibid., 7332.

30. WM 116 (39) 7, CAB ibid. Wuorimaa, op. cit., p. 119. On the reactions of the Soviet Government and of Ribbentrop, see Schulenburg to Ribbentrop, 9 Dec. 1939, tel. no. 903, and Ribbentrop to Schulenburg, 10 Dec. 1939, tel. no. 1939 in *DGFP* nos. 432 and 435 with notes.

31. Minute by F. Maclean, 13 Dec. 1939; FO 371/23695/7353. Author's italics.

32. WM 116 (39) 7.

33. The following description dealing with the question of Finland at the League of Nations in December 1939 is based, unless otherwise stated, on my article 'Suomen kysymys Kansainliitossa joulukuussa 1939' in *Historiallinen Aikakauskirja*, No. 4, 1971, pp. 323-38.

34. Memorandum concerning the negotiations of the Nordic foreign ministers in Stockholm, 18-19 Oct. 1939, during the meeting of the Nordic heads of state; UA 109 C1. Corresponding memorandum by the Norwegian Foreign Ministry; NUD 47 C 2.

35. Holma 6 Feb. 1940, r. no. 2; UA 109 5 Cb.

36. James Barros, *Betrayal from Within: Joseph Avenol, Secretary-General of the League of Nations*, 1933-1940. New Haven, Conn. 1969.

37. J. Paul-Boncour, *Entre deux guerres, Souvenirs sur la IIIe République: Sur les chemins de la défaite*, 1935-1940. Paris 1946, p. 184.

38. Author's italics. When Koht allegedly phoned Tanner on 5 Dec. and remarked that certain quarters had proposed the expulsion of the Soviet Union from the League of Nations, Tanner gave a sullen laugh and said, "What good is it for us?" Minute by Koht, 5 Dec. 1939; NUD 35 G 2, III.

39. Barros, pp. 203-4. Cf. Halvdan Koht, *For fred og fridom i krigstid* 1939-1940. Oslo 1957, pp. 112-15.

40. see Michel, p. 224.

41. Barros, p. 199, and sources mentioned.

42. Paul Reynaud, *Au coeur de la mêlée*. Paris 1951, p. 364. See Michel, pp. 56 and 193, and Shirer, pp. 578-80 and 596-601.

43. William C. Bullitt's Papers, which are deposited at Yale University, New Haven, Conn., are still closed for this period.

44. The United Kingdom LN delegation at Geneva to F.O., 11 Dec. 1939, tel. no. 27; FO 371/23695/7331. Cf. Paul Boncour, pp. 187-9. Author's italics.

45. Memorandum signed by A. W. G. Randall 4 Dec. 1939; FO ibid., 23694/7111.

46. Minute in Halifax's own hand, 7 Dec. 1939; FO ibid., 7123. Cf. the similar reactions of Sir A. Cadogan, Permanent Under-Secretary at the FO, on 4 December: David Dilks (ed.), *The Diaries of Sir Alexander Cadogan*, 1938-1945, London 1971, p. 235 (*Cadogan Diaries*).

47. Memorandum by R. A. Butler, 5 Dec. 1939; FO 371/23695/7222.
48. Butler's speech at the Council of the League of Nations, 14 Dec. 1939; Council of the League of Nations: Minutes of the 100th meeting, p. 8, Butler's report, 22 Dec. 1939, from Geneva; FO 419/34. Cf. Barros, p. 204.
49. Barros, p. 201. Cf. Koht, p. 115.
50. Representatives of the following countries were chosen as members of the committee: Bolivia, Canada, Egypt, France, India, Ireland, Norway, Portugal, Sweden, Thailand, United Kingdom, Uruguay and Venezuela. Norway and Sweden which, together with Ireland, stood for a moderate view, had difficulties in making the committee accept the tactical decision to appeal once more to the conflicting parties to stop the hostilities and start negotiations. This measure, approved by Finland in advance according to Unden, who made the initiative, was useless in itself: it was hardly to be expected that the Soviet Union would give an affirmative answer, at least not within twenty-four hours as demanded in the Secretary-General's appeal, even to Chamberlain's indignation. Société des Nations: Journal de la Vingtième session de l'Assemblée no. 2, 12 Dec. 1939, p. 2. *The Times*, 15 Dec. 1939.
51. Cf. Nevakivi article, p. 336. Author's italics.
52. Cf. Koht, pp. 113-15.
53. Georges Bonnet, *Le Quai d'Orsay sous trois républiques*, Paris 1961, p. 317.
54. Michael Foot, *Aneurin Bevan, a biography, I: 1897-1945,* London 1962, p. 312.
55. Cf. Niukkanen, p. 242; Paasikivi, op. cit., p. 128, and Tanner, p. 108.
56. Undated minute by Sir A. Cadogan; FO 371/23696/7581.
57. Barros, p. 205.

Chapter IV, pp. 62-74

1. WM 111 (39) 6, CAB 65/4, PRO.
2. FO 3H/23695/7224, ibid.
3. WM 116 (39) 8, idem. It should be added that even Lord Beaverbrook, though in many ways of the same thinking with Churchill and consequently careful when dealing with Russia, had in the middle of December written to Churchill, Hoare and Hore-Belisha, suggesting that the United States should be urged to back the forming of a Scandinavian front, possibly with the assistance of Czechs, Poles and even Canadians, in support of Finland, and eventually even to join the war against the Soviet Union. A. J. P. Taylor, *Beaverbrook*, London 1972, p. 400.
4. Memorandum by Halifax, 15 Dec. 1939, "Situation in Scandinavia and the possible results of the invasion of Finland"; WP (39) 164; CAB 67/3.
5. WM 118 (39), ibid.

6. Medlicott 1952, p. 181. Matérial concerning the discussions on the prevention of Swedish iron ore reaching Germany in general: group CAB 21/1387.
7. Ibid. Cf. Derry, op. cit. 11.
8. Medlicott 1952, pp. 186-8. On Thyssen also Paul Reynaud, *Mémoires II: Envers et contre tous*, Paris 1963, p. 317.
9. Churchill, p. 420.
10. Cf. ibid., pp. 430-2, Derry, p. 9, and Medlicott 1952, p. 147.
11. Churchill, pp. 543-4, and Harold Macmillan, *The Blast of War*, London 1967, p. 25.
12. Churchill, pp. 430-3.
13. Sir Ronald Campbell, British Ambassador in Paris to FO, 21 Dec. 1939, tel. no. 950; FO 371/23696/7745, PRO. Holma to UM, 7 January 1940, r. no. 1; UA 109 C2 e. On Flandin's opinions in particular, see Michel, pp. 226-9.
14. Gamelin, op. cit. 205. The late General Stehlin told the present writer that his impression of Daladier was similar. Cf. Michel, op. cit. p. 231.
15. Aladar Paasonen, *Marsalkan tiedustelupäällikkönä ja hallituksen asiamiehenä*, Tapiola 1974 (Col. Paasonen's memoirs), p. 84. Steinhardt, US Ambassador in Moscow, to Foreign Secretary Hull, 2 Feb. 1940, tel. no 130; *FRUS* 1940, I, pp. 590-1. It appears from French diplomatic archives that Ambassador Naggiar strongly recommended the breaking off of diplomatic relations, if not actual hostilities with the Soviet Union, and stressed that Moscow should not be given the opportunity to choose the moment of rupture.
16. On Daladier's character and activities in the winter of 1939-40; See Pertinax, *Les Fossoyers: Défaite militaire de la France, armistice, contre-révolution, I: Les derniers Chefs de la IIIème République, Gamelin, Daladier, Reynaud*, New York 1943, pp. 110-11 and 133-4.
17. Bullitt to the Foreign Secretary, 14 Dec. 1939, tel. no. 2973; *FRUS* 1939 I, p. 535.
18. Memorandum by Halifax, 16 Dec. 1939; FO ibid., 7568.
19. Chamberlain's report on the 4th meeting of the Supreme War Council to the War Cabinet, 20 Dec. 1939: WM 120 (39) 9. Cadogan's minute 21 Dec. 1939; FO 371/23696/7521. Cf. *Cadogan Diaries*, p. 238, and Clark, op. cit. 82-5.
20. Supreme War Council Conclusions 19 Dec. 1939; FO idem, 7842.
21. Holma to Tanner, 20 Dec. 1939, tel. no. 329 and, 31 Dec. 1939, letter no. 249. UM to Paris, 22 Dec. 1939, tel. no. R. 244, and the same date tel. no. L390 to London. Tel. no. c 114 to Stockholm and Oslo; UA 109 C2 e. Gripenberg to UM, 24 Dec. 1939, tel. no. 775; ibid. Cf. Carlgren, op. cit., p. 83.
22. Pakaslahti, op. cit. 234-5. Gripenberg's diary 23 Dec. 1939, VA.
23. Tanner's diary 7 March 1940; UA/VA. Cf. Paasonen, p. 88. Gripenberg to Foreign Minister, 24 Dec. 1939, tel. no. 775; UA 109 C2 e. Cf. Gripenberg, pp. 106-7, and *Cadogan Diaries*, p. 239.
24. MC 10 (39) 2, CAB 83. Cf. Clark, op. cit. pp. 85-7.
25. Ibid. and WM 122 (39) 1, p. 4; Conf. ann. CAB 65/4.

26. WM 122 (39) 1, (pp. 2 and 11) ibid.
27. Ibid., pp. 6 and 11-13.
28. *The Ironside Diaries, 1937-40* (=*Ironside Diaries*), ed. R. Macleod and Denis Kelly, London 1962, p. 188.
29. Comments by O.E. Sargent, 20 Dec. 1939, and by A. Cadogan, 21 Dec. 1939; FO idem, 7521. More on Sargent's views on Finland in *Cadogan Diaries*, p. 259.
30. WM 123 (39) 1; Conf. ann., CAB idem.
31. Ibid. Minute by Collier 27 December 1939; FO 371/23646/7933. Cf. Clark, pp. 90-1.
32. Original text of memorandum handed by Halifax to Prytz 27 Dec. 1939, pp. 10-11. Original text of memorandum handed by the French envoy in Stockholm to Günther 28 December 1939, pp. 11-12 in UD documents: *Handlingar rörande Sveriges politik under andra världskriget; Förspelet till det tyska angreppet pa Danmark och Norge den 9 april 1940* (=*Förspelet*), Stockholm 1947.
33. Erkko to UM 23 Dec. 1939, tel. no. 199; UA ibid.
34. Prytz to UD, tel. dated 5 Jan. 1940; *Förspelet*, p. 17. Author's italics.
35. See Woodward, op. cit., p. 23, and Koht, op. cit., pp. 132-4. Material concerning Norway: NUD 38 D 2/40; concerning Sweden: *Förspelet*, pp. 22-6.

Chapter V, pp. 75–95

1. C.O.S. reports, 31 Dec. 1939, "Military implications of a policy aimed at stopping the export of Swedish iron ore to Germany" (WP [39] 179) and "Stoppage of the export of iron ore to Germany: Balance of advantage between the major and minor projects" (WP [39] 180); CAB 80/6, PRO.
2. WP (39) 179, p. 6.
3. Ibid., p. 7
4. Ibid., p. 5. *Ironside Diaries*, p. 218.
5. WM (39) 123, 1, Conf. annex, CAB 65/4. My italics.
6. WP (39) 179, pp. 5 and 11.
7. Ibid., p. 23. Cf. Sir A. Cadogan's comment 21 Dec. 1939; FO 371/23696/7521, PRO.
8. WP (39) 179, p. 18.
9. Ibid., p. 21.
10. Cf., e.g., Chamberlain's speech at War Cabinet meeting 22 Dec. 1939: WM 122 (39) 1, Conf. ann.
11. Minute by Sargent 27 Dec. 1939, FO ibid., 7578. Author's italics.
12. "Le conflict russo-finlandais", anonymous undated memorandum, no. 17 in the publication by the German Foreign Ministry: *Die Geheimakten des französischen Generalstabes* 1939/41, Berlin 1941, which gives photocopies and German translations of a number of French general staff documents seized by the Germans during the campaign in France in 1940 and returned after the German collapse to the

Army Historical Section at Vincennes. As it appears (see below, fn. 43), the text concerned is the first part of *a memorandum written by the Finnish Colonel Paasonen.*

13. Tel. no 503 by Seeds, 6 Dec. 1939; FO 371/23694/7132. Minute by Collier 31 Dec. 1939; idem, 7945. However, Corbin's report on Sir Alexander's views, which the present writer has found in the official French archives, seems not to be in conformity with the latter's diary entries of the time: see e.g. *Cadogan Diaries*, p. 244.

14. WP (39) 179, p. 19. Author's italics.

15. Gripenberg's diary 2 Jan. 1940, VA.

16. Ibid., 14 Feb. 1940.

17. Cf. Gripenberg, op. cit., pp. 89 and 121-2, and Gripenberg's diary, 13 and 14 Dec. 1939 and 13, 19, 20, 24 and 26 Feb. 1940.

18. Gripenberg's diary 9 January 1940, and Gripenberg, pp. 156-7. Erkko to Premier Rÿti, letter of 12 January 1940; Ryti Papers 1, VA. Pajari, op. cit. p. 150.

19. Pajari, pp. 150, 262-3, and 268-9.

20. British air attaché in Stockholm (Johnson) to Monson, 7 Dec. 1939, letter no 38; FO 371/23645/7419. Niukkanen, op. cit. pp. 166-7, and Pajari, pp. 150-1 and 228.

21. Snow to Halifax, 21 Dec. 1939, tel. no. 238; FO 419/33 no. 208. Gripenberg's memorandum presented to Cadogan 28 Dec. 1939; FO 371/23646/7951, and Gripenberg's diary 28 Dec. 1939. Finnish Legation in London to Erkko, 22 Feb. 1940, tel. no. x-305; T 19932/35, SA, and Pajari, p. 201.

22. On the Allied armament deliveries to Finland in general, see the material in groups CAB 21/1291 and 1292, as well as in the Hankey Papers CAB 63/151. C. Barclay's memorandum, 27 Dec. 1939, which was delivered to the French; FO ibid. 7880. Cf. Gripenberg, pp. 89 and 154-5, and Niukkanen, p. 169.

23. The shipping reports in group T 19932/35 and Niukkanen, p. 168. Memorandum by Allied Military Committee, 8 Jan. 1940, "French War Material for Finland", appendix in memorandum by the War Cabinet military co-ordinating committee 10 Jan. 1940; MC (40) 10, FO 371/24797/680. Paasonen, op. cit., pp. 86-8, gives somewhat exaggerated figures, tending to include in these fourteen shipments items which did not reach Finland before the end of the hostilities.

24. Snow to Halifax, 10 Jan. 1940; FO 419/34.

25. On Ling's and Ganeval's trip to Finland the material in group UA 109 C2 c, especially Gripenberg's tel. no. 829, 31 December 1939. The envoy reported that, allegedly, Ling *had been instructed by Ironside "to discuss with Mannerheim not only the supply of war materiel but also the naval landing at Murmansk as well as political pressure on the Soviet Union".* More on Ling in Gripenberg's diary, 29-30 Dec. 1939, and 13, 15, 18 Jan. 1940, as well as in Gripenberg, pp. 97-8. Ling's r. 13 January 1940 and Collier's memorandum on discussion; FO 371/24796/606. On Ganeval's description, see Gamelin, op. cit, pp. 197-8. Cf. *Ironside, Diaries* p. 210.

26. WM 122 (39) 1 (p.7), Conf. ann.
27. WM 3 (40) 9, Conf. ann., CAB 65/11. Hore-Belisha's statement in WM 3 (40) 6, CAB 65/5. At the previous meeting on 2 January Hore-Belisha had demanded that the expeditionary force composed of regular troops be directed, instead of to Norway, to Finland by way of Petsamo whence he thought it would later be more convenient to assume control over the northern ore fields [WM 2 (40] 1). Author's italics.
28. WM 3 (40) 6.
29. MC (40) 2nd Meeting; FO 371/24796/505. Quotation from Sir Orme Sargent's speech.
30. WM 9 (40) 1, ibid, *Ironside Diaries*, pp. 196-7. UD memorandum on Wallenberg's report cabled from London, 12 January 1940: *Förspelet*, pp. 27-8. Cf. Carlgren, p. 90.
31. WM 15 (40) (with F.O. comments) and Gripenberg's diary 15-16 Jan. 1940.
32. Ibid, and F.O. to Dormer, 28 Jan. 1940, tel. no. 50; FO 371/24798/952. Cf. Pajari, pp. 153, 211 and 234.
33. MC (40) 6th Meeting Minutes.
34. *Ironside Diaries*, p. 212.
35. WM 31 (40) 1, Conf. ann. Author's italics.
36. Nevakivi, op. cit., 85-7, 90-1, and 192-3.
37. Snow's tel. no. 224, 13 Dec. 1939; FO 371/23645/7366. See also Tanner, op. cit., pp. 190, 209 and 229.
38. Tanner to Gripenberg, undated letter in Tanner's handwriting and signed by him; Gripenberg Papers, 79, VA.
39. Tanner to Gripenberg, 14 Dec. 1939, tel. no. L 376, and Gripenberg to Tanner, 16 and 18 December 1939, tels. nos. 713 and 737; VA 109 C2 d. Admiralty to F.O., 18 December 1939, letter no M/P. D. 08241/39; FO ibid., 7629.
40. Snow to F.O., 21 Dec. 1939, tel. no. 238; FO, ibid., 7675. Minute by Sargent, 22 Dec. 1939; FO ibid, UM to Holma, 23 Dec. 1939, tel. no. R. 246, and Holma to UM, 27 December 1939, tel. no. 249; VA idem. Memorandum by the French envoy in London, 23 Dec. 1939; FO ibid., 7773.
41. Daladier's statement to General Sikorsky: memorandum by Colonel Kedzior, Sikorsky's Commander-in-Chief, on the signing of the treaty between France and the Polish provisional government, 4 Jan. 1940; Archives of the Polish provisional government, file: treaties, no. 242, A IV 1/5, Sikorsky Institute (=SI), London. See Corbin's memorandum to F.O. 5 Jan. 1940: appendix in Letter no. 42 by Halifax to Campbell, 5 Jan. 1940, FO 371/24796/264. Cf. Gamelin, p. 198. Author's italics.
42. Daladier to Corbin, 17 January 1940, tel.; *Geheimakten*, no. 18. The corresponding *aide-mémoire* by Corbin to F.O. in Further Correspondence etc., XXXIII, no. 25; FO 419/34.
43. Holma to Tanner, 30 Jan. 1939, letter no. 432. Copy in Finnish of the mentioned memorandum of 24 Dec. 1939 (Ryti Papers 23) is, according to a statement by the late Colonel Paasonen to the present writer, in a letter dated 4 March 1972, drawn up by him. Its French version

(Appendix in letter no. 106/II of Colonel Melander to Foreign Minister, 11 February 1940, wherein Paasonen's letter no. 22/P/40/15 Jan. 1940) is evidently *the same document of which the German Foreign Ministry has published the first part in Geheimakten as the above-mentioned French document no. 18.*

44. Mentioned memorandum in Finnish, 24 December 1939, 'Venäjän ja Suomen selkkaus' (The Russo-Finnish conflict), pp. 3-4. Author's italics.

45. Minutes of the COS. meetings 24 and 25 January 1940; COS (40) 14-16, CAB 79/3 and memorandum by same, 2 February 1940, "French Proposals for Allied Assistance to Finland" with supplements; WP (40) 41, CAB 66/5. Cf. Jacques Minart, op. cit., p. 171 and note 1 therein.

46. Ibid., and Holma to Tanner, 18 January 1940, letter no. 231. Holma to UM, 30 January 1940, tel. no. 123; UA 109 C2 e.

47. French Proposals, WP (40) with supplements and WM 31 (40) 1 Conf. ann. Campbell to F.O. tel. dated. 28 Jan. 1940, enclosure in E.E. Budges' [COS.] letter to Cadogan, 29 January 1940, FO 371/24798/1193, and mentioned COS minutes of meetings on 24 and 25 Jan. 1940.

48. Halifax's report in the War Cabinet 2 Feb. 1940; WM 31 (40) 1, Conf. ann. and Campbell's mentioned tel. of 28 Jan. 1940. Daladier seems to have promised, even on 13 January, to Holma and Paasonen that, in London were to put up political obstacles to the operations of the Polish Navy in Petsamo, he would offer the vessels a base in France; Paasonen to foreign section of the headquarters, 22 Jan. 1940, r. no. 30/P/40; enclosure in Melander's mentioned letter to Tanner 11 February 1940. Author's italics.

49. Cf. Chamberlain's statement in the War Cabinet, 29 Jan. 1940; WM 28 (40) 7, CAB 65/5. Likewise the discussion at the War Cabinet meeting 2 Feb. 1940; WM 31 (40) 1, ibid. Negative answer of the navy Chief-of-Staff concerning the use in the Arctic of the sub-marine proposed to be delivered to the Finns; appendix in minutes of military co-ordinating committee 15 Jan. 1940; MC (40) 26.

50. On the Soviet submarines: COS. report Allied Assistance to Finland; WP (40) 36, CAB 65/5.

51. Macmillan, op. cit., p. 36.

52. Mannerheim op. cit., p. 389. See Gripenberg to Tanner, 27 Jan. 1940, tel. no. 280; UA 209 C2 e. The French Admiralty sent as liaison officer to Finland *Capitaine de frégate* Peltier, who has mentioned the Petsamo preparations in his memoirs: M. Peltier, *La Finlande dans la tourmente*, Paris 1966, pp. 109-11. Cf. Minart, p. 171, note 1. According to Peltier's own report in the French military archives, the planned operations were, at least by 20 Feb. 1940, never studied in detail.

53. Letter (unnumbered) from headquarters, signed by Lieutenant General L.O. Oesch, Chief of General Staff, to Foreign Minister, 6 Feb. 1940; UA 109 C2 c.

54. Holma's rs. 31 Dec. 1939 and 14 Jan. 1940; UA C2 e. Cf. Pertinax, op. cit. p. 133.
55. Holma's r. 14 Jan. 1940 and Gamelin, p. 198, Minart, p. 171, and Reynaud 1951, p. 366.
56. Cf. e.g. Pertinax, p. 134.
57. Tanner's tels. nos. L85 and R39, 3 Feb. 1940; UA ibid.
58. Tanner, p. 144. On the Swedish indignation cf. Carlgren, p. 126 and note 195.
59. Bullitt to Foreign Secretary, 15 Jan. 1940, tel. no. 80; *FRUS* 1940 I, p. 277. Cf. Holma's r. no. 1, 7 Jan. 1940; UA ibid. My italics.
60. Gamelin, pp. 196-7 and note 1 on the latter. Minart, pp. 171-5. A. Bethouart, *Cinq années d'espérance, Mémoires de guerre 1939-1945.* Paris 1968, pp. 9-21.

Chapter VI, pp. 96-120

1. *Ironside Diaries*, op. cit. 213.
2. Mentioned COS report French proposals for Allied Assistance in Finland, 2 Feb. 1940. Ironside's statement in the War Cabinet 2 Feb. 1940; WM 31 (40) 1, Conf. ann. CAB 65/4 PRO. Cf. Clark, op. cit., pp. 135-6. Author's italics.
3. Gamelin, op. cit., p. 200. Author's italics.
4. French material in the Vincennes archives. Chamberlain's statement at the War Cabinet meeting 7 Feb. 1940; WM 35 (40) 1, idem.
5. Churchill, op.cit., 442-3, *Ironside Diaries*, pp. 214-15. Cf. *Cadogan Diaries*, pp. 252-3, and Clark, pp. 137-43.
6. *Ironside Diaries*, p. 215.
7. Cf. WM 1 (40) 1, Conf. ann. 'If this recommendation was accepted, Scandinavia would have to be regarded, for the time being, as the decisive theatre of war. Subject to being secure at home and in France, all else would have to be relegated to second place.'
8. COS r. 14 Feb. 1940 "Intervention in Scandinavia: Plans and Implications"; WP (40) 35, CAB 66/5.
9. COS r. 14 Feb. 1940 "The Employment of Allied Land Forces in Scandinavia and Finland"; WP (40) 51.
10. Ibid., p. 2.
11. Joint report by COS and FO 18 Feb. 1940 "Scandinavia — Assistance to Finland, The Time Factor", especially p. 5; WP (40) 59.
12. Chamberlain's statement in the War Cabinet 7 February 1940.
13. Cf., however, Woodward, op. cit. 25.
14. WP (40) 59, p. 1. Author's italics.
15. WM 35, (40) 1, Conf. ann. CAB 65/11.
16. See Chew, op. cit., pp. 140-4, and 157-78; Cf. Upton, op. cit., pp. 83-5, 89-90 and 107-11. According to Meretskov, Soviet superiority as compared to the Finnish forces was in March only 23:10 in infantry and 28:10 in artillery, but absolute only in tanks: op. cit., p. 107.

17. War Cabinet minutes 9 Feb. 1940; WM (40) 37, 5 and 12 February 1940; WM 39 (40) 6, idem. The final instructions to Ling, 18 Feb. 1940, as supplement to War Cabinet minutes WM 45 (40) 1, idem.

18. WM 39 (40) 6, ibid. Cf. Gripenberg's Diary 10 February 1940, VA.

19. Comte de Vaux Saint-Cyr, 'Ma mission en Finlande, Souvenirs', *Revue Deux Mondes* 15 Oct. 1953, p. 724.

20. Blücher, op. cit., pp. 165-8, Tanner, op. cit., pp. 117-23. Memorandum by O. G. Sargent, 19 January 1940; appendix in Halifax's memorandum 'Volunteers for Finland' 22 January 1940; WP (40) 29, FO 371/24798/937. PRO. Upton, pp. 92-7.

21. For a concise description of the diplomatic developments in January 1940 see Upton, op. cit. (1974), pp. 92-7.

22. Tanner, p. 125. Cf. Wahlbäck 1964, pp. 267-9.

23. Tanner, p. 149 and especially pp. 150-1. Tanner's diary 8 Feb. 1940, UA and VA. Author's italics.

24. Tanner, pp. 152-3 and diary of same 9-11 Feb. 1940.

25. Tanner, pp. 153-7. Tanner's diary 11-12 Feb. 1940. Text in *Helsingin Sanomat*, 12 Feb. 1940. Cf. Schoenfeld to the foreign secretary, 13 Feb. 1940, tel. no. 87; *FRUS* 1940 I, p. 289.

26. Tanner's minutes of the meeting of the foreign affairs committee 12 Feb. 1940; appendix to Tanner's diary. Tanner, pp. 154-5.

27. Tanner's diary 13 Feb. 1940. Tanner, pp. 157-60.

28. Tanner's diary, 20 Feb. 1940, and Tanner, pp. 160-3.

29. Tanner's diary, 23 Feb. 1940, and Tanner, pp. 170-2.

30. WM 7 (40) 8, Conf. ann. Cf. WM 8 (40) 1, ibid.

31. Cf. Koht, op. cit., 126-7, and Carlgren, op. cit., pp. 91-2.

32. Halifax's report in the War Cabinet 6 Jan. 1940; WM 6 (40) 8, Conf. ann. Memorandum by Foreign Affairs Counsellor Jens Bull, 13 Jan. 1940, and minute by Foreign Minister Koht, 15 Jan. 1940; NUD 38 D 2/40 I. Cf. Premier Hansson's diary entry of 5 March 1940 in Krister Wahlbäck, *Regeringen och kriget, ur stadstradens dagbocker 1939-41,* Stockholm 1972 (=Wahlbäck 1972), p. 64—V.A.L. Mallet had succeeded Monson as British envoy in Stockholm 26 Jan. 1940.

33. WM 10 (40), p. 115, Conf. ann.

34. WM 16 (40) 6.

35. English text of Halifax's statement to Prytz, 19 Jan. 1940, and its Swedish translation; see *Förspelet*, pp. 35-9, and Further Correspondence, etc., XXXIII, no. 33; FO 419/34. Memorandum of Halifax's corresponding statement to Colban in the latter's letter no. 196 to UD, 19 Jan. 1940; NUD 38 D 2/40 I. Memorandum by Koht 15 Jan. 1940, ibid. On Prytz's assurances see Gripenberg's diary 20 Jan. 1940.

36. Tanner, p. 116, and Mallet to Halifax, 19 Jan. 1940, letter no. 20; FO 371/24798/1048.

37. Wahlbäck 1964, pp. 268-70 and 278.

38. Cf. ibid., p. 358, *Ironside Diaries*, p. 225, and Collier's memorandum 30 Nov. 1939; FO 371/23694/667, and Gripenberg's diary, 19 Nov. 1940.

39. Derry, op. cit., pp. 13-14; Churchill, pp. 443-7; Koht, pp. 164-9. Discussion of Daladier's proposal in the War Cabinet 22 Feb. 1940;

WM 49 (40) 5, ibid. Cf. Daladier's tel. to Corbin 21 Feb. 1940; *Geheimakten*, no. 21.

40. WM 6 (40) 8, ibid.
41. Ironside's statement 21 Feb. 1940; WM 48 (40) 6, Churchill's statement 3 Jan. 1940; WM 2 (40) 1.
42. Mentioned WP 35 (40), pp. 2 and 3, and *Ironside Diaries*, p. 221.
43. Minutes of the Finnish Cabinet meeting 25 February 1940.
44. Mentioned tel. by Daladier to Corbin 21 Feb. 1940.
45. Minute by Gunther 2 March 1940. *Förspelet*, p. 119. Carlgren, pp. 113-14. Cf. copy of handwritten instructions by Daladier 19 Jan. 1940; *Geheimakten*, no. 19.
46. Paul Stehlin, *Témoignage pour l'histoire*, Paris 1964, p. 215, and author's interview with General Stehlin.
47. Daladier's instructions of 19 Jan. 1940. Memorandum of 22 Feb. 1940, headed by 3rd section of the major French headquarters, 'Etude sur une action destinee a priver l'Allemagne et l'U.R.S.S. des ressources en petrole du Caucase,' *Geheimakten*, no. 22. On the Allied plans of intervention in Russia, in general, see the following study published only when the present study was going to press: Hans-Joachim Lorbeer, *Westmachte gegen die Sowjetunion 1939-1941* (Freiburg-im-Breisgau, 1975).
48. On the formation of Weygand's force, see Gamelin, pp. 206-14.
49. Henri de Kérillis, *De Gaulle Dictateur, une grande mystification de l'histoire*, Montreal 1945, pp. 363-4.
50. Reynaud 1951, pp. 372-3.
51. *Geheimakten*, pp. 212-15, 227-64, and 278-80. COS report dated March 1940 'Military Implications of Hostilities with Russia,' pp. 9-12; WP (40) 91, CAB 66/6. Cf. VM 70 (40), p. 120 and Reynaud 1951, pp. 369-71. According to the US Ambassador in Moscow, the Soviet Government had in fact moved additional troops into the Caspian Sea area in order to meet the Allied threat: Steinhardt to Secretary of State, 9 March 1940; *FRUS* 1940 I, pp. 276-7.
52. Reynaud 1951, pp. 371-4. Author's italics.
53. Steinhardt to Secretary of State, 8 Feb. 1940, tel. no. 151; *FRUS*, ibid., pp. 591-2. Cf. Maisky, op. cit., pp. 43-4.
54. Daladier's instructions to Naggiar seen by the present author in French diplomatic records. Souritz was pronounced *persona non grata* probably on the pretext that, after the conclusion of the peace of Moscow, he had sent Stalin an open telegram congratulating him on the victory over the 'plutocracies' (the Western Powers). Cf. Chargé d'affaires Murphy to Secretary of State, 19 March 1940, tel. no. 306, and Steinhardt to same, 27 March 1940, tel. no. 331; FRUS, ibid., pp. 593-4. Also cf. Maisky, op. cit. p. 44. Cf. Holma's r. no. 1, 7 Jan. 1940; UA 5C 6.
55. See Ernst Wigforss, *Minnen III: 1932-1949*, Stockholm 1954, p. 148.
56. Maisky, pp. 42-3.
57. Colin Cooke, *The Life of Richard Stafford Cripps*, London 1957, pp. 258-62. Cf. Clark, pp. 106-8 and 156-8.

58. Halifax's report of the discussion; WM 28 (40) 2, CAB 65/5. Maisky, p. 48. Woodward, pp. 29-30.
59. Cf. Clark, p. 110.
60. Maisky, p. 48. Author's italics.
61. Ibid. and Halifax's statement to War Cabinet 23 Feb. 1940; WM 50 (40) 2.
62. Cf. p. 255. Butler's memorandum on the discussion, 24 Feb. 1940, as appendix A in Halifax's memorandum (same date) 'Finland and Russia'; WP (40) 72, CAB 66/6. Maisky, p. 49. On the peace terms see Tanner, pp. 276 and 304. Author's italics.
63. Butler's memorandum 24 Feb. 1940. Cf. Maisky, ibid.
64. Halifax's memorandum 24 Feb. 1940 and Tanner, pp. 275-276 and 304.
65. *Istoriya diplomatii*, op. cit., IV, p. 30. *Cadogan Diaries*, p. 255. Corbin's reports in the French diplomatic records. WM 61 (40) (p. 40), CAB 65/6.
66. See Collier's memorandum, 13 Jan. 1940, on the discussion with Ling; FO 371/24796/606.
67. Ryti Papers 2.
68. Coulet, op. cit. pp. 70-1, Pertinax, p. 190.
69. Annales de l'Assemblée Nationale, ibid., 19 March 1940, p. 60. Author's italics.
70. See Gamelin, p. 194, fn. 3, Stehlin, p. 217, and Vaux de Saint-Cyr, mentioned article, p. 721.
71. See memoirs of an officer of the reserves in Béthouart's brigade: M. J. Torris, *Narvik*, Paris 1963, p. 28. Author's interview with General Béthouart. *Ironside Diaries*, op. cit., 217. COS 42 (40) 2, Conf. ann. (29 Feb. 1940) CAB 79/85. Cf. minutes of War Cabinet 13 Feb. 1940; WM 40 (40) 6, Conf. ann. Progress Report, week ending...28 Feb. 1940, appendix WM 55 (40), ibid.
72. Halifax's statement in the War binCaet 17 Feb. 1940; WM 44 (40) 5, ibid. *News of the World*, 18 and 25 Feb. 1940.
73. WM 45 (40) 1, Conf. ann.
74. Ibid. and Progress Report, 28 Feb. 1940. General Audet, 'L' Expédition de Norvège: Namsos février-mai 1940,' *Revue historique de l'armée*, no. 1, 1957, p. 104.
75. Audet, pp. 104-7.
76. Annales de l'Assemblée Nationale, idem, 9 Feb. 1940.

Chapter, VII pp. 121–45

1. Minutes on Foreign Affairs Committee meeting 23 Feb. 1940 at 6 P.M Supplement in Tanner's diary, ibid. UA and VA. On developments at the Isthmus front, see esp. Upton, op. cit. (1974), pp. 111-19.
2. Vilhelm Assarsson, *I skuggan av Stalin*, Stockholm 1963, p. 16. Cf. Wahlbäck 1972, p. 65.
3. Heinrichs, op. cit. p. 157.

4. Paasikivi, op. cit. p. 152.
5. Foreign Affairs Committee minutes, 23 Feb., ibid.
6. Tanner, op. cit., pp. 175-8, agrees almost word for word with Tanner's diary 24 Feb. 1940. Cf. Vereker to FO 25 Feb. tel. no. 141; supplement WM 52 (40) 7, Conf. ann. CAB 65/11, PRO.
7. Tanner, p. 178, also his diary.
8. Ibid, pp. 284-5, Tanner's diary 24 Feb. 1940. Tudeer's minutes of Cabinet meeting 25 Feb. 1940 at 3 p.m., supplement in Tanner's diary. Vereker's version of the discussion in his tel. no. 142, 25 Feb. 1940; supplement WM, ibid. Vereker mentioned that he had stated the number of the auxiliary force at 20,000 men.
9. Ryti's statement 25 Feb. 1940; Minutes of the Finnish Cabinet, ibid.
10. Idem. On President Kallio, Tanner, p. 179. Author's italics.
11. Tanner, pp. 180-6, especially p. 293.
12. COS 41 (40) 3/27 Feb. 1940; CAB 79/85.
13. WM 52 (40) 7.
14. Tanner's diary 28 Feb. 1940; Tanner, pp. 187-8.
15. Minutes on cabinet session 29 February 1940 at 4 P.M. especially pp. 1 and 5; Tanner's diary, 19 Feb. 1940, Tanner, pp. 193-5
16. Ibid., especially p. 194. Pakaslahti, op. cit., p. 260. Magny's instructions as they appear from French official archives.
17. Urho Kekkonen, 'Pekka Peitsi silloin ja tänään,' *Suomen Kuvalehti* 3 Dec. 1966.
18. Pakaslahti, pp. 263-4. Tanner's diary and Tanner, pp. 191-3. Tanner's minutes of Diet Foreign Affairs Committee meeting 29 Feb. 1940 at 6 P.M. supplement in Tanner's diary.
19. Pakaslahti, p. 259.
20. Ibid., p. 258.
21. Ibid., p. 259.
22. Halifax's memorandum presented at War Cabinet meeting 29 Feb. 1940 on discussion between Sir Alexander Cadogan and Ambassador Corbin the same morning; WM 55 (40) 6, Conf. ann. CAB 65/11. Holma's tels. nos. 254 and 255, 29 February 1940; UA 109 C2 e. Author's italics. As demonstrated by Holma's r. of 8 March 1940, the envoy still considered that he had acted on the instructions he had received. Communication no. 1141, UA, ibid.
23. Holma's mentioned tels. and Holma to Ryti 29 February, tel. no. 258; UA idem. Tanner, pp. 202-3, and Pakaslahti, p. 259.
24. Ironside's statement at War Cabinet meeting 28 February 1940; WM 54 (40) 4, Conf. ann. CAB, ibid. On French military assistance, Holma to Tanner 16 February 1940, letter no. 694; UA ibid., and Daladier's statement at the secret session of the Chamber of Deputies 19 March 1940; Annales de l'Assemblée Nationale, ibid. Reactions of the War Cabinet at meeting 1 March 1940; WM 56 and 57 (40) 1, esp. the latter, p. 5. Conf. ann. CAB 65/12.
25. WM 55 (40) 6.
26. Ibid., p. 4.
27. Chamberlain's statement at War Cabinet meeting 1 March 1940; WM 56 (40) 1.

28. Ibid. and WM 57 (40) and Gripenberg's diary 1 March 1940.
29. Vereker's tel. no. 170 of 4 March 1940 as reported by Halifax at War Cabinet meeting 4 March 1940.
30. Halifax's report at War Cabinet meeting 1 March 1940; WM 57 (40) Gripenberg to UM 3 March 1940, tel. no. 682; 109 C.
31. Cf. King Salter's tel. no. 5, 2 March 1940; WM 60 (40) 6; Conf. ann. CAB, ibid.
32. Gripenberg's diary 26 Feb. 1940, VA, and War Cabinet minutes 27 Feb. 1940; WM 53 (40) 11, CAB 65/5.
33. WM 53 (40) 11 War Cabinet minutes 1 March 1940; WM 57 (40), p. 7. Author's italics.
34. WM 56 (40) 1, esp. p. 4. Author's italics.
35. Ibid. Memoranda of British and French Legations in Oslo to the Norwegian Foreign Ministry 2 March 1940; NUD 35 G 2, VIII. The former and memorandum of British Legation in Stockholm to Swedish Foreign Ministry 2 March 1940 with its Swedish translation; *Förspelet*, pp. 120-2.
36. WM 56 (40) 1, esp. pp. 4 and 5. Gripenberg's diary 3 March 1940. Cf. *Cadogan Diaries*, p. 257.
37. WM 59 (40), esp. p. 10; Conf. ann. CAB ibid. Cf. *Cadogan Diaries*, p. 258.
38. WM 57 (40), esp. p. 4; Conf. ann, CAB ibid.
39. Halifax's statement at War Cabinet 2 March 1940. WM 58 (40) 4, Conf. ann. CAB ibid.
40. WM 59 (40) 6, and WM 60 (40) 6, ibid.
41. Gripenberg's diary 5 March 1940.
42. WM 58 (40) 4 and WM 60 (40) 6 with supplements.
43. WM 58 (40) 4; Tanner to Gripenberg, 5 March 1940, tel. no. L 188 UA 109 C 2 e. Cf. Öhqvist, op. cit., p. 317. Gamelin, op. cit. 197-8. The quotation of Ganeval in a private letter written in his own hand and deposited in the Vincennes archives. The opinion expressed therein was confirmed by General Ganeval in a personal interview with the present writer. Author's italics.
44. Tanner's diary 3 March 1940 and Tanner, op. cit., pp. 202-3.
45. Minutes of the Finnish Cabinet meeting 3 March 1940 at 11 a.m. in Tanner's diary. Cf. *Cadogan Diaries*, p. 258.
46. Same on 3 March at 4 p.m. Tanner, pp. 203. Cf. Paasikivi, op. cit., p. 168.
47. Minutes of the Finnish Cabinet meeting on 5 March 1940 at 10 a.m., pp. 2 and 3. Heinrichs, op. cit. pp. 166-7.
48. Minutes of the Finnish Cabinet, ibid., p. 2.
49. WM 61 (40) 5, Conf. ann. CAB 65/12. Cf. Cadogan, 6 March, on the Finns seeking peace, 'Secretly, I shall be glad....'; *Cadogan Diaries*, p. 259.
50. WM 62 (40) 7, ibid.
51. Foreign Minister to Gripenberg 8 March 1940, tel. no. L 194; UA 109 C 2 e, and WM 62 (40) 1. Author's italics.

52. See Paasikivi, p. 176, and Pakaslahti, p. 271. Tanner to legation in Stockholm (further to Moscow) 8 March 1940, tel. no. 1; UA ibid.
53. Legation in London to Foreign Minister 5 March 1940, tel. no. 707; UA ibid. Minutes of Finnish Cabinet meeting 6 March 1940 at 11 a.m., p. 3. Paasonen, op. cit., p. 99.
54. Pakaslahti, p. 274. Tanner's diary 7 March 1940. Cf. Tanner, pp. 219-20. Paasonen, pp. 100-1.
55. Pakaslahti, ibid. Cf. Mannerheim, op. cit., 385-6. Memorandum of 7 March 1940, on title page in Tanner's hand 'Paasonen 7 March 1940'. Tanner Papers 27, VA. The memorandum draws attention to the fact that it was now exaggeratedly promised that the British 24th Guards Brigade and the ski troop collected by Ironside would also be sent to Finland, while it had earlier been intended to leave them at Narvik and in the Kiruna-Gällivare area. No military reports given to the Cabinet give any evidence that these forces, not to speak of the three full-strength divisions of the second echelon, would really have been destined for Finland.
56. Mentioned memorandum of 7 March 1940, p. 2. Ryti's report at Finnish Cabinet meeting 6 March 1940 at 11 a.m. Mentioned minutes, p. 3. Cf. *Ironside Diaries*, 224.
57. Memorandum of 7 March 1940, pp. 4 and 8.
58. Tanner's diary 8 March 1940. Tanner, pp. 353-4. Cf. Pakaslahti, p. 276. Note written in Pakaslahti's hand and signed with his initials 8 March 1940, UA, ibid, and Mannerheim's letter to the Foreign Minister 8 March 1940 at 7 p.m.; Tanner Papers 27. UM to Mannerheim 9 March 1940, tel. no. 5105; UA ibid. Mannerheim, p. 387.
59. Mentioned minutes 6 March 1940 at 11 a.m., p. 3.
60. Ryti's draft memoirs, p. 187; Ryti papers, VA.
61. Tel. of Swedish envoy in Paris to Swedish Foreign Ministry; *Förspelet*, p. 133. Holma to Ryti, mentioned letter no. 114, 8 March 1940.
62. Halifax's report at the War Cabinet meeting 9 March 1940; WM 64 (40) 5, p. 1, Conf. ann. CAB 65/12. Ambassador Steinhardt to Secretary of State Cordell Hull 9 March 1940, tel. no. 264; *FRUS* 1940 I, pp. 306-7. Holma to Finnish foreign ministry 8 March 1940, tel. no. 316; Tanner Papers, ibid.
63. WM 66 (40) 2, p. 8; Conf. ann., ibid.
64. Journal Officiel du 13 Mars 1940; Débats parlamentaires no. 24; Chambre des députés, Séance du mardi 12 mars 1940, p. 508. Annales de l' Assemblée Nationale, ibid., 16 March 1940.
65. Journal Officiel du 13 Mars 1940, ibid., p. 508.
66. Halifax's report at War Cabinet meeting 8 March 1940; WM 62 (40) 7, p. 4; Conf. ann. Gripenberg's diary 7 March 1940; WM 63 (40) 4; Conf. ann. Report on Gripenberg's and Halifax's discussion; WP (40) 88, CAB 66/6.
67. WM 63 (40) 4, Conf. ann. Gripenberg's diary 9 March 1940. Cf. Gripenberg 1960, pp. 137-8.
68. Cf. Gripenberg, pp. 135-6. Pakaslahti, pp. 279-80. Memorandum in English 9 March 1940; appendix in Tanner's tel. no. S 109 dated 10

March 1940 at 2.15 a.m.; copy in UA 109 C 2 e. Cf. Mannerheim, p. 387.

69. WM 63 (40) 4, Conf. ann.
70. Pakaslahti, ibid. Cf. Tanner, pp. 233-4. Halifax's report at War Cabinet meeting 11 March 1940; WM 65 (40) 6, pp. 1 and 9; Conf. ann. Gripenberg's diary 10 and 11 March 1940.
71. Gripenberg to Finnish Foreign Ministry 9 March 1940, tel. no. 726, and telegram thereon of general headquarters (Melander) to Foreign Ministry of same date; UA 109 C 2 e. Minutes of Finnish Cabinet meeting 9 March 1940 at 2 p.m., p. 6, ibid. Cf. Pakaslahti, pp. 282-3. Gripenberg, pp. 137-40. Discussion on the matter at War Cabinet meeting 11 March 1940; WM 65 (40) 6; Conf. ann. See *Cadogan Diaries*, p. 261.
72. Chiefs-of-Staff Committee meeting 11 March 1940 at 3 p.m., CAB 79/85.
73. Halifax's report of War Cabinet meeting 12 March 1940; WM 66 (40) 2, pp. 7-8; Conf. ann. Cf. Tanner, p. 236. See *Cadogan Diaries*, pp. 261-2.
74. Text of note of British legation 12 March 1940, see *Förspelet*, p. 153.
75. Tanner's Diary 12 March 1940, and Tanner, p. 248. Stockholm (and later Moscow) was not informed until 13 March at 1.20 a.m. by tel. no. 14; UA 109 C 2 e. For the peace conditions see Upton, pp. 148 and 153-5.

Chapter VIII, pp. 146-63

1. See Clark op. cit., 185-6 and the sources quoted therein. War Cabinet decision on the instructions 12 March 1940; WM 66 (40) 2, pp. 1-2; Conf. ann. CAB 65/12, *PRO*. Cf. *Ironside Diaries*, op. cit., 226-8, WM 66 (40) 2, p. 6, and COS report on assistance to Finland: COS (40) 264 (S), CAB 66/6. Author's italics.
2. Same. Quotation: COS (40) 51st meeting/12; Conf. ann. CAB 79/85. Author's italics.
3. Tryggve Lie, *Leve eller dφ, Norge i krig*. Oslo 1955, pp. 80-1, and sources mentioned therein.
4. Hubatsch, op. cit., p. 47, note 11.
5. Admiral Auphan, 'A propos de l'expédition du Norvège', *Ecrits de Paris*, no. 47, Sept. 1948, p. 46. Béthouart, op. cit., p. 20.
6. Minutes of War Cabinet meeting 14 March 1940; WM 68 (40) 4; Conf. ann. Gripenberg's diary 13 March 1940, VA. See *Ironside Diaries*, p. 229. Author's italics.
7. Minutes of War Cabinet meeting 15 March 1940; WM 69 (40) 5; CAB 65/6. Gripenberg 1960, pp. 143-4.
8. WM 69 (40) 5, ibid.
9. WM 93 (40) 13, ibid. WM 71 (40) 12, CAB 65/6.
10. Churchill's memorandum on effects of the Soviet-Finnish peace on naval situation 14 March 1940; WP (40) 96; CAB 66/6. War Cabinet minutes 1 March 1940; WM 56 (40) 1, p. 3; Conf. ann. (CAB 65/12).
11. Same 4 March 1940; WM 59 (40) 6, p. 9; ibid. War Cabinet minutes

14 March 1940; WM 68 (40) 4, p. 1, ibid. Cf. Churchill's memorandum 14 March 1940.

12. Same, esp. pp. 4-5, and Medlicott 1952, p. 192.
13. See WM 68 (40) 4, pp. 4-5, ibid., and WM 70 (40) 10, CAB 65/6.
14. Macmillan, op. cit., pp. 53-59.
15. Reports of Swedish envoy in Paris to Swedish foreign ministry 12-15 March; *Förspelet*, pp. 155-62.
16. Halifax's report at War Cabinet meeting 17 March 1940; WM 70 (40) 5; CAB 65/6.
17. Undated French draft memorandum; Dok. no. 29 in *Geheimakten*, op. cit. 253. The English translation of the note in Further Correspondence, etc. (part XXXIII), pp. 142-3; FO 419/34. Author's italics.
18. Same, p. 254, and draft resolution in French of the Supreme War Council sixth session 28 March 1940; Dok. no. 30, ibid., p. 255. The English draft: doc. no. 135 in Further Correspondence, etc. FO 419/34. Cf. Mallet's letter to Gunther 5 March 1940; *Förspelet*, p. 235. Cf. Clark, p. 243.
19. Holma's report no. 5, 20 March 1940; UA 5 C 6.
20. Report no. 3 of same, 17 March 1940, ibid. Halifax's report on General Gamelin's statement at War Cabinet meeting 18 March 1940; WM 71 (40) 12; CAB 65/6. On return of the French trainers, see Béthouart, op. cit., p. 59.
21. See Pertinax, op. cit. 192-6. Reynaud 1951, pp. 375-6. Cf. Holma's report no. 4, 21 March 1940; UA ibid.
22. Annales de l'Assemblée Nationale, ibid., 19 March 1940, p. 71.
23. Just before the German aggression on Scandinavia the French proposed to London that the return of no material delivered to Finland should be requested. See Halifax's memorandum on the question; WP (40) 125; CAB 66/6. Cf. Holma to Foreign Minister Rolf Witting 30 March 1940, letter no. 1786; UA reports: Paris. Cf. Clark, op. cit., pp. 242-3. Cf. on Reynaud, however, Carlgren, op. cit., p. 136.
24. See Derry, op. cit. pp. 25-6 and 39-41. Cf. Churchill, op. cit., pp. 467-473.
25. Derry, pp. 60-3. Béthouart, pp. 21-4. Audet, mentioned article, p. 121.
26. Derry, p. 63.
27. Ibid, pp. 83-9. Béthouart, pp. 24-7. Stehlin, op. cit., pp. 242-9. Cf. Audet, pp. 121-4.
28. Stehlin, pp. 250-4.
29. Béthouart, p. 27. Stehlin, p. 248. Derry, pp. 88, 196, 198-201, and 209-11. On the resumption of the ore transports, same, pp. 211 and 229.
30. Quotation from Mackesy's official report: Derry, p. 151. On the equipment situation, ibid., pp. 149, 157, 159 and 233.
31. Ibid., pp. 150 and 194.
32. Ibid., p. 176.
33. Cooke, op. cit., p. 258.
34. *Istoriya Kommunistitseskoi Partii Sovetskogo Soyuza, V: 1938-1958,* Kniga pervaya (1938-1945). Moscow 1970, p. 74.
35. Noted at the second meeting of the negotiations on 14 October 1939

by the secretary of the Finnish delegation and retold in his recently published memoirs: Johàn Nykopp, *Paasikiven mukana Moskovassa,* Helsinki 1975, p. 56.
36. Gripenberg's diary 23 March 1940.
37. Hubatsch, p. 154.
38. Draft memoirs, p. 186; Ryti Papers 9.
39. See Meretskov, op. cit., p. 116. *Istoriya velikoi otechestvennoi voini Soviet-kogo Sajuza 1941-1945,* II, Moscow 1961, p. 266. Cf. Steinhardts, cable to Secretary of State, 9 March 1940; *FRUS* 1940, I, pp. 276-7, and Carlgren, p. 129.
40. WM 59 (40) 6, p. 9; Conf. ann. (CAB 65/12).

Chapter IX, pp. 164-84

1. Medlicott 1968, p. 239.
2. *Daily Mail,* 2 Dec. 1939.
3. W. P. and Zelda K. Coates' noteworthy pro-Soviet booklet *The Soviet-Finnish Campaign, Military and Political, 1939-1940* was not published until 1942.
4. Gripenberg, op. cit., pp. 91-2.
5. Clark, op. cit., p. 41.
6. Same, p. 42. Dalton, op. cit., p. 293.
7. Minutes of the executive meeting of the Socialist International in Brussels 23-25 Feb. 1940, translated into Finnish in Kalle Lehmus, *Talonpoika suurten sakkilaudalla.* Helsinki 1969, pp. 137-40 and 143.
8. Dalton, p. 293.
9. Cf. Gripenberg's diary 13 March 1940, VA and Clark, pp. 41-2. More about public opinion in Britain during January-February, see Clark, pp. 126-7, and esp. pp. 130-9. We may add the warnings by B. H. Liddell Hart against provoking a conflict with Russia which were strongly polemicized by Mr. Voigt in the March 1940 issue of *The Nineteenth Century and After.*
10. Sir Walter Citrine, *My Finnish Diary.* London 1940, pp. 12-13. Cf. Dalton, p. 293.
11. Citrine's book as well as Pritt's were both published in the Penguin Special series.
12. Travel report of Labour delegates according to Citrine. Halifax's statement at War Cabinet meeting 12 Feb. 1940; WM 39 (40) 8, CAB 65/5, PRO. Cf. Dalton, p. 293.
13. Noel-Baker's memorandum on the Finnish armament needs and peace prospects 14 Feb. 1940, appendix in Halifax's memorandum 'Military Assistance to Finland', WP (40) 58, CAB 66/5.
14. Noel-Baker's memorandum, p. 7. Author's italics.
15. See War Cabinet minutes 19 Feb. 1940; WM 46 (40) 5.
16. Macmillan, op. cit., pp. 28-33.
17. Ibid., pp. 34-8.
18. Ibid., pp. 39-43, and esp. pp. 42-3.
19. Ibid., pp. 44-6.
20. Ibid., pp. 46-9. Cf. Carlgren, op. cit., p. 114.

21. Macmillan, op. cit., pp. 53-9.
22. Gripenberg's diary 3 and 5 Jan., and 2 Feb. 1940. Cf. Tanner, op. cit., p. 174.
23. Serlachius to Ryti 30 Dec. 1939. Ryti Papers 4, VA. The booklet *British Relief to Finland Feb.-Oct. 1940* ed. Henry Bell, Helsinki 1940.
24. Cf. Potiemkine, op. cit., p. 672, and Holma's report no. 733, 20 Feb. 1940; UA 109 C 2 e.
25. See e.g. Shirer, op. cit., pp. 210-13.
26. Dalton, p. 292, on Blum's Brussels speech. Lehmus, pp. 131-3, esp. p. 133.
27. Statement given to Japanese newspapermen in March 1940; Holma's tel. no. 275, 3 March 1940; Tanner Papers 27.
28. Pakaslahti, op. cit., 232. Peltier, op cit., 116. Annales de l'Assemblée Nationale, ibid., 19 March 1940. See Shirer, pp. 212-3.
29. Interviews with Generals Ganeval and Stehlin; Peltier, pp. 110-17.
30. Ibid., p. 113. Coulet, op. cit., p. 70. Pakaslahti, p. 238. Interviews with Generals Oesch and Airo.
31. Cf. Gamelin, p. 198.
32. 'A certain amount of volunteers have been available, but most of them have been in Red Spain, so they cannot be taken into consideration..' Col. Hiisi to Col. Melander, 18 Dec. 1939, letter no. 262/9/39; T 17522/9, SA.
33. Tel. no. C-124 of 31 Dec. and no. 19 of 16 Jan. 1940 by Finnish Foreign Ministry; UA and Tanner 27.
34. Col. Gibson's letter to Halifax 2 Jan. 1940; FO 371/24796; 'Official Report on the Finnish Aid Bureau and the British Contingent of the International Volunteer Force for Finland' signed by same 30 Sept. 1940 (hence 'Gibson's r.'), p. 1; UA 109 C 3 d: Britain and Ireland. WM 3 (40) 6, CAB 65/5. Gripenberg 1960, pp. 100-1, and his diary 3 Jan. 1940.
35. WM 3 (40) 6, WM 10 (40) 1 and WM 16 (40) 6, CZB idem, MC (40) 2 and 6; FO 371/24797/505. Gripenberg's diary, 8 Jan. 1940.
36. Interview with Commander Gröndahl. Gibson's r., p. 1. Gripenberg's diary, 22 Jan. 1940.
37. WM 24 (40) 4, Conf. ann. Lord Halifax's memorandum 26 Jan. 1940; WP (40) 33; FO 371/24798/1090.
38. Chamberlain's remark at War Cabinet meeting 3 Nov. 1940; WM 3 (40) and WM 39, 42, 43, 49 and 52 (40); CAB 65/5.
39. Gripenberg 1960, pp. 100-1.
40. Ibid., pp. 99-101, and Gibson's r.
41. Gibson's r. See Clark, p. 246.
42. Ibid.
43. See WM 37 (40) 6; CAB 65/5. Gripenberg 1960, pp. 102-3.
44. Gibson's r.
45. Ibid. and Clark, p. 208.
46. Ibid. and the material in UA 109 C 3 c and d in general.
47. The Finnish Government paid the last ones sick compensation until the 1950s. Material in UA 109 C 3 d. Clark, pp. 209-210.
48. Minister Orde to FO 11 Dec. 1939, tel. no. 147; FO 371/23695/7361. Memorandum of Lieut. Col. Tadeusz Rudnicky (General Sikorsky's

special representative) 'The negotiations with Finland' 22 Feb. 1940; PRM 16, p. 1, SI. Mannerheim, op. cit., p. 389.

49. Minister Hoare's tel. no. 884, 18 Dec. 1939; FO ibid. 23645/7618. Holma's letter 30 Jan. 1940; UA 109 C 2 e. Young's memorandum 8 Feb. 1940; FO ibid.

50. Noel-Baker's letter to Ryti 5 March 1940. Ryti Papers 3.

51. Mannerheim, p. 389.

52. Rudnicky's memorandum 22 Feb. 1940.

53. Holma to Foreign Minister, letter 30 Jan. 1940 and letter no. 798, 23 Feb. 1940; UA ibid. Rudnicky's mentioned memorandum.

54. Memorandum by Col. Kedzior, the Polish Chief-of-Staff, on the conversation between Daladier and Sikorsky on 4 Jan. 1940; A IV 1/5, S.I. The proposal of the chairman of the ministerial council approved 25 Jan. 1940; PRM-16, p. 1, ibid.

55. Sikorsky to Daladier 24 March 1940, letter no. 540/XIV; PRM, idem.

56. Memorandum by Col. Kedzior 21 Feb. 1940; PRM, ibid.

57. Ibid. Cf. Sikorsky to Foreign Minister Zalesky 22 Feb. 1940, letter no. Prez. Par. 499. VII. 40; PRM, ibid.

58. Minart, op. cit., pp. 175-6. See Derry. op. cit., p. 63.

59. Sikorsky's letter to Gamelin 19 Feb. 1940. Report of the listening centre (Centre d'écoutes) 4 Feb. 1940 on the French broadcasts of Radio Moscow, dated at the registry of the Provisional Polish Government 19 Feb. 1940, no. 464/XVIII, ibid.

60. Sikorsky's letter to Gamelin 19 Feb. 1940.

61. Same to Zalesky 22 Feb. 1940.

62. Same to Daladier 24 Feb. 1940.

ADDENDUM

Chapter V, p. 95

61. In March 1976, after the first proofs of this book were printed, a doctoral dissertation on almost the same theme was defended at the Faculty of Social Sciences of the University of Helsinki (*Maaliskuusta maaliskuuhun: Suomi Englannin politiikassa* 1939-1940 by Martti Häikiö in Finnish with summary in English.

The auther claims, contrary to the conclusions drawn above, that "the change in the situation of Northern Europe took place in the first part of December [1939], when both the Allies and the Scandinavian countries adopted the policy which they pursued during the whole Finnish war" (op. cit., p. 114). It is obvious that when insisting on December instead of January he thinks more of decisions in principle than of actual operational preparations—the very factor of change, according to my opinion. It should be stressed that in the decisions of December, Finland figured only as a side-show, whereas towards the end of January it tended to become an essential target of intervention. As to the role of the Scandinavians, their counteraction no doubt became effective only after they had got wind of the Allied plans in Christmas week (see above, pp. 68-9 and 74)—and this brings us definitely to January.

BIBLIOGRAPHY

I. *Unpublished Primary Sources*
(abbreviations in parentheses)

(1) ARCHIVES OF FINNISH FOREIGN MINISTRY
(Ulkoasiainministeriön arkisto=UA), HELSINKI
Group   5 C : Reports 1939-40 from legations: Berlin, Geneva
Copenhagen, London, Moscow, Oslo, Paris, Stock-
holm, Washington
Group   109 : Finnish-Soviet negotiations October-November 1939
and the war 1939-40
A 1 : Reports from legations
— 10: Other information and assessments of the situation
B 1 : Military reports of the legations
C 1 : Finland-Britain
Finland-France
Finland-Germany
C 2 : Assistance from Poland and the Western Powers
C 3 : Volunteers
G 1 : Minister Tanner's notes with supplements (Minutes of
the Finnish cabinet [VN] and the foreign affairs com-
mittees of cabinet and diet during the war)
(2) FINNISH   NATIONAL   ARCHIVES   (Valtionarkisto=VA),
HELSINKI
Material of the Foreign Ministry (UM 15) League of Nations Depart-
ment
Documents of the German Foreign Ministry (photocopies)
The Gripenberg Papers
The Harri Holma Papers
The Risto Ryti Papers
The Väinö Tanner Papers
(3) MILITARY ARCHIVES (*Sota-arkisto*=SA), HELSINKI
T 17522/9 : Finnish military attaché in Paris 1939-40
T 19932/35: Finnish military attaché in Stockholm 1939-40
(4) ARCHIVES OF SWEDISH FOREIGN MINISTRY (*Svenska utrikes-
departementet* = SUD), STOCKHOLM
HP 20 a: The question of Åland 1939
(5) ARCHIVES OF NORWEGIAN FOREIGN MINISTRY (*Norske
utrikes-departementet* = NUD), OSLO
35 D: Norwegian territorial waterways
35 G 2: Soviet-Finnish relations 1939-1940
PIL/VIII: The Finnish-Soviet conflict
(6) PUBLIC RECORD OFFICE (PRO), LONDON
Cabinet Office (CAB): War Cabinet (incl. Chiefs-of-Staff Committee
and Military Co-ordination Committee)
documents, groups 21, 23, 63, 65, 66, 79,
80 and 83

Foreign Office (FO) : Group FO 371, General correspondence
—documents from the groups 23072, 23643-9,
23692-7 and 24798
Group FO 419:
—/33, Further correspondence respecting
Scandinavia and the Baltic States
(part XXXII)
—/34   „   „   (part XXXIII)
(7) INSTITUT HISTORYCZNY im. GEN. SIKORSKIEGO, LONDON
(Sikorsky Institute = SI):
Groups A. IV. 1/5 and PRM-16: Documents of the Polish Provisional Government
(8) In addition, the author had special permission to use the archives of
the French Foreign Ministry in Paris and the French Embassy in
London, as well as those of the army Historical Section at Vincennes,
without quoting from or referring to individual documents.

*Information derived in 1971-2 from personal interviews and reports to
the author by the following:*

Lieutenant-General A. F. Airo, Heinolan mlk., Finland
Général d'armée Antoine Béthouart, Paris
Général de corps d'armée Jean Ganeval, Paris
Ambassador G. A. Gripenberg, Helsinki
Commander Holger Gröndahl, Helsinki
Lieutenant-General Lennart Oesch, Helsinki
Colonel A. A. Paasonen, Flourtown, Pa., USA
Général d'armée aerienne Paul Stehlin, Paris
Major-General K. M. Wallenius, Helsinki

II. Published Primary Sources

L'Assemblée Nationale, Annales de ... Comités secrets des 5 février, 19
mars et 19 avril 1940. Paris 1949.

Débats parlementaires no 24: Chambre des Deputés, Compte rendu in
extenso, 28e séance 12-3-1940. *Journal Officiel* 13-3-1940.

Documents on British Foreign Policy, Third Series IV, V and VII. London
1951-2 and 1954 (=*DBFP*).

Documents on German Foreign Policy, Series D, vol. VIII: The War years
1939-1940, Washington 1954.

Dokumenty vneshnei politiki SSSR, 16 (1933) Moscow 1971

Foreign Relations of the United States 1939, I, Washington 1956, and 1940, I,
Washington 1959 (=*FRUS*).

Kungl. Utrikesdepartementet, *Handlingar rörande Sveriges politik under andra
världskriget: Förspelet till det tyska angreppet pa Danmark och Norge den
9 april 1940*, Stockholm 1947 (=*Förspelet*).

Auswärtiges Amt, *Documents rélatifs à la politique franco-anglaise d'extension de la
guerre*, 1940 Nr 4, Berlin 1940.

Die Geheimakten des französischen Generalstabes 1939/41, Nr 6, Berlin 1941 (=*Geheimakten*).

Jane Dégras (ed.), *Soviet Documents on Foreign Policy 1917-1941*, III, London 1953.

Finnish Ministry for Foreign Affairs, *The Development of Finnish-Soviet Relations During the Autumn of 1939—In the light of official documents* (=*Blue-White Book*), Helsinki 1940.

Finnish Foreign Trade Directory 1950, Helsinki 1950.

III. *Newspapers*

The Daily Mail, London, 1939
The Evening Standard, London, 1939
Helsingin Sanomat, Helsinki, 1940
Suomen Kuvalehti, Helsinki, 1966
The Times, London, 1939-40
The Yorkshire Post, Leeds, 1939

IV. *Literature, Memoirs and Studies*

(In order to distinguish between more than one work by the same author the source gives, in case of repetition, the year of publication in addition to the author's name.)

Assarsson, Wilhelm, *I skuggan av Stalin*, Stockholm 1963.

Audet, Gen., "L'Expédition de Norvège: Namsos, février-mai 1940", *Revue historique de l'armée*, No. 1, 1957.

Auphan, Amiral, 'A propos de l'expedition de Norvège', *Ecrits de Paris*, No. 47, Sept. 1948.

Barros, James, *Betrayal from within, Joseph Avenol, Secretary General of the League of Nations, 1933-1940*, New Haven 1969.

Beaufre, André, *Le drame de 1940*, Paris 1965.

Bell, Henry, *British Relief to Finland, Feb.-Oct. 1940*, Helsinki 1940.

Béthouart, Gen. Antoine, *Cinq années d'esperance, Mémoires de guerre 1939-1945*, Paris 1968.

Blücher, Wipert von, *Gesandter zwischen Diktatur und Demokratie*, Wiesbaden 1951.

Boheman, Erik, *På vakt, kabinettsekreterare under andra världskriget*, Stockholm 1964.

Bonnet, Georges, *Fin d'une Europe*, Paris 1949.

Butler, J.R.M., *Grand Strategy* (History of the Second World War), II, London 1952.

Cadogan, Sir Alexander: *see* Dilks, David.

Carlgren, Wilhelm, M., *Svensk utrikespolitik, 1939-1945*, Stockholm 1973.

Chew, Allen F., *The White Death: The Epic of the Soviet-Finnish Winter War*, Ann Arbor, Mich., 1970.

Churchill, Winston S., *The Second World War: I, The Gathering Storm*, London 1948.

Citrine, Sir Walter, *My Finnish Diary*, London 1940.

Clark, Douglas, *Three Days to Catastrophe*, London 1966.
Cooke, Colin, *The Life of Richard Stafford Cripps*, London.1957.
Coulet, François, *Vertu des temps difficiles*, Paris 1967.
Dalton, Hugh, *Fateful Years, Memoirs 1939-1945*, London 1957.
Derry, T. K., *The Campaign in Norway* (History of the Second World War, United Kingdom Military Series) London 1952.
Dilks, David (ed.), *The Diaries of Sir Alexander Cadogan, 1938-1945* (=Cadogan Diaries), London 1971.
Eagle, Elvire, and Lauri Paananen, *The Winter War: the Russo-Finnish Conflict 1939-1940*, London 1972.
Feiling, Keith, *The Life of Neville Chamberlain*, London 1947.
Foot, Michael, *Aneurin Bevan, a Biography I: 1897-1945* London, 1962.
Gamelin Maurice, *Servir — La guerre, septembre 1939-19 mai 1940*, Paris 1947.
Gripenberg, G. A., *Finland and the Great Powers: Memoirs of a Diplomat*, Lincoln, Nebraska 1965.
Heinrichs, Erik, *Mannerheim Suomen kohtaloissa*, II, Helsinki 1960.
Hubatsch, Walther, *"Weserübung," Die Deutsche Besetzung von Dänemark und Norwegen 1940*, Göttingen 1960.
Ironside: *see* Macleod-Kelly.
Istoriya diplomatii, IV, Moscow 1975.
Istoriya Kommunistitseskoi Partii Sovetskogo Sayuza, V: 1938-1958, 1 (1938-1945), Moscow 1970.
Istoriya Ordena Lenina Leningradskogo Voennogo Okruga Moscow 1974.
Istorya Velikoi Otechestvennoi Voiny Sovetskogo Sayuza 1939-1945, I, Moscow 1960.
Istoriya Vtoroi Mirovoi Voiny 1939-1945, III (Moscow, 1974).
Jakobson, Max, *The Diplomacy of the Winter War*, Cambridge, Mass. 1961.
Kekkonen Urho, 'Pekka Peitsi, Silloin ja tänään,' *Suomen Kuvalehti*, 3 Dec. 1966.
Kérillis, Henri de, *De Gaulle dictateur*, Montreal 1945.
Kirke, Gen. Sir Walter, Preface to *Finland's War of Independence* by J. O. Hannula, London 1939.
Koht, Halvdan, *For fred og fridom i krigstid 1939-1940*, Oslo 1957.
Korhonen, Keijo, *Suomi neuvostodiplomatiassa — Tartosta talvisotaan, 2, 1933-1939: Turvallisuuden pettaessa*, Helsinki 1971.
Krosby, Hans-Peter, *Finland, Germany and the Soviet Union, 1940-1941, The Petsamo Dispute*, Madison, Wisc. 1968.
Lehmus, Kalle, *Talonpoika suurten shakkilaudalla*, Helsinki 1969.
Lie, Trygve, *Leve eller dø. Norge i krig*, Oslo 1955.
Lorbeer, Hans-Joachim, *Westmächte gegen die Sowjetunion 1939-1941* (Einzelschriften zur militärischen Geschichte des Zweiten Weltkrieges, Bd 18, Freiburg-im-Breisgau 1975).
Macleod, R., and Denis Kelly (editors), *The Ironside Diaries, 1937-1940* (=Ironside Diaries), London 1962.
Macmillan, Harold, *The Blast of War*, London 1967.
Mannerheim, C.G.E., *The Memoirs of Marshal Mannerheim*, London 1953.
Mead, W.R., *Finland*, London 1968.

217

Medlicott, W.N., *The Economic Blockade*, I (History of the Second World War, United Kingdom Civil Series), London 1952.
————, *British Foreign Policy since Versailles*, London 1968.
Meretskov, K.A., *Serving the People*, Moscow 1971.
Michel, Henri, *La drôle de guerre*, Paris 1971.
Minart, Jacques, *P. C. Vincennes, secteur 4*, Paris 1945.
Nevakivi, Jukka, *Muurmannin legioona — Suomalaiset ja liittoutuneiden interventio Pohjois-Venajalle 1918-1919*, Helsinki 1970.
————, "Suomen kysymys Kansainliitossa joulukuussa 1939", *Historiallinen Aikakauskirja*, No. 4, 1971.
Niukkanen, Juho, *Talvisodan puolustusministeri kertoo*, Porvoo 1951.
Nykopp, Johan, *Paasikiven mukana Moskovassa*, Helsinki 1975.
Paasikivi, J. K., *Toimintani Moskovassa ja Suomessa 1939-41*, Porvoo 1959.
Paasivirta, Juhani, *The Victors in World War I and Finland: Finland's Relations with the British, French and the United States Governments in 1918-1919* Helsinki, 1965.
Paasonen, Aladár, *Marsalkan tiedustelupäällikkönä ja hallituksen asiamiehenä*, Tapiola 1974.
Pajari, Risto, *Talvisota ilmassa*, Porvoo 1971.
Pakaslahti, Aaro, *Talvisodan poliittinen näytelmä, UM:n poliittisen osaston päällikön päiviä ja öitä*, Porvoo 1970.
Paul-Boncour, J., *Entre deux guerres — Souvenirs sur la IIIe République: Sur les chemins de la defaite, 1935-1940* Paris 1946.
Peltier, M., *La Finlande dans la tourmente*, Paris 1966.
Pertinax, *Les Fossoyers: Défaite militaire de la France, armistice, contre-revolution, I: Les derniers Chefs de la IIIème république, Gamelin, Daladier, Reynaud,* (New York 1943).
Polvinen Tuomo, *Venajan vallankumous ja Suomi 1917-1920*, II, Porvoo 1971.
Potiemkine, V. (ed.) *Histoire de la diplomatie*, III: 1919-1939, Paris 1947.
Pritt, D. N., *Must the War Spread?*, London 1940.
Reynaud, Paul, *Au coeur de la melée*, Paris 1951.
————, "*Memoires II: Envers et contre tous*, Paris 1963."
Roussilon, Didier de, *Vérites sur la Finlande*, Paris 1946.
Shirer, William L., *The Collapse of the Third Republic, an Inquiry into the Fall of France in 1940*, London 1972.
Stehlin, Paul, *Témoignage pour l' histoire*, Paris 1964.
Strang, Lord, *Home and Abroad*, London 1956.
Suomi, Juhani, *Talvisodan tausta. Neuvostoliitto Suomen ulkopolitiikassa 1937-1939. I: Holstista Erkkoon*, Helsinki 1973.
Soderhjelm, J. O. *Kolme matkaa Moskovaan*, Tampere 1970.
Tanner, Väinö, *The Winter War*, Stanford, Calif. 1957.
Taylor, A. J. P., *The Origins of the Second World War*, London 1961.
————, *Beaverbrook*, London 1972.
Torris, M. J., *Narvik*, Paris 1963.
Upton, A. F., *The Communist Parties of Scandinavia and Finland*, London 1973.
-————, *Finland 1939-1940*, London 1974.
Vaux Saint-Cyr, Comte de, "Ma mission en Finlande, Souvenirs", *Revue Deux Mondes*, 15 Oct. 1953.

218   *The Appeal that was never made*

Wahlbäck, Krister, *Finlandsfrågan i svensk politik 1937-1940*, Stockholm 1964.
———, *Regeringen och kriget, ur stadsrådens dagbocker 1939-41*, Stockholm 1972.
Watt, D. C., "Anglo-German Naval agreement of 1935; an interim judgement", *Journal of Modern History*, June 1956.
Wigforss, E., *Minnen III:*1932-1949, Stockholm 1954.
Woodward, L., *British Foreign Policy in the Second World War*, I, London 1970.
Wuorimaa, Aarne, *Lähettiläänä Hitlerin Saksassa*, Keuruu 1967.
Öhqvist, Harald, *Talvisota minun näkökulmastani*, Porvoo 1949.

INDEX

143-7, 150-1, 170-1, 175, 178-81;
threat of Soviet invasion, 62-3, 72,
73n., 77-9, 105-6, 114, 144, 149;
threat of German invasion, 62n.,
63, 72, 73n., 105-7; iron ore
transports to Germany, 63-6,
68-78, 105, 118-19, 144, 149;
policy of neutrality, 21, 51, 55, 60,
64-6, 73, 104-5, 120, 195(n.51);
Swedish assistance to Finland, 80,
84, 102-8, 120, 124, 138, 150, 171;
Swedish peace mediation between
Finland and U.S.S.R., 102-4,
114n., 136, 139

Tanner, Väinö, second Finnish delegate at the Moscow negotiations
in Oct.-Nov. 1939; Foreign
Minister 1939-1940, 30, 54-5,
56n., 69, 87, 93-4, 102-4, 108,
121-6, 133-8, 142-4
Thyssen, Baron Fritz von, German
industrialist, 64, 68

Turkey, 32, 109-11, 123, 137

United States of America, 30-2, 34,
44, 53-4, 56n., 85n., 94

Vereker, Gordon, British Minister in
Helsinki 1940-1, 115, 121-4,
127-8, 134, 142-4
Viipuri (Viborg), 45, 106, 114n.
Volunteers, recruitment for Finland:
in Great Britain, 84, 174-9; in
France, 173-4

Walden, Maj.-Gen. Rudolf, Finnish
industrialist, representative, of
C.-in-C. in Ryti's cabinet 1939-40,
103-4, 121, 134
Wallenberg Marcus, Jr., Swedish
banker, 84
Wallenius, Maj.-Gen. K.M. (Finnish),
91
Weygand, General Maxime (French),
4, 78, 91, 109-10